A BATTLE-AXE IN THE BEAR PIT
Millicent Preston Stanley MP

Dr Wendy Michaels OAM

In this absorbing biography Wendy Michaels provides a rich and thoroughly researched study of the life and career of Millicent Preston Stanley, a pioneering Australian female politician whose story deserves to be better known.

- Honorary Associate Professor Caroline Webb, The University of Newcastle

Connor Court Publishing Pty Ltd

Published in 2025 by Connor Court Publishing Pty Ltd.

Copyright © Wendy Michaels

ALL RIGHTS RESERVED. This book contains material protected under International and Federal Copyright Laws and Treaties. Any unauthorised reprint or use of this material is prohibited. No part of this book may be reproduced or transmitted in any form or by any means, electronic or mechanical, including photocopying, recording, or by any information storage and retrieval system without express written permission from the publisher.

Connor Court Publishing Pty Ltd.
PO Box 7257
Redland Bay QLD 4165
sales@connorcourt.com
www.connorcourt.com

ISBN: 9781923224568

Cover Design by Maria Giordano
Cover illustration: Noel Rubie
Millicent Preston Stanley Vaughan c. 1945
National Portrait Gallery of Australia
Gift of Judi Preston-Stanley 2013

Printed in Australia.

CONTENTS

About the Author	v
Foreword: The Hon. Shelley Hancock OAM	vii
Introduction: A Pretty Useful Weapon	xi
1. An Impression (1883-1901)	1
2. Never Equalled in Brilliance (1902-1918)	9
3. Political Woman of the Future (1919-1924)	25
4. Advent of a Woman (1924-1925)	41
5. Sojourn in the House (1925)	57
6. A Trick and a Stratagem (1926)	73
7. Pass that Bill (1927-1930)	87
8. What Political Action Failed to Do (1931-1932)	103
9. The Final Factor (1933-1934)	117
10. A Citizen's Life (1934)	131
11. Peace and War (1935-1945)	145
12. Cold War and Camels (1946-1949)	161
13. The Forgotten Sex (1950-1954)	175
14. A Sad Retreat (1955)	189
Notes	195
Acknowledgements	223
Index	227

Dr Wendy Michaels OAM has had a distinguished career as an academic, educator, consultant, writer, and festival director. Before her retirement she was a lecturer in the School of Humanities at the University of Newcastle. Wendy's awards include an Order of Australia Medal for services to women and to the dramatic arts, a National Council of Women Award for Promoting the Status of Women, a JEDA Award for Drama Writing, Honorary Life Membership of Drama NSW for service to Drama in Education, and the Minister for Education Award for Excellence in Tertiary Teaching. She has published poetry, plays and stories for children and numerous articles and books including:

Building Plays (with Caroline Tarlington)

Inside Drama (with Peter Newham)

Playbuilding Shakespeare

Played Upon a Stage

Secret Smiles (illustrated Lisa Fitter)

The Playwright at Work

Up and Away with Picture Books (with Maureen Walsh)

When the Hurly Burly is Done: Shakespeare in the Classroom

Foreword

The building that serves as the home to the Parliament of New South Wales has existed in one form or another on Macquarie Street since 1811. It was first a hospital and in 1829 it became home to Australia's first Legislature and then in 1856 New South Wales' first Legislative Assembly. It is Australia's first and oldest parliament, and the most continuously used public building in Australia. However, it would not be until almost one hundred years after parliamentarians first sat in the building, in 1925, that the first female parliamentarian would grace the benches of either Chamber.

Prior to 2017, recognition and awareness of New South Wales' first female Member of Parliament, Millicent Preston Stanley, was minimal. Visitors to the Parliament, its members and staff knew little of this remarkable woman, her achievements and the trail she blazed for the women that would follow her.

As the first female Speaker of the NSW Legislative Assembly and the first female member for the state electoral district of South Coast, much of Millicent's own journey resonates with me. My admiration of and fascination with this remarkable woman was cemented upon learning that following accusations that she was a 'battle-axe', Millicent famously responded: 'once sharpened, a battleaxe could be as powerful as a sword'. I was also amazed by the courage she demonstrated entering the Legislative Assembly Chamber – known as the 'Bear Pit' – as its sole, and first woman.

In 2016, I initiated the commissioning of an exhibition celebrating not only Millicent, but the achievements of all women in NSW politics. It was through the process of developing the exhibition's content that I was introduced to this work's author, Dr Wendy Michaels.

Wendy's passion and dedication to recognising and raising awareness about Millicent and Millicent's colourful story were inspiring. Wendy described Millicent and her context so intimately, eloquently and in such detail that she was able to bring Millicent to life. The woman she described was a fierce feminist and suffragist, a committed community advocate and representative, and an adept debater and witty wordsmith. I am sure much of Millicent's life also resonates with and is embodied in Wendy. Therefore, I find it fitting that Wendy be the one to commit Millicent's journey and legacy to paper.

I can now proudly say that the Parliament has held its first exhibition to focus entirely on the contribution of women to political life in NSW. *A Fit Place for Women: NSW Parliament* highlighted more than a century of achievements by women as campaigners, protestors, voters, parliamentary officers, members, ministers, presiding officers and premiers, and at its centre was Millicent.

The exhibition was the Parliament's most successful to date in terms of visitor numbers, media coverage and audience feedback. Overall, the exhibition received almost 70,000 visitors. Furthermore, in honour of the significant contribution of all women to NSW political life, but particularly Millicent, the Parliament now also boasts a room named in honour of Millicent Preston Stanley. The room includes images of Millicent, segments of her inaugural speech and details of her time as a member, which I hope will serve as a lasting and more enriched dedication to this female pioneer within the parliamentary precinct.

Today, the lower house chamber is still affectionately referred to as the 'Bear Pit' and the robust debate it became infamous for still rages despite the many changes to the Parliament and NSW's democratic system over the years.

The term 'Bear Pit', or 'Bear Garden' as it has also been known, has its origins in the Westminster system of government and is often used to describe not only the NSW Legislative Assembly, but many lower houses throughout the Commonwealth such as the House of Commons in London and the Victorian Legislative

Assembly. It is of course a reference to the blood sport of bear baiting in which an audience from a raked auditorium would place bets upon the clash between dogs and bears in the arena below.

It is not known precisely when the term was first used to describe the NSW Legislative Assembly and much of the evidence of its historical use is anecdotal. Yet, it becomes clear from early newspaper articles that the term gained traction in the late nineteenth century and has entrenched itself within the culture and identity of the Parliament ever since.

It is a fitting descriptor for a chamber that for more than a century has hosted aggressive verbal and at times physical combat. In November 1886, the *Richmond River Herald and Northern Districts Advertiser* described the antics of the NSW lower house in such a way:

> The proceedings of the Legislative Assembly during the closing months of a long-protracted session have been of a kind to bring discredit on representative institutions. The House had lost its deliberative character, and had become converted into a bear-pit, where personal passion, foul language and riotous conduct appeared to be the natural elements. The Ministry was attacked with a vindictive bitterness beyond parallel, and as heat produces heat, so the retorts upon the Opposition were fashioned in the same form... some members found language an inadequate vent and on more than one occasion the chosen representatives of the people sought to settle their differences by a resort to fisticuffs.

Who would not despair for the person charged with the responsibility of presiding over and maintaining order in such a chamber!

While the chamber does enjoy a particular reputation for heated debate, it is paramount that we remember its role as our state's democratic forum from which many great ideas and pieces of legislation have also originated. A Speaker must carefully find the balance between ensuring a certain level of decorum applies, consistent with the respect and standards befitting the House and its members, and guaranteeing each representative can freely and fully advocate for their constituents, that their ability to discuss and debate is not hindered in any way.

From the outset my intention as Speaker has always been to ensure that members on each side treat each other fairly and with respect. Regardless of their gender, members within the Chamber are treated equally by all with none spared the heated argument or cutting comments, which are just as likely to originate from a female member as a male. Is this not a sign of growing equality within the Chamber?

It is my prediction that the passionate, lively, coarse and robust debate of the NSW Legislative Assembly will be a tradition maintained by many a future parliament and parliamentarian.

Outside of the chamber I have tried to remove what barriers exist for women within the parliamentary precinct. As the first female Speaker I viewed it as my responsibility to concentrate on lessening the inequities found in the traditions and infrastructure of the Parliament of New South Wales, a parliament created, built and designed at a time when a woman was not only unable to stand for election, she was unable to vote!

There will come a time in which being a woman in parliament and taking on a leadership role such as Speaker won't be special – it will just be the norm. However, we 'firsts' and those that follow us will always remember it was Millicent Preston Stanley who forged the way for us all.

The Hon. Shelley Hancock OAM
Speaker of the NSW Legislative Assembly 2011-2019
Minister for Local Government 2019-2021
Member for South Coast 2003-2023

INTRODUCTION

A Pretty Useful Weapon

A battle-axe is a pretty useful weapon if it's kept sharp and bright.

Millicent Preston Stanley

In 1925, Millicent Preston Stanley, an outspoken woman with the 'gift of eloquence',[1] became the first woman elected to the New South Wales Legislative Assembly. She arrived with a reputation as an activist, advocate and campaigner, who was not averse to firing witty retorts with the 'swift return of a punching ball'[2] at those who challenged her. On one occasion when a gentleman tossed the 'battle-axe' slur at her she riposted, 'a battle-axe is a pretty useful weapon if it's kept sharp and bright'.[3]

Millicent found that sharp, bright weapon useful in the NSW Bear Pit. Although the Legislative Assembly was Australia's Mother Parliament, there was nothing motherly about it. Not long after its establishment in 1856 it earned the name 'Bear Pit' because of the behaviour of members who regularly used abusive language and engaged in fisticuffs on the floor of the House. As one astute observer noted, members behaved more like 'chimney sweeps' than English gentlemen.[4]

No wonder parliament was not considered a fit place for a woman!

When Millicent entered those hallowed halls, some observers commented she might be the 'angel in the house', taming members' wild behaviours and one gentleman even suggested she might bring 'moral, material and spiritual welfare' to the parliament.[5] But that was not her mission. She was focused on enacting legislation that would make the nation a better place for women and children – and men. As one journalist put it, 'She had the cause of women and children at heart, and it is to help this cause that she has gone into parliament'.[6]

Millicent may have been a battle-axe but she rejected any battle between the sexes. Men and women were different but that did not make them opponents. She did not set out to challenge men's power but to provide a balance to their power so that women's issues, which by their very nature were beyond men's ken, would be dealt with in the parliament. In short, she saw her service as complementary to, not in opposition to, men's.

Millicent's life spanned two depressions, two world wars and the onset of the Cold War. The social turbulence of these times shaped her worldview and prompted her to work for peace and for a better world. She was engaged in political action long before she entered parliament and she would continue to be involved in politics long after her skirts ceased to rustle on those sacred benches.

Without the benefits of today's social media platforms this skilled networker engaged women's organisations in her campaigns. Keeping a tight veil over her private life, she engaged the press to report on her public activities, publish her articles, letters to the editor and verses, thus projecting her carefully crafted political persona to the public and for posterity. She hoped, above all else, she would be remembered as 'a politician of depth and understanding'.[7]

A Battle-axe in the Bear Pit: Millicent Preston Stanley MP paints a portrait of this trailblazing politician. Piecing together information about her family, political apprenticeship, employment in commercial and political associations, work in voluntary organisations, and her election campaigns, it traces her pathway into parliament, describes the misogyny she encountered there, outlines her attempts to advance her legislative agendas against the obstacles and obstructions in her path, and follows the twists and turns of her extensive post-parliamentary political career.

This biography pays homage to her relentless determination

to fulfil the Feminist Club manifesto, 'equality of liberties, status and opportunities between men and women in all spheres'.[8] But it is not a hagiography – it does not shy away from calling out her opportunistic and manipulative actions and criticising her obfuscations, miscalculations and misjudgements. Millicent was a remarkable woman but she was no saint to be placed on a pedestal and venerated.

This is the story of a significant early twentieth century Australian woman politician – a story with uncanny resonances for women politicians today.

1

An Impression
(1883-1901)

Her vivid personality ... her earnestness and wonderful organising faculties have inspired with unbounded confidence all with whom she has come in contact.

'An Impression: The Woman MLA' [1]

The front page of Sydney's *Evening News* on Monday 1 June 1925 reported on the state election the previous Saturday. It featured two columns of photographs – one, under the subheading 'Old Faces out of the House', identified the men who had lost their seats, while the second, headed 'New Faces in the House', showed the newly elected members of the Legislative Assembly. At the top of this column was the first Woman MP, 'Preston Stanley, Miss'.[2]

Other newspapers across the nation depicted the election of Millicent Preston Stanley as a triumph for the woman who had blazed the trail for women. While one presciently questioned how much a lone woman in a House of eighty-nine men could actually achieve,[3] another hailed her as an 'outstanding figure' in the political life of the State and, problematically, went on to declare she was a 'politician by heredity, ability and training'.[4] In truth, Millicent could not lay claim to any inherited political position like later 'political widows' May Holman, Lady Millicent Peacock and Dame Enid Lyons.

Mary Liddell's page six profile in the same edition was titled, 'An Impression: The Woman MLA'. Liddell compared Millicent to Lady Nancy Astor, the first woman to take a seat in the British House of Commons in 1919, who was renowned for her acerbic responses to hostile interjectors. Liddell assured her readers Millicent would deal with the 'verbal gladiators' in the NSW bear pit in a similar way,[5] a prediction that would prove accurate.

Liddell embroidered her profile of Millicent even more colourfully. At the age of sixteen, she declared, Millicent was as well-known to members of the parliament as the Speaker himself because she spent so much time as a 'spectator in the ladies' gallery'.[6] As a young woman, Millicent's observations from the parliamentary ladies' gallery led her to wonder at the 'vacuity of mind'[7] of so many of the old men in the Chamber. Liddell's claim, that Australian political leaders acknowledged Millicent 'as an authority on every phase of politics'[8] is problematic. She was respected by some political leaders but there were others, both in the Labor Party and amongst the Nationalist and Progressive parties who were, at best, sceptical, and at worst, hostile to her agendas. Some were overtly antagonistic to the idea of any woman sitting on 'the sacrosanct seats of the lords of creation'[9] as Millicent would soon discover.

Liddell was well credentialed to publish the profile of this prominent woman. She was one of the founders of the Society of Women Writers, served two terms as Vice President of the Institute of Journalists and was the only female to contribute to a Sydney University Diploma course in journalism.[10] She was a regular columnist for the two Sydney tabloids owned by Samuel Bennett, the *Evening News* and *Sunday News* and unlike many women journalists at this time, her columns were 'signature' pieces,[11] her by-line testament to her professional status. Liddell was no hack scribbler dabbling in the woman's angle but a serious reporter and columnist whose knowledge and expertise warranted readers' attention. Moreover, Liddell and Millicent were colleagues who had worked together in the Women's Loyal Service Bureau and the Feminist Club of NSW.

Despite Liddell's journalistic credentials and her professional relationship with Millicent, her profile contains errors that a journalist – even a tabloid journalist – would be expected to 'fact check'. Did Liddell verify her claims about Millicent's family story? Or did she not want to let the facts get in the way of a good story? Or, was she persuaded by Millicent's carefully crafted, false family story?

Contrary to Liddell's claims, Millicent was not born in Victoria but in George Street, Sydney on 9 September 1883. Her mother, Frances Ellen Preston (known as Fanny), was born in 1859 in the gold rush town of Ballarat, Victoria, to Jane Preston a servant, and Robert Roland Preston, a Ballarat Foundry worker. It is possible Millicent did not know her grandfather was dismissed from the Foundry for dishonest practices[12] but she did know Fanny had moved to Sydney after her own mother's death and lived with her older sister Ada. Fanny and Ada were close and remained so even after their respective marriages; Ada's death notice identifies Fanny as the 'beloved sister of Mrs Preston Stanley'.[13]

How much Millicent knew about her father and his family is unknown. Her father, Augustine Gregory Stanley was born in 1856, the son of a warehouse labourer James Stanley, who had been convicted of forgery – 'uttering base coin' – in the Lancaster Quarter Sessions, Liverpool in April 1831 and transported to the Colony of New South Wales on the convict ship, *Isabella*. Millicent never acknowledged her convict grandfather or her parents' shotgun wedding, which was conducted by Thomas W Unwin at St Luke's Church, Sussex Street Sydney on 11 May 1883. Millicent was born four months later, on 9 September 1883.

Regardless of what Millicent knew about her parents' marriage, she experienced life in a dysfunctional family, marooned in the working class – a situation that informed her life-long missions. When her parents met, her father was employed in Stanley and Murray grocers at 74 Pitt Street Redfern although at various times thereafter he changed his occupation from dealer to tea dealer to draper. With each change there was also a change of domicile for the growing family.

In June 1885 Fanny gave birth to a son, Frederick Charles, a sickly baby who died ten months later in March 1886. He had become dehydrated after two weeks of diarrhoea and vomiting. Millicent was only two years old and probably barely aware of his death other than as an absence. Nevertheless, she certainly became aware of the arrival of another sibling. On 26 January 1887, Fanny gave birth to another boy, Victor Charles. Millicent would turn four in September that year.

The Stanley family's life was probably little different to that of other working class families, particularly as Australia became gripped by drought and slipped into Depression in the 1890s. As banks failed and unemployment soared, poverty was rife. An astute child, Millicent would have been alert to the marital tensions even if she did not comprehend that the causes lay in her father's insecure income, his alcoholism, and his cruelty to her mother, behaviours that today would be labelled domestic abuse.

Millicent was barely eight years of age when Augustine deserted the family in 1891 'without just cause or excuse'. How her mother explained his absence to Millicent and Victor is unknown. Whether it was Fanny who created the fiction of his death or Millicent's own invention, she could hardly have been unaware of her mother's struggles to support them.

Three years later, in September 1894, Fanny took advantage of newly amended laws to file for divorce. In her affidavit to the Supreme Court, Fanny stated she was destitute – 'not worth the sum of twenty five pounds'. She claimed that prior to her husband's wilful desertion, he had for more than three years been an 'habitual drunkard' and 'habitually cruel' to her. She had not heard from him in twelve months, had enquired of various people about his present whereabouts, had written countless letters to him, which went unanswered and had attempted to trace him at his last known address in Victoria, all to no avail. Unbeknown to her, Augustine had moved from the Victorian to the Western Australian goldfields.

In February 1895 Fanny was granted a *decree nisi*. The judgement came with a warning that if she remarried before the decree was made 'absolute', she would be guilty of 'bigamy'. Marrying again was not on Fanny's agenda. Millicent, now twelve years old was not oblivious to the toll these years had taken on her mother and perhaps that influenced her own reluctance to marry. Although she never spoke publicly about her formative childhood experiences, they appear as an undercurrent in her campaigns, particularly those associated with temperance and infant health.

Millicent may not have known her father died in Fremantle Hospital, Western Australia, on 24 September 1913. She was then thirty years of age and had not had any contact with him since he deserted the family. However, Millicent would not have been surprised to learn the cause of his death; 'Apolectic [*sic*] Fit – Alcoholism'. She was not aware of Augustine's disreputable life in the west. In 1906, for instance, he was found guilty of stealing from his Kalgoorlie landlady, fined and required to pay costs with one month's imprisonment in case of default.[14] Throughout her life, Millicent did not refer to her father in any of her papers or public speeches; the fiction of his death was her means of publicly expunging him from her life, her story, her identity.

Similarly, Millicent made no mention of how her mother coped after her divorce was granted in 1895. It could not have been easy for a working class woman left destitute with two children in the last decade of the nineteenth century. Nevertheless, Fanny ensured her family was not stranded in poverty. She succeeded, somehow, to move them from their various domiciles in the working class suburbs of Surry Hills and Redfern to a flat in the middle class suburb of Darling Point.

Victor was somehow able to attend St Mary's, an Anglican school in near-by Waverley. He became a non-commissioned officer in its cadet corps and excelled at debating. After school he qualified as an accountant and worked with the State Wheat Board. Both Victor and Millicent enrolled in a Diploma of Economics course at Sydney University in 1913 although only Victor graduated.[15] Like Millicent, he was involved in liberal politics and became a prominent member of the National Association Debating Club where he was hailed as 'one of the leading platform speakers' representing NSW against other states.[16] Victor, who had been marked out as a probable Nationalist candidate for the 1920 state election, died suddenly at his home in the Blue Mountains in 1919, a victim of the influenza pandemic.

Millicent does not appear to have attended school despite the *Public Instruction Act* 1880 mandating compulsory, secular and free education for children from six to fourteen years of age. Nevertheless, she became an outstanding autodidact. She had access to public libraries, attended Workers Educational Association (WEA) public lectures and at the age of thirteen joined the School of Arts Debating Society. This movement provided education for Protestant members of the working class through libraries which were stocked with books, journals and newspapers and public lectures, debating, and amateur theatricals. Millicent revelled in these and recalled hearing men such as George Reid, William Holman and Edmund Barton speak there.[17] It may have been here that she first encountered Billy Hughes, an active member of the Debating Society, who would become Prime Minister in 1915 and one of Millicent's supporters.

These early life experiences shaped the future direction of this young woman's career. Determined to overcome the social restrictions associated with her origins, she plotted a pathway out of the working class. An important step was adopting an aristocratic-sounding name. Millicent later claimed she assumed the double-barrelled surname, Preston Stanley when she was twelve years old, although the veracity of that claim is open to question. What is clear is that by 1904 her mother and her brother had also added Preston to their surname. References to all of them in newspapers and Sands directories from this date show the name was only sometimes hyphenated.[18]

Millicent's adoption of this surname worked to conceal the reality of her working class background and to cement the impression of her supposed patrician lineage. In a class-based patriarchal social order the name also helped to prise open doors for her political career that might otherwise have remained closed. As she stepped across those thresholds, she embroidered her public persona so that even those with whom she collaborated closely were oblivious to the discrepancies in her family story.

In her *Evening News* portrait, while Liddell had, perhaps unwittingly, colluded with Millicent in propagating her story, she had correctly pinpointed the most significant influence on Millicent's life – her mother, 'Fanny'. For Millicent, a mother's duty was not only 'to cure' her children's 'colds and rub away their pains' but also 'to sweep evil from [their] path'.[19] She idolised her mother's 'fire and force', resilience and strength; her determination to protect her 'cubs' made her a tiger.[20]

If Jane Austen had observed the 'vivid personality' of the 'pretty and attractive' young lady that Liddell described, she might have declared Millicent must be in want of a husband. But not Millicent! Despite the attempts of handsome suitors to woo her, wrote Liddell, she was intent on the 'serious side of life' and would work for 'those who cannot fight for themselves'.[21]

2
NEVER EQUALLED IN BRILLIANCE
(1902-1918)

Miss Preston Stanley addressed a large attendance at the Oddfellows' Hall last evening. She held the audience throughout by a speech which has never been equalled in brilliance by any woman speaker ...

Miss Preston Stanley Speaks at Orange[1]

Australia became a nation on 1 January 1901 after Queen Victoria gave royal assent to the legislation that allowed the six colonies to form the Commonwealth of Australia. For Millicent, the new nation born in the new century brought the promise of new beginnings. The following year the federal parliament, passed the *Commonwealth Franchise Act*, which permitted women over the age of twenty-one to vote and to stand for election to the federal parliament. By contrast, when the NSW parliament passed the *Women's Franchise Act* 1902, it allowed NSW women over the age of twenty-one to vote but not to stand for election to the state parliament.

As a nineteen year old Millicent did not qualify for the franchise but she was determined to educate herself for the day when she would be able to vote and perhaps participate in the legislative process. She found the perfect mentor in Hilma Molyneux Parkes, a former Vice President of the Womanhood Suffrage League. Hilma established the Women's Liberal League (WLL), a women-only organisation independent of any political party, to foster liberalism and Empire loyalty, improve women's social position and support candidates who were 'liberal and patriotic citizens of high principles and ability'.[2] Women 'who join men's organizations', Hilma warned, 'lose their identity, sacrifice their point of view and ... become the blind tools of Party'.[3]

An expert recruiter and campaigner, Hilma was adept at using the press, particularly letters to the editor, as a mouthpiece for WLL. Millicent, from her early years was an avid newspaper reader and it was possibly in the pages of the *Herald* that she first encountered Hilma and WLL. Perhaps she read one of Hilma's letters prior to the 1903 federal election in which Hilma urged women not to 'put little value on so great, so glorious a privilege as the right to choose your lawmakers'.[4] Or, she may have read 'The Women's Liberal League Manifesto' published in the *Herald* prior to the 1904 NSW State election. Women must not reject the responsibility of voting simply because they share it with men, Hilma cautioned, and they must use their vote wisely. To emphasise her point, she assured her readers, liberals were 'ready to pass legislation for the better protection of women and children'.[5] Her message was an ideal fit for Millicent's view of women and children.

Millicent commenced her political apprenticeship in WLL and so impressed members that they elected her as Relieving Officer in March 1905 and the following year, as Reading Secretary.[6] WLL provided Millicent with a comprehensive education in the significant and contested political issues of the era and honed her debating skills. In the immediate post-federation period a key political issue *du jour* was socialism. While liberals expressed concerns about its dangers, Labor Party members argued the case for socialising the means of production, distribution and exchange. Billy Hughes (who would desert the Labor Party in 1916, forever after labelled a 'Labor Rat') even went so far as to assert 'socialism is inevitable'.[7]

On the other hand, conservative newspapers carried cautions about the dangers of socialism, ministers of religion delivered sermons about the social breakdown it would cause, and non-Labor politicians likened it to anarchy. When the NSW Minister for Works, Charles Lee, a leading anti-socialist warrior, addressed a WLL meeting in March 1905, Millicent took his message to heart.[8]

Combatting socialism became a key plank in her liberal feminist mission for the rest of her life.

In 1909, WLL moved into new premises in the Equitable Life Assurance Company Building at 350 George Street, Sydney. This sandstone edifice built in 1895, with its marble foyer and ornate leadlight atrium, had previously housed the Women's Federation League and Maybanke Wolstenholme's journal, *Woman's Voice* was published there. In March that year Hilma, aged just fifty, suddenly died.[9] Although Millicent had lost her mentor a new opportunity opened up for her.

This building was home to the San Francisco-based Viavi Company, established in 1891 by former book publishers turned entrepreneurs, brothers Hartland and Herbert Law.[10] They took advantage of women's lack of gynaecological and obstetric knowledge to capture a niche market with their remedies for 'diseases of women', a euphemism for conditions associated with the female reproductive system. The business plan involved direct sales to women by female agents, who marketed Viavi products with catchy advertisements: 'WHAT YOU NEED MOST! To make life worth living, is a knowledge of VIAVI, an educational pointer to the Science of Right Living', which will 'help you be "Nature's Helper".'[11] Their propaganda offered a medical and moral solution to women's woes.

The promise of an income may have lured Millicent to this company along with the claims that Viavi products assisted women's health and well-being and improved the human race. At the age of twenty-six, Millicent was appointed NSW Manager and she traversed the state promoting the 'Viavi Way to Health'. Viavi treatments served humanity, she declared, and if we are to produce 'a sound race of men ... we must evolve a race of mothers'.[12] This position offered her opportunities to develop her campaigning and public speaking skills and become familiar with the state's country regions.

It is unclear when or why she departed the Viavi company. Perhaps she became dissatisfied with the remuneration or disgruntled with the frequent travel away from Sydney, or preoccupied with her other political activities. Or, she may have reached a similar conclusion to that of the Perth journalist who alleged the products prejudiced women against the medical profession.[13] By 1913, her name disappeared from Viavi advertisements.

During her time with Viavi, Millicent had maintained her membership of WLL and, despite Hilma's warning about women being stifled in political organisations dominated by men, she had also joined the Liberal Reform Association. She had so impressed members of this Association that in 1912 they elected her Vice President of the newly formed Paddington Branch and gave her responsibility for the 'work in the city and suburbs'.[14] The following year, she took on the task of establishing branches to teach girls about 'the value and the importance of their suffrage' and to spread the 'word of Liberalism',[15] and established the Young Liberal Clubs with recreation rooms, libraries, gymnasia, writing and reading rooms.[16] Then in 1913, acknowledged as the Association's most valuable woman speaker, she became a paid organiser.

Millicent's first task in that role was to harness women's votes to help defeat the incumbent Labor government in the 1913 NSW State election. Her knowledge of the state's regional areas and public speaking skills made her an ideal campaigner and she attracted laudatory press notices. At the south coast town of Dapto she was deemed to have a fine grasp of the situation, delivering her message forcefully and convincingly;[17] in Albury, on the Murray River, her performance was extolled as the best achieved by any woman speaker;[18] at Molong in the central west, she was judged an eloquent and interesting speaker;[19] and in the near-by town of Orange, she gave an address 'never ... equalled in brilliance by any woman speaker'.[20] The journalists were impressed but whether that translated into votes for liberal candidates is a moot point – the Labor Party retained government.

Like many other WLL women, Millicent looked forward to the day when women would not be simply relegated to these support roles, but able to stand for election to state parliament. In 1914, she participated in a mock election campaign arranged by the Liverpool branch of WLL. Three members deemed to be possible future 'candidates' took on candidate roles; Mrs Leatham, a WLL organiser, was a Labor candidate, Margaret Dalrymple-Hay, a Law School librarian at the University of Sydney, was a Liberal candidate and Millicent, the Liberal Reform Association organiser, was an Independent. After the candidates made their speeches, the members voted. Despite the high calibre of her opponents, Millicent easily 'topped the poll'.[21] Nevertheless, she probably did not entertain the thought of ever standing as an independent candidate as she recognised the power that political parties now wielded.

As a valued 'Liberal Lady organiser', Millicent's next task was to campaign for Liberal candidates in the double dissolution federal election scheduled for 5 September 1914. With not a little bravado, Liberal Prime Minister Joseph Cook persuaded the Governor General Sir Ronald Munro Ferguson to dissolve both Houses and call an election, the first double dissolution election in Australian history. Although she had ignored Hilma's advice about joining men's political parties, Millicent did draw on Hilma's techniques for encouraging women to exercise their franchise wisely. In all her campaign speeches, she appealed to women to shed their 'apathy' and place their votes for the Liberal candidates so as to ensure the incumbent Cook government was returned to office.[22]

Unexpectedly, one month before the election, the world pivotted on its axis. Initially, the war that broke out between Great Britain and Germany was background noise to the Australian election campaign, but by election eve it had shifted centre stage and the campaign changed its focus from local issues to imperial concerns. While Cook promised a Liberal government would commit Australian resources to the 'preservation and the security of the Empire'.²³ Labor leader Andrew Fisher, more eloquently vowed that if Labor was elected, 'we Australians will help and defend Britain to our last man and our last shilling'.²⁴ For Millicent, Fisher's imperialist promise, delivered with such conviction by the man who had twice previously held the position of Prime Minister, provided some compensation for the Liberal loss.

Many Australians believed, or at least hoped, the war would be over by Christmas. Perhaps Millicent thought so too. How else to explain her announcement that she would sail, alone, across the Pacific Ocean in February 1915 to visit the Panama-Pacific International Exposition in San Francisco? The Waverly Women's Branch of the Liberal Association so admired her adventurous spirit, in acknowledgement of her contributions to the Association, they staged a farewell function at the home of their President, Mrs Edmund Playfair, and presented her with a set of 'toilet-table silver' for her personal grooming during her trip.²⁵

It is difficult to determine what enticed Millicent to undertake this voyage. She later offered two different explanations, neither particularly convincing. One was that she sought to study the means by which Hetty Green became America's richest woman through her Stock Exchange investments.²⁶ Green, nicknamed the 'Witch of Wall Street', was an eighty-one year old eccentric woman, who wore only black and was then living in New York. Millicent's other equally unconvincing account was that she was interested in pursuing a career in real estate. How this trip could assist either of these goals is a mystery. She did not pursue a stock broking career upon her return although she did later become a Director in Reginald Weaver's Martin Place real estate agency.

Weaver was also a politician who became one of Millicent's avid supporters. He was known for his hostility to trade unions and fervent imperialism, and his sharp tongue and ironic verses. His real estate and political interests were lampooned in a satiric verse of unknown authorship.

> In real estate at Neutral Bay
> An agent is the warlike Weaver
> Who looks bright-eyed towards the day
> When, as the UAP retriever
> Of fallen fortunes, past defeat
> He'll get the House, Macquarie Street.
> Not three score years of wear and tear
> Have dulled his fighting tongue's sharp edge
> Except for his once rufus hair,
> All Red's anathema to Reg
> Whose Democratic dreams to yell
> 'Vacate this House' to Bill McKell.[27]

In San Francisco, Millicent visited the Panama-Pacific International Exposition which was promoted as a comprehensive and representative contemporary record of human progress in celebration of the completion of the Panama Canal and the restoration of the city after the 1906 earthquake. Perhaps this was the hook that snared Millicent. Or perhaps it was the platform given to the Board of Lady Managers to celebrate the 'New Woman' and discuss issues about women's rights. Unfortunately she left no diary account of her journey but her subsequent passions suggest the trip provided another pivotal moment in her political career.

One significant component of the Exposition was the Palace of Education and Social Economy, which featured eugenics displays by prominent members of the American Eugenics Movement. Francis Galton's *Science of Eugenics* 1883, which outlined a case for improving human evolution and the British race, spawned the global eugenics movement. Despite contestations as to its veracity and validity, eugenics was widely embraced for some decades, only suffering an ignominious demise post-World War II after the atrocities it permitted the Nazis to commit were revealed.[28]

Prior to her San Francisco trip Millicent may have encountered this 'science' in talks by the educationalist Meredith Atkinson at the Workers Education Association (WEA), or sex educator Marion Piddington's lectures at the Feminist Club, or during her time working for the Viavi Company. Regardless, upon her return from the USA, she certainly was convinced of the value of eugenics. She immediately set about proselytising the message in public speeches, press articles and in her 1917 booklet, *The Production of Human Degeneracy*.[29]

In this publication, she refers to the work of prominent eugenicists, and poses the key question, 'what are we doing to prevent the propagation of degenerate human stock?'. Her answer is unequivocal; nothing was being done other than measures which were exacerbating the problem. Millicent employs the now discarded term 'feebleminded' to describe supposed inherited mental and moral deficiencies. Like most eugenicists, she believed 'feeblemindedness' was hereditary and therefore incurable. Her solutions to the dangers posed to the human race from the inheritance of feeblemindedness included segregation, marriage restrictions and the prevention of propagation, although, unlike some eugenicists of the time, she did not advocate sterilization.

Despite her unashamedly didactic approach, a *Sunday Times* reviewer later described her booklet as an 'exhaustive study of the problem of human degeneracy'. The reviewer praised her solutions and their cost savings for the 'courts, gaols, reformatories, hospitals, asylums and children's relief departments' and lauded the 'colossal' social gains that would follow.[30] Although she would later step back from this 'science', Millicent's initial embrace of eugenics was influenced as much by these social and economic issues as by her personal concerns about the moral deficiency of alcoholism. Like her mother and Hilma, she was an avid temperance advocate and became an active member of the NSW Alliance for the Suppression of Intemperance.

The 1916 Black Monday riots confirmed Millicent's commitment to temperance and her belief in the need for prohibition – or at the very least for tighter restrictions on alcohol sales. On Monday 14 February soldiers from the Australian Imperial Forces camps in Casula and Liverpool were involved in a protest march in the city, which climaxed in fights and skirmishes at Central Station with one soldier shot and six wounded. Newspapers and temperance advocates blamed the behaviours on excessive alcohol consumption, prompting the State Government to hold a referendum on the issue.

The Liquor Referendum, later referred to as the Early Closing Referendum, was held on 10 June. It asked voters to nominate the hour between 6.00pm and 11.00pm they believed hotels should close. President of the Alliance for the Suppression of Intemperance, Archbishop Francis Boyce, whose son Francis became Attorney General in 1927, published a manifesto, that argued the real 'evils' associated with drinking occurred 'after 6 o'clock', and urged voters to use that time slot to lift the nation 'to a more honourable and truer position'.[31] The campaigning in this referendum divided voters; workers and the liquor industry generally supported 9.00pm closing while 'six oclockers', mainly women and temperance advocates supported 6.00pm closing.

Millicent, a committed six oclocker, was eager to cast her vote on 10 June. However, when she presented at a polling booth to do so, the presiding officer declared she was not eligible – her name was not on the electoral roll. She promptly obtained a copy of the supplementary list and pointed out her name to the officer. Furious at the dismissive treatment she received, she wrote an acerbic letter to the editor of the *Herald* alleging 'a large body of voters, who were entitled to an expression of their opinion' were probably disenfranchised by such inefficiency.[32]

The following day, a letter from the electoral office signed by G C Bluett pointed the finger at her; Millicent had failed to disclose her 'hyphenated' name, he alleged.[33] Refusing to be publicly denigrated, she penned a further letter to the editor asserting the officer's error had nothing to do with a hyphenated name but his failure to properly consult the supplementary list.[34] There was no further response in the press. Her contretemps reassured her that, as a woman, she could and must demand her voice be heard.

The referendum result affirmed six o'clock hotel closing. Millicent was delighted, despite its unforeseen outcome – the 'six o'clock swill', a last minute rush by men to consume multiple glasses of alcohol before the barmaid called 'Time Gentlemen Please'.

Millicent now turned her attention to making a contribution to the war effort. With reports of growing casualty numbers in the war, fewer men were volunteering for service. Australian women were not permitted to fight on the war front although that did not prevent the eighteen-year-old Maud Butler from disguising herself as a soldier and twice stowing away on a troop ship bound for Egypt. She was arrested, charged and found guilty of wrongfully wearing military uniform. Maud then resigned herself to working on the home front, collecting money for the Returned Soldiers Association, although even there she found herself on the wrong side of the law when she wore an AIF uniform while soliciting funds.[35]

While Millicent might have admired Maud's spirit of adventure, she used her skills to assist organisations raising money for the war effort. She campaigned for the Sandbag Fund, which sent sandbags to the soldiers in the trenches on the Western Front. Sandbags provided cover from harsh weather, soaked up water on the trench floor, concealed soldiers from the enemy and protected them against rifle fire. She also campaigned for the Edith Cavell Memorial Fund, which aimed to provide a Home for War Nurses returning from the front lines. Edith Cavell, a British nurse had treated the wounds of both German and allied soldiers, before being executed by the Germans. Millicent appealed to women to follow Edith's example and 'make some sacrifice' of their own to help the nurses, who had also made sacrifices for the soldiers.[36]

Like many Australians, Millicent watched with concern as the situation on the front deteriorated. When Britain requested Australia send troop reinforcements of 5500 men each month to maintain operational levels, there was no question in her mind about how Australian men should respond. But, with recruiting down to 'zero',[37] Billy Hughes, who became Prime Minister after Andrew Fisher resigned in 1915, introduced a referendum seeking voters' approval to require men currently undergoing compulsory training to serve overseas. Pacifist organisations such as the Women's Peace Army, the Women's International League for Peace and Freedom and the Anti-Conscription League vigorously prosecuted the 'NO' case. Millicent did not hesitate to campaign for the 'YES' case, proclaiming men who went to fight were valiant patriots and women did not want to be the wives of men who 'failed the great test of manhood and patriotism', nor did they want to be the mothers of these men's children.[38] Despite the YES campaign's ardour, the referendum was defeated.

To Millicent's chagrin, this also proved to be the fate of a second referendum the following year. As unsustainable losses of men placed the Empire under threat, Britain requested Australia send a sixth Australian division to sustain imperial forces. Hughes proposed another referendum for 20 December 1917, this time seeking to recruit reinforcements of single men, widowers, and divorcees without dependents between 20 and 44 years of age for compulsory overseas service. In advocating the 'YES' vote, Millicent declared this was 'the greatest test that has ever been applied to the womanhood of any land'.[39] She exhorted women to prove 'that national pride and patriotism were no less the attributes of loyal women than they were of brave men' and, she warned that unless Britain won the war, the 'days of Australian democracy as a democracy are numbered'.[40] To make her message even more potent, she turned her campaigns into theatrical events and included patriotic songs such as *Land of Hope and Glory*.[41]

Millicent had cemented her reputation as a formidable speaker and her expertise was now in demand not only to support recruitment campaigns but also to raise funds for war bond initiatives. At a Win the War League meeting at the Mosman Town Hall,[42] speaking alongside returned soldiers Sergeants Sanders and Brown, she implored men to enlist for war service, and at the launch of the War Savings Certificates campaign, where she was the only woman speaker alongside several male politicians including Prime Minister Billy Hughes,[43] she emphasised the War Savings Certificates allowed everyone to assist in maintaining the Australian Army. Unwisely, she then went on to criticise extravagantly dressed women suggesting they should be 'made to feel uncomfortable', and even more provocatively declared a woman who paid 780 guineas for a fur coat was a 'criminal'.[44]

Understandably, Millicent's comments attracted public censure. Writing under the pseudonym, 'Senga', a journalist pointed out men's suits cost as much as women's fur coats,[45] and another unnamed journalist called her hypocritical because she spent money on her own wardrobe and then told young men to 'go to the war'.[46] Millicent prided herself on dressing well but she had neither the inclination nor the funds for extravagances such as fur coats. Her point was that women should make some sacrifices to support the men in the trenches.

In August 1917 when local food and fuel supplies and the transportation of cargo to the soldiers on the front were disrupted by a 'general' strike, Millicent, along with other women, was ready for action. The strike began in two Sydney railway yards after the introduction of the Taylor-inspired time-card system that required workers to clock on and off. Because this system enabled employers to measure individual output, the unions feared it would be used to sack workers. The strike spread swiftly from the railway yards to mining, transport and shipping with nigh on 100,000 workers walking off jobs across the eastern states. To alleviate the situation the NSW government called for volunteer male workers to register with a newly established National Service Bureau, located at 35

O'Connell Street Sydney.[47] Despite attracting the ire of the unions that labelled the volunteers scabs and blacklegs, men and boys willingly signed up to replace the striking unionists.

Inspired by their loyalty, Millicent collaborated with a group of influential and well-connected women, including Mrs Antill, Mrs Macarthur-Onslow, Miss Macarthur-Onslow and Dr Mary Booth[48] to persuade the government to allow them to establish a similar organisation for women – the Women's Loyal Service Bureau (WLSB). The Bureau took up residence in the Assembly Hall of the recently-completed Education Department Building in Bridge Street, adjacent to the O'Connell Street National Service Bureau. On 23 August 1917, newspapers announced the opening of the WLSB and invited women who could assist with jobs the strikers had vacated to apply in writing or in person to the secretary.[49] According to press reports, over 400 women signed up the first day; at the end of the first week there were 2000; and by the end of the second week 4000 women registered.[50] The Directors were delighted at the response of these women who were prepared to work for the welfare of 'our boys' in the trenches; like the men, they answered the call to serve God, King and Country.

The Bureau provided a pool of women workers for government instrumentalities and private employers. Newspapers reported a dozen women workers, including some 'society girls' were despatched to pack flour and jellies for one firm.[51] Other women worked as packers in meat works and grocery factories, and an interstate shipping company utilised fifty women as cooks, stewards and bakers. Apart from private employers, the Department of Labour and Industry engaged some as waitresses in the Central Railway Refreshment Rooms and others as cooks and waitresses on four of its steamers.[52] It is unclear how many women in total were employed, but it is evident that those who were, tended to be used only in those jobs normally reserved for women. The Directors were disappointed at the reluctance to place women in traditional male positions of motor mechanics, lorry drivers and tram fare collectors, despite many women wanting to take on these tasks.

The Government paid lip-service to the WLSB, but was sceptical about its worth beyond its propaganda value. George Beeby, nicknamed 'bumptious Beeby'[53], the Minister for Labour and Industry viewed the Bureau as a precautionary measure 'in the event of it being wanted'.[54] In the face of his response, the Directors published a manifesto declaring the one impulse that should unite all Australians at this 'supreme moment in our national history' was the need for national efficiency. Their manifesto criticised the 'disruption, mutiny, stagnation, [and] paralysis' which was preventing the democratically elected government from assisting the Allies and praised the 'magnificent expression of the loyal womanhood of the state'. It proposed the WLSB should work permanently with the Department of Labour and Industry in organising all female labour in the state.[55]

Needless to say, Beeby was not amenable to this proposition and he wound up the Bureau on 19 October 1917. At this last meeting with the Bureau directors, he thanked the women, dismissively noting 'members of the different volunteer camps are under a deep obligation for the services rendered, which resulted in making their conditions much more comfortable'.[56] Millicent was not alone in her displeasure at this rebuff of the women's patriotism – they had not set out to make conditions 'more comfortable' for the men in the camps but to make a contribution to the war effort.

On 11 November 1918, after Germany and the Allies signed the Armistice, the canons fell silent and a great peace settled over Europe. H G Wells' 'war to end all wars' came to an end. When the news arrived in Australia late in the evening, crowds pouring into Sydney's Martin Place as harbour ferries tooted their horns and cathedral bells pealed.

Two weeks later, the NSW parliament passed the *Women's Legal Status Act*. The lawyer Herbert Vere Evatt, who would also enter parliament in 1925, commented it was the 'main achievement' of a particularly fractious parliamentary session.[57] Millicent, along with many other women such as Annie Golding, Rose Scott and Kate Dwyer, who had been advocating for this legislation for years, was gratified that at last the more conservative members of the 'legislating brotherhood'[58] had not prevailed.

Despite the persistence of 'entrenched prejudices at the grass roots level',[59] the *Women's Legal Status Act* 1918 marked the beginning of a new era for NSW women. Attorney General David Hall claimed the Act was a tribute to the pre-eminent part women had played in the war effort and it would unlock those doors that had previously been bolted against them. That was only partially true; the Act did not permit women to be appointed to the Legislative Council or to sit on juries. However, women now did have the right to practise law, serve on municipal councils, and become justices of the peace.

Millicent was probably disappointed that Ada Evans, the first woman to graduate in law in 1902 was admitted to the bar in 1921, but declined to practise, 'deterred by the lapse of time since her graduation, indifferent health and compelling family commitments'.[60] However, in 1924 Sibyl Morrison became the first practising female barrister and Marie Byles the first practising female solicitor. It took until 1928 before a woman, Lilian Fowler, was elected to a Municipal Council but in 1937, Lilian was elected as the State's first female Mayor of Newtown Municipal Council. And, in 1921 Millicent, along with 60 other women celebrated their appointment as Justices of the Peace.

Although the Act did not permit women to be appointed as members of the Legislative Council, it did enable them to stand for election to the Legislative Assembly. With that door prised open at last, it only remained for a woman to step across the threshold. As Millicent reflected on her political apprenticeship did she consider herself ready to take that step?

3

POLITICAL WOMAN OF THE FUTURE
(1919-1924)

If Miss Preston Stanley is a fair sample of the political woman of the future then the present generation of male politicians will have to retire to the obscurity which befits them ... .

Morning Bulletin, 6 October 1919[1]

Towards the end of May 1919, a Melbourne gossip columnist, writing under the pseudonym 'Nimitybelle', announced that Millicent Preston Stanley was about to sail for Townsville to campaign for the Nationalist Party. The Northern National Political Union of Queensland had engaged Millicent to campaign in the referendum that Prime Minister Billy Hughes had scheduled in conjunction with the December federal election. The journalist opined that her 'knowledge and sound judgement' and her 'rare gift of holding an audience with a voice of magnetic sweetness' would be a 'tower of strength' for the party.[2] A few days later, 'The Nomad' – penname of a Brisbane journalist – reported the six months campaign of this 'fine capable speaker' was to begin in Townsville.[3]

Hughes was dubbed the 'Little Digger' for his leadership of the nation during the war, visiting Australian troops in hospitals in England and in the trenches in France. He returned from the Paris Peace Conference where he had demanded Australia be 'granted the status of a nation,'[4] and hoping to capitalise on his war time popularity, called an early election. He combined the election with a referendum designed to give him the authority to deal with profiteering, high prices and industrial unrest by extending government war powers over trade, commerce and monopolies.

Millicent's task was to campaign for the re-election of the Hughes government and the 'YES' vote.

It was no mean feat for a young single woman to venture into union-dominated Queensland towns such as Mackay, the 'Sugar Capital' of the north, and Mareeba the cattle and tobacco growing centre, to spruik the Nationalist anti-union agenda. However, the Party thought she was up to the task, and she was determined to demonstrate that she was.

By deliberately limiting your productive output with your 'ca'canny' or 'go-slow', she told the men at one Townsville rally, you hurt yourself and your families because you all end up paying higher prices for everything. This was not what the striking men wanted to hear and they were only too ready to challenge her statements. But she was well prepared to counter attack. 'This gentleman on my left', she pointed to one persistently noisy interjector, 'appears to have political wasps in his hat'.[5] The audience laughed, the gentleman scowled and the local reporters praised her capacity to 'speak better than any of the men'.[6]

Such retorts infuriated One Big Union (OBU) supporters. The OBU, promoted by Industrial Workers of the World (IWW), aimed to combine all unions into one global organisation to campaign for fewer working hours, better working conditions and higher wages. Millicent condemned the OBU for instigating the Brisbane Red Flag riots in May 1919, which had erupted between socialists and ex-servicemen, and when she denigrated the socialists charged with infringing the *War Precautions Act* for carrying the Red Flag, OBU member Edward Thomson challenged her to put her 'antagonistic views' to his members face to face.[7] Millicent did not respond to his letter, but the Nationalist Secretary, H G Bradley replied that her tight schedule prevented her from accepting his invitation. However, OBU members would be most welcome to attend Millicent's Townsville meeting.[8] Whether any did so is unknown.

Notwithstanding such hostile receptions, the local press lauded her performances. The *Northern Miner* reported that in Charters

Towers she commanded the 'silent attention' of a 'big attendance' for three hours, with 'interjection being conspicuous by its almost entire absence'. The absence of interjection may have been occasioned by Millicent's opening warning; she had 'no objection to reasonable interjection' but if they turned her meeting into a 'bear garden' she would call on the police to protect those who had come to hear her.[9] Bear garden was an apt description of some of her meetings. In Cairns, when a unionist, John Cunningham leaped on to the platform to harangue her, Senior Constable Murphy arrested him. The following month at another Cairns meeting, another unionist, Snowy Williams acted in a 'disorderly manner', was arrested, charged and, when he did not appear in court, his case was heard *ex parte* and he was found guilty.[10]

Fortunately, there were rewarding moments for the young campaigner. Part of her role was to persuade women to participate in the liberal cause. At a meeting in the gold mining town of Charters Towers, she painted a vivid picture of the war-time jobs English women undertook in industry and munitions factories, managing hydraulic presses and driving overhead cranes. Now that the war was over, those same women were redirecting their 'splendid energies' to the peace process.

Australian women were just as capable as English women of making contributions to the nation, she assured them. The old-fashioned ideas that were once trotted out, *ad infinitum*, about women's natural function being marriage and motherhood were passé, but, she went on, in order to move beyond them women needed access to education, training, motherhood endowment and equal pay and this would never come under a Labor government. Her speech struck a chord with her audience who promptly formed a women's branch of the Northern National Political Union.[11]

Although Queensland voted 'Yes' in the referendum the vote was not carried nationally. However, the Nationalist Party was re-elected with Billy Hughes returned as Prime Minister. Millicent had not contemplated seeking election to federal parliament since the issues that most concerned her were state matters. Perhaps, as she sailed for Sydney in December 1919, having demonstrated her political campaigning skills, she may have envisaged herself as a candidate in the NSW State election scheduled for early 1920.

If she was intending to offer herself as a candidate, she would have considerable support. In early 1920, Miss Jessie Macdonald, the Principal of Morven Garden School, a coeducational boarding school run by the Theosophical Society, presented Millicent with a petition requesting she accept nomination as a candidate. In a 'vigorous speech', Jessie urged Millicent to comply with the request of the 'several thousand men and women electors' who had signed the petition. Millicent acknowledged she had a 'very keen interest' in the possibility of becoming a candidate but she could not acquiesce at this time because of 'urgent personal reasons'.[12] She did not elaborate on those reasons; perhaps they were connected with her brother's death during the influenza epidemic, while she was away in Queensland.

Four women nominated as candidates for the 1920 election, the first time women could do so after the passing of the Women's Legal Status Act, 1918. The independent feminist Dr Mary Booth had collaborated with Millicent in the Women's Loyal Service Bureau and the Soldiers and Citizens Party candidate, Grace Scobie OBE worked with her in the Win the War League. There were two Socialist Party candidates, Daisy Loughran and Annie Toohey.

In reporting on the election campaign, journalists tended to gloss over the political party connections of the women candidates. Some applauded them while others warned they would split the vote because women would vote for women regardless of their political affiliations. Unlike Millicent, Rose Scott, who thought women should not be aligned with any political party, certainly hoped all women would vote only for women candidates. But that was not to be; none of the women was elected.

If Millicent had regrets at not standing for parliament at that election, she was not going to wallow in them. Instead she turned her attention to her other roles, particularly her presidency of the Feminist Club of NSW. The Club had been established in 1914 by Mrs Baker-Young to provide a place for women to discuss political, social and economic issues. By 1920 membership was waning, so Millicent set about expanding the lecture program, including topics such as 'Dreams and Psychoanalysis', 'Women as Freemasons', and 'The History of the Child'. She engaged notable lecturers such as Clara Neale OBE, an officer with Queen Mary's Army, Madame Soubeiran, founder of Alliance Française and H V Evatt, a prominent lawyer who spoke about women's legal status. She also invited renowned singers such as Dame Clara Butt DBE and Dame Nellie Melba GBE to present recitals.[13] Under her presidency membership of the Club increased; 'nearly every woman of note in the literary, artistic, and political world', exclaimed one journalist, became a member.[14]

With Club secretaries, Mary Liddell and Ruby Rich, Millicent (who now identified herself as O M Preston Stanley), revamped the Club's logo, motto and charter. They produced a pamphlet outlining the Club's *raison d'être* which featured the newly designed logo – the toga-clad Roman goddess of Justice, bearing the justice scales minus sword and, like the statue atop London's Old Bailey, without blindfold. This image was set against the rays of a rising sun encircled by the motto, 'Equality, Fraternity, Humanity, Service'.

The Foreword amplified the 'Fraternity' message of 'Brotherhood' – word choices that pre-date awareness of sexist language, but which also signalled that any man who was committed to securing 'equality of liberties, status and opportunities in all spheres between men and women' would be welcomed as a Club member.[15] While this might have surprised some feminists, Millicent would later say that sometimes a man can be a better feminist than a woman.[16] The lofty ideals of the manifesto situated the Club as a non-discriminatory, political organisation with both a local and transnational focus. The Club would work for 'the improvement in conditions of women and children', 'the representation of women in Parliament' and the collaboration of women's organisations. Millicent envisaged the Club as a political organisation lobbying governments to implement the reforms needed to improve the lives of women and children.

Millicent's long-standing concern with the feebleminded featured prominently in the new Charter so it is not surprising she organised a deputation to lobby for amendment to the *Lunacy Act, 1898*. Reginald Weaver introduced the deputation to John McGirr, Minister for Health and Motherhood, who informed the women a committee of specialist practitioners was currently working on a draft bill. Millicent already knew this since her colleague Dr Mary Booth was a member of that committee. At Weaver's suggestion McGirr invited Millicent to join the committee, an appointment that allowed her to claim she was an authority on the feebleminded.[17]

As well as deputations to government, Millicent broadened the Club's Working Platform to include community based programs that supported women and children. The Home Companion Scheme was designed to improve the 'Status of Domestic Service' by supporting the migration to Australia of educated English women for employment in rural towns.[18] In 1922 Millicent engaged the club in salvaging the Little Citizen's Kindergarten.[19] She supervised the Kindergarten's move to new premises in Surry Hills and established a fund to raise £300 per year to maintain it.[20] These initiatives, according to one enthusiastic journalist, put the Feminist Club 'well ahead of anything along the same lines in Australia'.[21] Her vision not only enhanced the Club's status but also expanded her political networks and cemented her political ambitions.

During the early 1920s Millicent expended her energy in many organisations. Perhaps the most vital one for her was recruiting new members, particularly new women members, to the Nationalist Party. Before long she had established several new Party branches in the Eastern Suburbs electorate. Her success in attracting members convinced some in the Party that she should be preselected as a candidate for the Eastern Suburbs electorate for the March 1922 state election.

However, as she discovered, Party endorsements were complicated by faction-fighting in the newly-established coalition of the Nationalist and Progressive Parties.[22] The Nationalist Party, perhaps unsurprisingly, endorsed four men as their candidates – Harold Jaques, Charles Oakes, Hyman Goldstein and William Foster – and the Progressive Party endorsed the sitting member James MacArthur-Onslow to its one allotted slot. Millicent missed out on pre-selection.

The opportunity to add her name arose when MacArthur-Onslow was appointed to the Legislative Council, thereby creating a vacancy on the Coalition ticket.[23] Millicent entered the electoral fray as the fifth endorsed candidate for the Eastern Suburbs electorate and her colleague, Ruby Rich became her campaign secretary.

If Millicent expected general approval from Party members and the wider community she was disappointed. One journalist criticised her as an intruder into the male realm, suggesting she was butting into the limelight reserved for men because she selfishly wanted to share in 'the loaves and fishes'.[24] Missing the moral of that parable about sharing, this journalist's criticism reflected the view that women had no right to the same privileges as men.

Opposition to her candidature in some Party ranks was bitter. Captain Marks, who had unsuccessfully sought pre-selection, was a vocal opponent. Her candidature was an affront to all women, he declared, since 'women's ennobling sphere is encompassed by the four walls of her home'. Millicent believed women's ennobling capacity could be just as well employed within the four walls of the House as in her home. As she pointed out in a letter to the editor, unless women could leave those four walls they could not attend a polling booth to vote.[25]

Marks was not the only one to voice his disapproval of Millicent's candidature. Vice-President of the Waverly branch of the Party, George Overhill, was outraged at what he considered Millicent's creation of 'mushroom branches' in the electorate to prop up her candidature. The term, mushroom branches, which connotes shady deals to recruit members to unfairly advantage a candidate, has since been replaced by the term, branch stacking. Millicent did not have the financial means for branch stacking even if her moral code permitted it. Florence Gordon from the North Randwick Branch, publicly countered Overhill's criticism, claiming Millicent's name had not been the only enticement for everyone to join the new branches; some had joined the Party to support other candidates.[26]

There were also those on the other side of the political divide who were critical of her campaign. Mr Nyland, a lawyer with Labor sympathies challenged the veracity of her statements about the OBU, AWU and the Labor government. Always ready to carry out her verbal assaults in public, Millicent counter-challenged Nyland to meet her in her electorate so that she could demonstrate the truth of her statements.[27] Her battle-axe reputation – a strong, opinionated woman with well-developed rebuttal skills, and moreover a woman who would not crumble under attack – apparently deterred him from doing so.

Strategically, Millicent declared she was not standing for election exclusively as a women's candidate representing only women's issues. But, she asserted, she would bring perspectives other than those of the businessman to the legislative process. Although some journalists lauded her as the 'best platform candidate' who enunciated her policies, others either accused her of seeking to only represent women's issues or merely seeking 'a man's job and honors [sic] at a man's pay'.[28] This misperception would follow her throughout her career.

There was only one other woman candidate in the 1922 State election. Mrs Clare Meta Wilson, an Independent Progressive candidate standing in the Western Suburbs electorate, was described as a picturesque lady but disparaged as the 'silent woman candidate' who let others speak for her. However, she did stage one gutsy photo-op, entering the lion's cage at Wirth's Circus clad in sea-green satin, covered with shimmering beads.[29] In one version of the story, Clare stroked the mane of the most savage lion[30] and in another version, the four 'slightly bored' lions 'wondered why such an attractive morsel' had been tossed into their cage when it wasn't 'meal time'.[31] If this spectacle was designed to suggest she was capable of surviving the Bear Pit, it was unsuccessful. She only received a small number of votes.

On the other hand, there was a sense of optimism that Millicent would become the state's first female MP at this election. Some journalists confidently touted her as a probable new member and *The Sun* featured photos of five possible new members, with Millicent, the only woman, prominently placed under the headline, 'New Faces in Parliament – Certainties and Perhapses'.[32] Despite gaining nearly four thousand first preference votes, Millicent did not become one of the 'Certainties'. Opinion was divided between those who saw her defeat as appropriate because she wanted 'to push her political barrow',[33] and others who considered she should have won the seat since she was the best candidate.[34]

The Sun's female journalist, writing under the pseudonym Fanella assessed the implication for Millicent's future election:

> Her great fight at the last election ... will not be forgotten soon. In the words of her political opponents and those prejudiced against her on the general grounds that 'we don't want women in politics' – it was a magnificent fight. But her victory belongs to a future election: the riper time when she will have profited by the mistakes made while still earning a sufficiently substantial number of votes to put her name in the second selection.[35]

Fanella did not elaborate on whether the mistakes were made by Millicent, her campaign team or the electors, but her future success was inevitable, she declared, because of her sound arguments for better health measures, an end to child labour, equality for the sexes and reforms of the laws that visit injustice upon women. Her stance in promoting 'better birth, better parents, better education, and better social conditions' was sensible since, 'In the Australian cradle lies our greatest wealth, security, and glory as a Commonwealth'.[36] No doubt Millicent was disappointed with the result, as were her supporters, although their disappointment was somewhat ameliorated by the defeat of Labor and the return of the Nationalist government.

One setback did not diminish Millicent's determination to play a role in improving the lives of women and children. The next three years became a time of almost frenzied activity in multiple organisations. In addition to her presidency of the Feminist Club, she took on the presidency of the Business Women's Prohibition League and paid organiser for the NSW Temperance Alliance. When the American Prohibitionist W E 'Pussyfoot' Johnson visited Australia bringing his 'Special Message from American Women', Millicent appeared as a speaker alongside him to support the Temperance cause.[37] Prohibition was an unlikely eventuality but Millicent remained optimistic that one day such a measure might be introduced to curb the evils of drink and its disastrous effects on women and children.

Millicent used her status as one of the first women gazetted as a Justice of the Peace, to further advance these reform agendas. In 1922, she invited Western Australian feminist Bessie Rischbieth to speak about her work with Western Australian women justices at a meeting of NSW women justices. They were so impressed they formed the NSW Women Justices Association with Millicent duly elected Vice-President and in 1923, President.

Under her leadership, the Association lobbied government to extend women's participation in the justice system – particularly in jury service. It was a gross injustice, Millicent proclaimed, that a woman could be arrested by a male policeman, prosecuted by a male attorney, found guilty by a jury of men, sentenced by a male judge and imprisoned by male gaolers. She organised another deputation to the Minister of Justice Thomas Ley, and argued he should amend the legislation to allow women to serve on juries as this would alleviate some of this blatant discrimination. Ley, however, pointed out a serious problem with this proposition; women could not serve on juries because they could not be locked up overnight like male jurors, since they had to go home and 'cook dinner for their husbands'.[38] Ley further pointed out that allowing women to serve on juries would require legislation, although he gave no indication he intended to introduce it.

Since NSW women had yet to cross the threshold into the legislature, their sole means of making their voices heard was through their organisations. As Millicent appreciated, women's voices were more powerful when they collaborated. Her executive positions in several organisations facilitated such collaboration. Millicent organised a meeting of women's organisations to mount a campaign aimed at reducing high rates of infant and maternal mortality. The campaign sought the establishment of a Chair of Midwifery at Sydney University, specialised midwifery hospitals in regional areas, better midwifery training for medical students and nurses, and the removal of entry fees for midwifery training.[39]

When their demand for a Midwifery Chair was rejected by the University and a Veterinary Chair established instead, Millicent rebranded the campaign, 'Horses Rights for Women', borrowing the slogan from the American judge, Ben Lindsey who had used it to support women's claims for the same welfare rights as horses.[40] She then mustered a multi-organisation deputation to put their demands to the Minister for State, Charles Oakes, one of the Nationalists who had opposed her 1922 candidature.[41] This provided her with one of her more successful campaign tales, which she delighted in retelling on numerous occasions.

Amidst Millicent's successes there were, of course, personal disappointments and political failures. Millicent had positioned the Feminist Club in a transnational context, even including the goal that 'women be represented on all bodies set up in connection with the League of Nations'. She perhaps entertained the possibility of being included on one of those international bodies and she was pleased when the Feminist Club and the Women Justices Association nominated her as the National Council of Women (NCW) representative at the League. However, Prime Minister Stanley Melbourne Bruce selected historian Jessie Webb, as Australia's 1922 representative ahead of Millicent and Margaret Dale. Nevertheless, Millicent, not one to let personal disappointment overshadow the occasion, fêted Jessie at the Feminist Club upon her return from Geneva.[42]

One of Millicent's political failures that did disturb her was the campaign to amend the Crimes bill. Millicent headed another deputation to Attorney General Thomas Bavin, the man who would become leader of the Nationalist Party in 1925. The deputation sought the removal of clauses in the bill that would adversely affect women – photographing, body searching, and invasive medical examinations. The deputation also argued for the reinstatement of capital punishment for the offense of rape of a girl of ten years of age. On this issue Bavin replied, politely but firmly, that he did not want youths led astray by the 'wantonness' of loose girls with no moral sense to hang for rape.[43] Once again, the women found themselves confronted by the apparently benign but malignant face of patriarchal misogyny.

Nowhere, Millicent believed, was the face of patriarchy more damaging to women and children than in child custody cases. Despite minor amendments made to guardianship legislation in 1899 and 1916 as a result of lobbying by Maybanke Wolstenholme and Rose Scott, the ancient common law father-right principle that vested child custody in the father remained. A mother could be granted custody of her children only in cases where the father had forfeited his 'natural' right through proved misconduct that rendered him unfit for 'paternal control'.[44]

Millicent, who knew her mother gained custody because her father had forfeited his natural right, ensured the Feminist Club Charter included concise statements about equal custody; the mother should have the same 'rights' as the father over children 'born in wedlock' and the father should have the same 'responsibility' as the mother for children 'born out of wedlock'. While the term 'wedlock' is now obsolete, the intention of these clauses was to ensure that married women had equal rights in their children and that the fathers of unmarried women's children should take equal responsibility for the offspring they sired. Much to Millicent's chagrin, these were not values shared by all men at the time, as the Ellis case (commonly referred to as the Polini case) would demonstrate.

When Justice John Musgrave Harvey handed down his judgement in the *Ellis v Ellis* custody case in April 1924, Millicent, like many other women, was incensed. The mother, English actress Emélie Ellis (née Polini), had sought custody of her two year-old daughter Patricia. Justice Harvey heard the Supreme Court case in camera, thereby excluding the public and the press from hearing the evidence. On 10 April he handed down his judgement in open court. He refused the mother's application and awarded the father custody of the child.[45] From Millicent's perspective, Harvey's judgement represented an intolerable injustice inflicted by the patriarchal system on this mother and by implication on all mothers.[46]

Emélie's successful Australian stage career amplified the poignancy of her story. She had met and married Harold in a whirlwind ship-board romance, had supported him from her stage earnings in the first years of their marriage, and had contributed to the purchase of his property in Hartley Vale. When the property failed just before Patricia's birth, they reached a two year separation agreement. Emélie would return to the stage, support Patricia and a nurse to reside with Harold's parents and he would go to Queensland to acquire jackerooing skills. After the two years' separation they would resume the marriage. Emélie kept her side of the agreement but Harold did not. With no income other than his meagre allowance as a returned soldier he moved in with his parents.

In late 1923 Emélie asked Harold to send Patricia and the nurse to live with her during her two month Melbourne season, but he refused and dismissed the nurse. It was a wronged-woman story worthy of the stage, made more bitter by Harvey's justification for his judgement.

In refusing Emélie custody of her daughter, Harvey said she had 'mixed motives' in leaving her husband 'to shift for himself', had 'never allowed her maternal affection to interfere with the calls of her profession', could not tolerate a 'life of domestic drudgery and poverty', nor reconcile herself to a 'humdrum life with a husband who had not come up to her hopes and expectations'. On the other hand, he excused Harold's 'muddling incapacity', his 'want of candour' and the 'hopeless muddle' of his financial situation that had led to their property being resumed by the mortgagee.

Emélie responded in a public statement affirming she would 'endure with some measure of fortitude the blow which it has fallen to my lot to receive', but urging women to ensure NSW laws were 'so altered that no other mother receives treatment as cruel as that which has been meted out to me'.[47] She followed this by meeting with Premier Sir George Fuller,[48] and in a follow-up letter to him reiterated the need to amend the Act that 'robbed' mothers of their babies.[49] At the end of April she left Australia, never to see her daughter again.

Millicent was infuriated that NSW law, unlike English law, did not require the court to take the mother's wishes – only her 'conduct' – into consideration. That the male-only court determined what was in the child's best interests without any reference to the mother, was intolerable. In the absence of any guidelines in the Act, Harvey's determination of Patricia's best interests rested on his personal belief in a 'settled' home and the inability of an actress-mother to supply it because she needed to travel for work. This judgement transgressed the 'sacred bond' between mothers and their children.

Under Millicent's direction, the Feminist Club leapt into action, drawing up a petition demanding a woman 'should be regarded as the natural guardian of a child of tender years, providing there was nothing against her character; and that it should not be considered sufficient justification should she have to go abroad to earn a living, to remove from her the custody of the child'.[50]

Within three weeks, Millicent led a deputation to Minister Ley and presented their petition with its 20,000 signatures. Once again, Millicent experienced Ley's intransigence as he responded that it was 'not the practice in English-speaking countries to bring in legislation especially for the purpose of upsetting a decision of a Judge'.[51] For Millicent this was red rag to a bull. She would not let this matter rest until the legislation was amended – however long that took.

It was not only Millicent who was incensed by the injustice of this case. Dr Robert Stopford, the Nationalist Party Member for Balmain (1922-1925), a general practitioner, known as the 'children's friend', who ran free clinics for slum children, declared the case a 'disgraceful incident'. In his view, 'a woman in such circumstances has a right to her child' and the legislation must be amended so that mothers could 'feel that they are human beings, and not creatures of laws made by men who sometimes don't know how to make them'.[52] Stopford was a lone male voice crying in the parliamentary wilderness – and regrettably, one that was lost to the parliament when Evatt defeated him at the 1925 election.

Child custody became one of the defining features of Millicent's political career. It was not merely a *cause célèbre* but pivotal to her conception of motherhood; mothers had an indissoluble bond with their children, a bond that fathers did not, and could not, have. That any man-made law allowed this bond to be severed was insufferable. This man-made law must be changed – but for that change to occur, a woman must be seated on those sacrosanct seats of the lords of creation.

4

ADVENT OF A WOMAN
(1924-1925)

For the first time in our history members of the Legislative Assembly were not all men. At long last a woman had penetrated to the precincts of a chamber hitherto sacred to the misnamed lords of creation.

Sydney Morning Herald, 27 June 1925[1]

In September 1924, a *Sun* journalist bemoaned, 'With one exception, the efforts of women to enter Parliament in Australia constitute a chapter of failures.' That one exception, Edith Cowan, had just lost her seat in the West Australian state elections. However, the fault for this chapter of failures, wrote the journalist, did not lie with women but with men; even when women put themselves forward as candidates, 'preference is shown to the men'.[2]

Not everyone shared this view. Carlotta Smith, an Adelaide journalist was upbeat at the 'number of women in the field of prospective candidates' for the next NSW election. This, she wrote, would 'add a great deal of mettle to the campaign for a woman in Parliament'.[3] Harrie Nowland, a Queensland journalist who was keen to see the end of 'teacup politics' singled out one candidate for special mention, the 'well-known propagandist' Millicent Preston Stanley. However, she sounded a note of caution; some of Millicent's ideals were not yet included in her Party's platform – an insightful comment on Millicent's position in the party. Nevertheless, Nowland expressed confidence that Millicent would bring 'intelligent feminine influence from within'.[4]

As Nationalist Party members jostled for pre-selection the hype surrounding this candidate predicted she would gain her Party's nomination. A Labor newspaper even acknowledged the Party would select her because she was one of the most outstanding 'lady platform speakers in Australia'. However, it also added, she 'prattles too much'.[5] After her experience with the Party's pre-selection process for the 1922 election, Millicent may not have been so confident. In a moment of doubt, she told a Women Justices Association meeting, women were willing to 'honour good and great men' but reluctant to support 'the good women of the world'.[6]

Needless to say, she was destined for disappointment. The Nationalist Party announced the five candidates selected from the nine vying for the Eastern Suburbs seat. Millicent expected the three sitting members, Hyman Goldstein, Harold Jaques and Charles Oakes, would be selected, but she had hoped that her long years of work for the party would be rewarded. But no! The committee chose two men for the remaining two places – J R Robinson, President of the Eastern Suburbs and Wentworth Conferences and George Overhill, the man who had criticised her 'mushroom branches'.[7]

If the Party members thought that was the end of the matter, they underestimated Millicent. She lodged an appeal to the Council. There was considerable opposition to having a woman candidate – politics was after all men's business – but Millicent had a very large following, particularly among women and that was not a minor consideration since voting was not yet compulsory and many women still resisted exercising their franchise. The Council declined to make a decision and forwarded her appeal to the Executive, which noted she had polled well in the 1922 election. Somewhat begrudgingly the Executive decided 'she should not be deprived of the opportunity to try again'.[8]

Millicent joined the other five Nationalist Party men competing for the five Eastern Suburbs seats. Her nomination attracted approval from some journalists. Her 'resonant, Clara Butt-like tones' impressed one journalist,[9] while another lauded her as 'a fine platform speaker and an excellent campaigner'.[10] She was 'an indefatigable worker in all causes affecting woman' claimed one,[11] while another predicted that if she is elected 'the alleged weaker sex will have a very powerful spokeswoman'.[12]

Although Millicent was already on the campaign trail, the pre-selection saga was not over. When Charles Oakes accepted a life appointment to the Legislative Council, William Foster, who had also challenged his omission from the original Nationalist pre-selection, advertised himself as 'Mr Oakes's successor'.[13] Reginald Weaver, Millicent's campaign manager, 'an implacable foe of socialism'[14] and an uncanny political operator who thrived in 'the thick of the political hurly burly',[15] initiated a countermove. 'Don't be fooled by false Advertisement', counselled the fliers he distributed in the electorate – 'give your No 1 vote to Millicent'.[16]

The press turned their attention to predicting the election date. The Fuller government would return for a short session, speculated some, before calling an autumn election; others placed bets on dates ranging from April 25 to the end of May. Several papers counselled readers to enrol, informed them about the recently introduced preferential voting system,[17] and reminded them Election Day was held on Saturday for the convenience of voters. Their advice was, of course, partisan. The *Herald*, instructed electors to 'vote Nationalist' to prevent a Labor and Communist takeover of the state,[18] while *The Australian Worker* advised readers that 'No Labor man or woman, with the cause at heart, will fail to make provision for voting' – and of course vote Labor.[19] It even urged those in the Balmain electorate to vote 'in the interests of the home, of women workers, child welfare, cheaper living, and better industrial conditions' for Labor candidate Kate Dwyer.[20]

The novelty of women as both candidates and voters invited opportunities for journalistic creativity. 'The woman who can remember all the things that go into a plum pudding', wrote *The Australian Worker*, 'need have no fear of recording a vote'.[21] The *Sunday Times* devoted one of its regular 'Dear Ruth'/'Yours Naomi' columns to criticism of the woman who merely 'makes her little mark in the space opposite the name chosen by her menfolk' and how 'heartbreaking' that is for women who 'are trying to do something for their own sex'.[22]

Mildred Muscio, Acting President of the National Council of Women (NCW) NSW commented on how shameful it was that Australia, which was in the vanguard of women's suffrage, was well behind other countries in electing women to parliament. Democracy, she argued, was premised on direct representation and sound legislative decisions must be made by men and women. In this election, she counselled, women should vote for women candidates because they had expert knowledge about children and household economies that men did not, and could not, acquire.[23]

With the election date set for 30 May, Millicent officially launched her election campaign in the Sydney Town Hall on 11 May. She promoted herself not simply as a woman but as a feminist, and emphasised her feminism 'does not work against men' but works for men by 'helping the cause of women and children'.[24] The Rev Robert Hammond, rector of St Barnabas Church on Broadway, a committed Temperance Advocate, praised her as 'a woman whose brain was equal to that of any man' and who had 'more political ability than any candidate for the same electorate'. Sir Frederick Waley told the audience that women made up half the population and therefore should be represented by their own sex in parliament.

As her campaign progressed, she was supported by other distinguished men. At a meeting at the Randwick Town Hall, former Prime Minister Billy Hughes praised her as a 'student of public affairs' with 'the personality, the character, and the ability to make a good legislator'.[25] He went on to say that Millicent had 'mental equipment as good as any male member of Parliament'.[26]

Notwithstanding this support, Millicent's candidature was not universally applauded. *The Catholic Press* weighed in with derogatory, almost defamatory accusation that she lent her 'little pink ear to fablespinners' – listening to and repeating idle, inaccurate gossip – and should she ever be elected her contribution would amount to 'Much Ado about Nothing'.[27] *The Freeman's Journal* dismissed her as the 'lady with the compound name' who was merely chasing votes and had little chance of being elected,[28] while *The Australian Worker* denounced her as a 'bitterly prejudiced Tory' whose 'eloquence had failed to land her a winner' at the previous election and was unlikely to do so this time.[29] The following week it also criticised her as a fraud because she wasn't married, wasn't a mother and claimed (incorrectly) that since she did not come from the working class, she was not qualified to 'pose as an authority' on working women.[30]

One journalist incorrectly positioned her as representing the 'feminist party',[31] while others reproached her for supporting policies that only benefitted women and others accused her of seeking special privileges because she was a woman. No, Millicent responded; her policies would benefit men as well as women and she was not asking electors to vote for her on the basis of her sex but on the merits of her policies.[32] A *Daily Telegraph* journalist did acknowledge her 'force, personality' and 'well-ordered and well-stocked mind', but declared she was 'too honest, too outspoken, to cajole the male vote'.[33] Millicent did not wish to cajole the male vote, but to persuade voters – men and women – about the importance of the issues affecting women and children that were too often neglected by the members of parliament.

Despite her supposedly 'masculine control of her feelings',[34] this constant carping probably took its toll on her confidence. Perhaps her mother, who shielded her from an intrusive journalist the morning after the election,[35] supplied the emotional support she needed during the campaign.

Or perhaps it fell to Weaver to ensure she was not discouraged by these slings and arrows hurled at her. Amongst her papers in the

National Library is an anonymous verse based on Rudyard Kipling's poem, 'If', which encourages Millicent not to give up the fight:

> If you can grab the Votes when all about you
> Are losing them, and crying out at you
> For taking them – and frankly I don't doubt you
> Have taken them, and mean to keep them too!
> If you can keep your end up over Friday –
> If you can fight till then, believe you me
> You'll top the Eastern Suburbs poll, my lady!
> If you do this – you'll be a She MP.[36]

While the conservative press evoked the bogey of Bolshevism in its attacks on the Labor campaign, Labor-aligned newspapers reciprocated by targeting Nationalist leaders. The Nationalist Party, crowed *The Australian Worker*, welcomed 'every self-seeker and deserter' – a snide reference to the 'Labor Rat' Billy Hughes – and described Premier, Sir George Fuller as the 'enemy of the people' and 'white-anter of industry' who was determined to 'keep the workers from their rights' and to 'bludgeon' anti-strike laws through the parliament.[37]

Cartoonist Will Donald was also on the attack with a 'Babes in the Wood' cartoon that depicted Nationalist and Progressive Party members as vultures about to seize their prey, two innocent children, a 'Small Farmer' and a 'Worker'. Donald inverted the sixteenth century English folk tale of robins protecting abandoned children in the woods, to suggest the Nationalist government wanted to devour the electorate. 'We should escape quickly', the boy tells the girl or 'those birds will smother us with dead leaves'. This cartoon suggested the NSW electorate is a wake-up to the Nationalist predators – they will vote Labor.[38]

Election Day, Saturday 30 May 1925, dawned bright and clear. Polling booths around the state opened their doors at eight o'clock. There was traffic congestion on Sydney's north shore as political parties ferried their loyal voters to polling booths in motor cars. In the eastern suburbs Millicent was praised for engaging 'only six cars' for her supporters while her opponents were 'said to have employed six or seven times that number'.[39] Throughout the day, a steady stream of electors made their way past the campaigners handing out how to vote cards to the tables where officials sat ready to mark off their names.

Seven women located in five city and two country electorates and two hundred and seventy four men contested the ninety seats in the state's Legislative Assembly. In the Eastern Suburbs electorate the fifteen candidates were listed alphabetically on the ballot paper, with Millicent second last. Nationalist Party supporters were advised to number six of the fifteen candidates in order of preference despite there being only five seats in this electorate.

The choice for these electors was captured in another anonymous satiric verse, 'The Woman Will Win'.

> Have your mind made up when you reach the ballot gate
> The barrier falls at eight o'clock, so don't be running late.
> See the fifteen candidates all canter around the course,
> A different coloured ribbon tied around every blooming horse.
> O'Halloran and Alldis with the communistic red,
> Melville, Crick and Anderson are Bolshevistic bred.
> 'Pretty Joey' Robinson whose hair is white you know
> Thinks he still is young enough to give the game a go.
> While Randwick's own Mayor Goldstein will be certain for a place,
> Hedgers like old Foster, never ought to run a race.
> That one with green's not trying – he may get there just the same,
> For he's a Roman Catholic and Fallon is his name.
> Sectarianism saves him from being in the lurch,

He cannot play a lone hand, as he leans upon the Church.
Next comes Marks, like Shylock, in a coat of gabardine,
Who failed to gain selection, so is hedging in between.
Jaques and Gillespie will win, that's as certain as can be,
Whilst the last to leave the stable is the greatest certainty.
For that is Preston Stanley – one who can't help running straight,
For though she is a woman – she's the worthiest candidate.
Just glance at her fine record, see the work that she has done,
Surely she is worthy – why not give her number one?
She's good for any obstacle, on the flat or Overhill,
Has a fine determination and the character to will.
Take your pick from off this program, back six starters for a place.
There are only fifteen running, and they can't all win the race.
Give your one to Preston Stanley – is the straight out tip from me
Preston Stanley's out for principle, so that's your guarantee.[40]

The writer of this verse is not identified and it does not appear to have been published in the press. However, after the election one journalist claimed 'Woman will win' was Millicent's campaign slogan.[41] Despite the lack of poetic refinement, the verse's prediction was accurate; the woman did win.

Monday 1 June 1925 was cloudy and cool. Although the election result was not immediately clear, for those who hoped the Fuller government would be returned, a bleak winter appeared to be setting in. As the counting of votes continued over the next two weeks, newspapers predicted a hung parliament or a narrow majority for one side or the other. On Monday 15 June, Sir George Fuller handed the Nationalist Coalition Government's resignation to the Governor, Sir Dudley de Chair.

The press had a field day with headlines such as 'A Song of Defeated Tories', 'Lang's Jubilation', 'Mr Lang Takes Charge' and 'Labor Takes over the Reins'. However, little attention was paid to Labor's slim majority of one seat – a situation that would become problematic for Premier Lang as his term unfolded.

Journalists had also forecast two women, Millicent and Labor's Kate Dwyer, would be elected. Kate was unsuccessful but Millicent was eventually declared the winner of the fifth Eastern Suburbs seat. Victory for this 'noted feminist and social reformer' was a 'triumph for all women who had worked for public welfare', declared *The Sun*.[42] She had 'business ability', 'genuine enthusiasm', a 'fine speaking voice', and an 'impressive personality'.[43] Like Edith Cowan and Lady Nancy Astor she was a flag bearer and a trailblazer who would purify proceedings in the bear pit. She would be a 'force in the parliament', although her 'gift of words' would 'probably startle quite a number of men'.[44] Another journalist pointed out she would be only one female voice in the House, but she had 'the cause of women and children deeply at heart' and a 'fine body of women as sympathisers' to support her.[45]

Millicent probably felt mixed emotions as she surveyed the 'shoals and quicksands of political life' ahead of her. At one victory celebration she pledged to maintain her 'sincerity of purpose' and her 'courage of opinion' and reiterated her goal of improving the lives of women and children. She promised to introduce a motion for the appointment of a commission to inquire into maternal and infant mortality rates and to push for the introduction of a bill for the 'segregation of feebleminded persons'.[46]

Those in her audience were pleased to hear these women's issues articulated by the woman they expected to achieve so much. 'At last a woman has broken down the barrier that made the legislature a sacred preserve from which women were excluded', said Dame Mary Hughes, second wife of Billy Hughes. Her election was the 'crowning of the efforts of an army of women', said Mary

Liddell while Mrs Jamieson Williams, one of the unsuccessful independent women candidates, urged all women to stand firmly behind Millicent.[47] This was a noble, if naive call.

When Millicent arrived at parliament house she encountered the first of many obstacles that would be placed in her path. Unlike the other new members, she was not allocated an office in the main building but relegated to the parliamentary annex, Richmond Villa,[48] which was situated in a row of colonial terrace houses behind Parliament House and connected to it by a pathway, Domain Terrace.

This meant she could not readily engage in informal discussions with colleagues in the lobbies or corridors and did not have easy access to the services of parliamentary staff. Fellow Nationalist Sir Thomas Henley later criticised the Government's lack of 'chivalry' in locating Millicent 'in a part of the building' where she had 'to run five minutes to get in the House when the division bells were rung'.[49] Millicent did not publicly articulate frustration with her isolation but she probably felt slighted.

Her office looked out across the Domain[50] towards the Botanical Garden and Woolloomooloo Bay. She appended her name to the door and decorated the room with grey wall paper and a fine Wilton carpet in an Eastern design creating an elegant 'office boudoir drawing room'.[51] It was 'as delightful a retreat for a woman as those heavily-furnished sanctums which have been the sole privilege of man for so many years'.[52] For Millicent it was a workplace, a sanctuary from the vicissitudes of the Chamber, and a parlour in which to entertain her guests.

The 27th parliament began briefly on Wednesday 24 June 1925. The Clerk read the proclamation summoning Members of the Legislative Assembly to the Legislative Council Chamber for the reading of the Commission by the three senior Members appointed by the Governor, Dudley de Chair. Men and women in the galleries would usually sit quietly during this ceremony, but today they had come to witness the first woman's skirts rustling on those sacred benches, so they applauded when Millicent entered and sat between Walter Wearne and John Lee – a 'rose between two thorns'.[53] The President read the Commission to the assembled members of both Houses:

> We have it in command from the Governor to let you know that, it being necessary that a Speaker of the Legislative Assembly be chosen, it is his Excellency's pleasure that you, *gentlemen* [my italics] of the Legislative Assembly, repair to your own Chamber, and there, after members shall have been sworn, proceed to the election of one of your number to be your Speaker.

As several journalists pointed out, whoever was responsible for drafting this Commission had overlooked the presence of a woman amongst the 'gentlemen' of the Legislative Assembly. This was not the only time Millicent's presence demanded revision to parliamentary language. The Sergeant-at-arms' customary announcement of the Speaker's entrance in the Assembly, '*Gentlemen*, Mr Speaker' did not meet the 'demands of chivalry' required by a woman's presence and was amended to '*Honourable* Members, Mr Speaker'.[54]

When the members of the Legislative Assembly returned to their Chamber, Millicent signed her name in the Roll of the House and shook hands with Premier Lang to enthusiastic acclamation from the women in the gallery. She was now a fully-fledged member of the Legislative Assembly – the first female MP in the NSW Bear Pit. Two days later the first session of parliament was prorogued until 21 July, and on 17 July further prorogued until 12 August. Premier Lang was giving the Labor Party as much time as possible to formulate its legislative platform before the official opening.

Wednesday 12 August was cold, wet and windy. Traffic banked up outside Parliament House in Macquarie Street as crowds assembled for the momentous official opening of the first parliament in NSW in which a woman would be seated amongst the eighty-nine men. Members and guests arriving at Parliament House were bedecked in their finery, with mackintoshes and umbrellas shielding them from the rain. The inclement weather did not dampen the enthusiasm of the visitors and journalists who jostled up the stone steps and into the parliamentary galleries to obtain the best seats.

Prior to the ceremonial opening, Mrs Flowers, wife of the President of the Legislative Council, held a VIP reception in the President's Rooms. Amongst her guests were the Governor's wife, Lady de Chair and her daughter, Miss Elaine de Chair, the Premier's wife, Mrs Lang and her daughters, Mrs Dooley wife of the Speaker, and Mrs Willis wife of the Deputy President of the Legislative Council. Millicent held her own reception in her Richmond Villa office for the women who had supported her candidature.

The ceremonial opening of the 27th Parliament was bedecked with the customary displays of gold braided uniforms and grand pomp and ceremony. As His Excellency the Governor, Sir Dudley de Chair arrived at Parliament House a twenty-one gun salute rang out across Sydney Harbour. The Governor entered the Legislative Council Chamber, escorted by the President, also in ceremonial dress. Members of the Legislative Assembly were summoned to the Council, and followed in procession behind the Speaker Mr Dooley, who chose not to wear the traditional Speaker's wig and robes.

When Millicent appeared, the women in the ladies' gallery tapped their umbrellas on the floor to welcome the first woman parliamentarian, then settled back in their seats.[55] Millicent was resplendent in a black Ottoman silk[56] gown with gold and Oriental *entre deux* stitching, cloche hat with latticed gold braid and pearl necklace, and she carried an envelope-style patent leather 'vanity bag'. The press scrutinised her attire and declared she resembled the renowned English actress Irene Vanbrugh.[57]

His Excellency took his place in the President's chair and

delivered the opening address, outlining the Labor Government's legislative agenda and, as was customary, ended with the invocation:

> I now invite your earnest consideration of the matters proposed as the subjects of your deliberations, and pray, that, under the guidance of Divine Providence your labours will conduce to the well-being and prosperity of the State.

After these formalities, the members of the Legislative Assembly adjourned to the green Chamber and Millicent took her seat in the back row of the Opposition benches on the right of Harold Jaques, also a member for the Eastern Suburbs electorate.[58] In the public gallery, according to one journalist, Hyam Goldstein, the 'astute political engineer' who had not been re-elected, watched her with 'pained eyes' as she took the seat he had once occupied.[59]

Premier Lang then caught Opposition members by surprise. He moved an adjournment of the Legislative Assembly until 1.30pm. Members, who had anticipated the usual adjournment until 4.30pm raised various objections – it was not traditional practice, there were no sessional or standing orders directing it, they had been given no advance notice, and, most importantly, resuming at 1.30pm did not allow them sufficient time to examine the Governor's speech before the Address in Reply debate commenced. Eventually Lang agreed to a compromise and the House adjourned for lunch.

During the adjournment, Millicent's mother, attired in black velvet, assisted her to play host to the stream of visitors who made their way to her office in Richmond Villa. These women no doubt concurred with the journalists who opined that the parliament would provide 'ample scope for her intellectual energies and gifts of oratory' and that since she had a voice worth listening to and gave 'frank and forceful utterance' to her views, she could go far – 'Premier perhaps – possibly Speaker'.[60] That utopian notion would not come to fruition.

It was 2.00pm when the Speaker resumed the chair. At 2.15pm Millicent, now without her cloche hat, slipped in to the Chamber, not as unobtrusively as she may have wished. The removal of her hat caused consternation. Some commentators pondered how the Speaker might respond if she were to address him in that hatless state. Recently in the British House of Commons, they mused, a hatless woman member had addressed the Speaker, and he had roundly rebuked her for her impropriety.[61] Would this Speaker respond in the same way? Millicent did not attract any rebuke. She sat throughout the afternoon session, listening and taking notes, using her vanity bag as a support for her writing pad.[62]

The session began with the usual formalities followed by questions without notice. One of these was posed by Jaques, and again it highlighted the problem of gendered language. Jaques asked about pensions for widows who were 'maiden ladies'. According to one journalist, Millicent had a whispered conversation with Jaques who amended his question – 'maiden ladies' was replaced by 'elderly unmarried widows'.[63] It is not possible to know precisely what Millicent whispered to him, but perhaps she pointed out the virgin connotations of the word 'maiden' that were at odds with the state of widowhood.

Throughout the afternoon session of the parliament, Millicent's presence was commented on by speakers from both sides of the Chamber. She would later observe that 'the advent of a woman in the Parliament of this country is not exactly to be considered a popular innovation'.[64] Ironically, it was a fellow Nationalist, Albert Bruntnell, who initially voiced some of the strongest disapproval. Declaring he was not 'an enthusiastic supporter' of women entering the 'hurly-burly of political life' and 'gracing' the parliamentary benches he expressed the hope Millicent might, perhaps, bring some benefit to 'the moral, material and spiritual welfare of the people of this State'.[65]

On the other hand, Labor member Dr Evatt, who was accorded the privilege of moving the Address in Reply, applauded her presence and expressed regret she was not on his side of the House. He went on to assert that she would support his government's measures for women and children, including the 'payment of pensions to widows'.[66] In that Evatt was mistaken. While Millicent was in favour of widows' pensions she would oppose the government's bill because it discriminated against those who had no children.

The following day, Thursday 13 August 1925, George Fuller outlined the Opposition's response to the Government's program. The opposition would not support some of the measures, including the restitution of the forty-four hour week, taxation, revenue manipulation, compulsory unionism and the restoration of seniority to the 1917 strikers. Fuller criticised Lang's political appointments to the Public Service Board and the forced resignation of Bertram Stevens, the under-secretary and director of finance at the State Treasury, who had an impeccable reputation for efficiency and probity.

As the session moved through the Address in Reply Millicent observed and made notes, perhaps formulating her forthcoming 'maiden' speech.[67] She was conscious of the attention paid to first speeches and aware her own speech would attract special interest as the first ever made by a woman in that parliament. Surveying those seated in the galleries above, one day, she spotted Kate Dwyer, the defeated Labor candidate for Balmain, and made her way out to greet her. They adjourned to Millicent's office for tea.[68] Their conversation would make fascinating reading today but unfortunately there is no record of the matters they discussed.

When pressured by journalists to indicate when she would make her maiden speech, Millicent said she would try to catch the Speaker's eye on Tuesday 25 August.[69] On Sunday 23 August newspapers suggested Premier Lang would shortly close the Address in Reply debate. Whether Millicent could catch the Speaker's eye before then became a topic of speculation in the press. If she attempted to do so on 25 August as she had indicated, she was not successful. Time was running out. Would the Speaker give her the call based on the 'chivalrous principle of ladies first'?[70] Or, was she deliberately holding out to gain attention? One journalist suggested it was natural for her to wait until the last day, as a 'woman always wants the last word'.[71]

Millicent did not get the last word in this debate, but the first words of the first woman to speak in the NSW parliament on 26 August 1925 certainly had a galvanising effect on the parliament and on the public.

5

Sojourn in the House
(1925)

Miss Preston Stanley, MLA has spoken. With a sea of male faces around her, and only the bright smiles and approving nods of a packed ladies' gallery to cheer her, she launched her attack. A sizzling, caustic, cutting, logical onslaught, with mere men as the target.

The Sun, 26 August 1925[1]

On Wednesday, 26 August 1925, women filled the parliamentary gallery expecting this to be the day Millicent Preston Stanley made history. The atmosphere in the Bear Pit was electric as the Speaker gave her the nod. She stood sedately in her grey suit at the end of the back row, scanned the women in the gallery above, surveyed the men seated around her, then commenced her maiden speech.

> In rising to address this Assembly for the first time one is necessarily conscious of a thrill of enthusiasm for the echo of issues long settled are still here, the romance of great personalities long silent still linger, the traditions of a century that is gone are still evergreen and inspiring, making this Chamber the most historic spot in all Australia. It is a privilege to share in the traditions of this House – it is a greater responsibility to maintain them unsullied.[2]

Millicent may have been a novice in the House, but she was no neophyte orator and for the next ninety minutes she held her audience in thrall. It was a long maiden speech, a point some members commented upon – albeit not favourably.[3] But, as the first woman to speak in that Chamber since its establishment in 1856, she was determined to make a mark not only for herself but for all women.

If her audience expected her to make a demure, diplomatic maiden speech, they were destined for disappointment. After her sedate opening Millicent launched into an address that made the men sit up and take notice.[4] She demolished the false assumptions held by men who were 'blinded and poisoned by their own prejudice' and 'enwrapped in the moth-eaten trappings of an age that is gone'. Women did not lack 'logical faculty' and 'capacity for reason', nor did they need men to protect them from the 'hurly burly of politics'. While some women may not be 'fit to sit in Parliament', that was true of some men and, if parliament was 'no fit place for women', that was a serious indictment of the men who had made it so. Millicent critiqued Labor's intention to abolish the Legislative Council, which was still an appointed chamber. She would normally applaud appointing women but Lang's action in doing so was a 'barren honour' since they would be put there 'to chop their own heads off'. Her guillotine image was a reminder Lang expected these women to vote for the Council's abolition.

Most importantly, Millicent declared, women's issues affected not only women but the nation as a whole – women's questions were national questions and national questions were women's questions.

Like her fellow opposition members, Millicent's role in the Address in Reply debate involved critiquing the government's agenda and she intended to carry out that task with the same vehemence as other opposition members had done. The government's agenda, she declared, was filled with 'flimsy things' and totally lacking in the 'crying needs of the State'. The reintroduction of the forty-four hour week was a mere 'millstream' compared with the raging 'Niagara Falls' of three hundred maternal deaths annually and, moreover, the restoration of the 1917 strikers' seniority was a middling 'Mount Lang' compared with the massive 'Mount Vesuvius' of annual infant deaths. Her comparison of Vesuvius, an Italian volcano with Mount Lang, a minor peak in the Victorian Grampians was particularly potent because of her implied reference to the Premier's name.

Not only was the government's agenda filled with insignificant things, she continued, but it omitted those very issues that mattered most. Public health required 'vitally necessary' reform to prevent disastrous outcomes for babies, school children and men in industry. She listed the Acts that needed reform and if the Health Minister 'can find his department, and understand all its ramifications and limitations,' she sniped, 'he is a very clever and ingenious man'. In retrospect she might have been wiser not to position herself in such an antagonistic relationship with George Cann so early in her parliamentary term.

At the beginning of the session the Speaker had reminded the House about the 'time honoured custom'[5] that new members be heard in silence but Millicent had already seen that custom honoured more in the breach than in the observance. As she continued her tirade the women in the gallery applauded but the men in the Chamber squirmed and mumbled. In response Millicent commented that she didn't mind them interjecting but would rather their comments were audible.[6]

Millicent was, perhaps, surprised the first audible interjection came from her side of the House. James Arkins, a Labor 'Rat' and serial interjector challenged her statements about maternal mortality, implying she did not know what she was talking about. She dismissed him, saying she would 'deal with the matter in my own way' and her way was to draw on her extensive reading of the medical literature in order to explain why there was a need for a commission of inquiry into maternal and infant mortality. Her response indicated she would not be treated as an inferior in this Chamber by any man. For a few moments, members lapsed into silence, probably wondering how much longer she would continue with her 'lecture'. They did not have to wait long before she again threw down the gauntlet: 'man is the nation's greatest wealth'.

They chorused, 'Hear, hear!' but Millicent reminded the 'hilarious gentlemen' that the generic term 'man' includes 'woman'!

Millicent then turned her attack on Labor's policies. Just as the 1919 Queensland strike had increased the cost of goods, so Labor's proposed forty-four hour week would also increase costs, make NSW uncompetitive, even bankrupt the state. Moreover, working men's wives worked much longer hours than their husbands and then they had to put up with a 'bear of a husband' when he came home.

She condemned the Party's 'spoils for the victor' practices and accused the party of corruption. The evidence was clear. The Union demanded the removal of Mr Justice Edmonds from the bench because he had given an adverse judgement against it and the abolition of the Water Sewerage and Drainage Board because its policies were at odds with Labor policy. Moreover, unions had been infiltrated by communists, and the worst of these infiltrators was a woman, Adela Pankhurst Walsh,[7] who maintained the 'worker who is thrifty betrays his own wife and children'. 'What Bedlamic theories!' Millicent declaimed.

Next she turned on Alick Kay, blasting him because he supported Labor despite being elected as an Independent. Hansard does not record Kay's interjection but the *Herald* reported it as, 'I will support this Government for three years'. In a letter to the editor, Kay maintained he actually said 'I can keep a government in office for three years'.[8] In any case it was an assertion of the power this unaligned parliamentarian could wield with his vote – a situation that enraged Millicent.

Members were now unconstrained in their interjections. She was not a genuine representative of women, shouted one member to whom she swiftly riposted she was not a representative of women but of voters in the Eastern Suburbs electorate. Another accused her of 'playing up to the people'; and another derided her lack of 'facts' and 'logic'. Would she vote for the Widows' Pension bill, bellowed another. Yes, she responded, (laughter). But only as long as there was no 'serious objection' (derision). Labor's advertisements were a sham, she responded, because they falsely depicted it as a pension for all widows – when it was only intended for widows with children.[9]

Afterwards Millicent admitted she had felt nervous, but she showed no obvious sign of unease at the time. She almost seemed to be revelling in the skirmish as she batted back their interjections – 'that is your point of view; it is not mine' and 'this is not a laughing matter; I will tell you why' – sounding rather like a mother scolding recalcitrant children or a school ma'am reprimanding unruly pupils. Finally, tiring of their Bear Pit antics, she declared that some honourable members appeared to 'imagine that they have only to hit back and tell me some Government somewhere, at some time, did something and I will immediately collapse'.

Millicent had no intention of collapsing. She had chosen to make her statements in the same manner as male members and she expected them to treat her as a member not as a woman. She assured them she required no special treatment because of her sex but, she asserted, during her time in the House she would continue to pursue those 'great questions which are of supreme importance to women'. She then brought her oration to a demure close;

> I only hope, realising as I do that every woman's question is a national question, that every national question is a woman's question, I shall be able to make a slight contribution to the bettering of the conditions of the people of this State as a result of my sojourn in this House.

Her speech had the 'galvanising' effect she intended and her supporters had anticipated.[10] The women in the gallery were jubilant, rejoicing in a triumph in which they could vicariously share. Her fellow Nationalists, even those who doubted the wisdom of allowing a woman into the hurly burly of politics, were impressed and many shook hands with her.

No sooner had she resumed her seat, than various members took the opportunity to critique her speech. Nationalist John Fitzpatrick was the first to offer his assessment; he had some 'kindly regard for the lady folk' and could tolerate 'their lectures', but not this one.[11] Labor Member Hugh Connell acknowledged the 'very eloquent' speech given by the 'new lady member', which members had listened to sympathetically because her 'oratorical ability is far above the average'. But, he asserted, she was a hypocrite since she only put the case for 'a certain section of the women of our community' and she had positioned herself 'in political company' that does nothing for workers. Moreover, she had no personal understanding of the working class.[12]

Millicent was probably not surprised when another Labor member Cecil Murphy[13], a forthright, aggressive debater, rose and declared that, despite her 'eloquent language', her conclusions were neither 'stamped with the hallmark of logic' nor 'on a par' with those of male members and she supported a party which was 'guilty of the breach of faith' in respect to women. He brushed aside Millicent's interjections and when another member challenged his *ad hominem* attack he retorted that if his comments hurt it was because 'they happen to be only too true'.[14] Murphy turned his attack on other opposition members, and perhaps for Millicent one bright spot was his denigration of Theo Hill, with whom she would clash before the year was over. Hill was 'old', 'dirty and miserable', a 'political misfit' and a 'cur', shouted Murphy. The Speaker ordered Murphy to withdraw the un-parliamentary word, 'cur', and promptly adjourned the debate.

At long last, a woman's voice had echoed in the parliament and journalists set about recording history's first draft. Most of the mainstream press trumpeted Millicent's fluency and ease of delivery and her notable contribution to the debate. Many judged her speech a fine oration and 'better than even her most ardent admirers expected.'[15] Her vibrant voice, dignified demeanour, expressive gestures and the frankness of her 'racy, crisp, and breezy' speech was refreshing for those accustomed to listening to politicians use language 'to conceal rather than to express what they have in their minds'.[16] Her introduction of matters never before dealt with in a 'serious fashion' in a Parliament 'composed entirely of men' was admirable.[17] She handled important matters with sheer common sense and was less concerned with party politics than with the 'well-being of the community'.[18] She was a 'force to be reckoned with', who would render 'great service not only to her own sex but to the nation'.[19] Millicent told Frances Taylor, founder of *Woman's World*, that 'she felt the terrible responsibility of being a pioneer in Parliament for her sex' and she was aware many men 'wanted to laugh' at her, and newspapers 'were looking for a humorous touch of copy'.[20]

Some newspapers not only found humorous copy but projected a less than favourable impression of this first woman parliamentarian. Millicent had shown herself to be 'a formidable adversary' with 'quick wit, power of retort, and fearlessness in speech' and this would inevitably make members think twice before they tackled her in 'a warfare of words' again, or so one journalist opined.[21] According to another, the air was 'electrical' as Labor members hurled interjections and Opposition members demanded the Speaker throw the interjectors out,[22] although Hansard does not record these demands. Millicent 'squelched every interjector', lashed Labor members and demolished the government agenda, or so it was reported.[23] Metaphors such as 'lash' that left a 'sting' and interjectors writhing as she 'ripped' them open with her 'stiletto' tongue positioned her as a harridan. Headlines such as 'Sizzling Shots', 'Fireworks from Miss Preston Stanley' and 'A New Terror' further reinforced this image of a belligerent woman.

Not surprisingly, *The Bulletin*, the weekly journal emblazoned with 'Australia for the White Man' on its masthead, was less than complimentary, condemning her 'blistering remarks' and 'withering scorn'.[24] Sydney scandal sheet *Truth*, went one step further declaring the 'lady legislator' failed in her one chance to 'make history', because she had discarded her position as a 'feminine idealist' and was 'hobbled in the strangling habiliments of party'.[25] The *Labor Daily* criticised her for failing to acknowledge the 'band of Labor women pioneers' who had 'blazed the trail toward the proper care of mothers and children'.[26] The following day that paper carried a letter from a 'Tired Mother' who, oblivious to Millicent's family background, stated she was not from the working class and could not understand the plight of 'working mothers'.[27]

Three days later, the *Sunday Times* published an article under the headline, 'Sex Disability in Public Life. How Australia Stands Condemned'.[28] 'The growing realization that woman should take her place alongside man in all the serious business of life', stated the writer, 'is by no means exclusive to Australia' and yet Australia remained amongst the most 'benighted of nations'. Other nations were moving forward but Australia was still stuck in old patriarchal traditions. The growing inclusion of women in legislatures in other parts of the world compared poorly with Australia's reluctance which was a 'blot on the escutcheon of democracy'. Australians must realise 'intellect has no sex', 'all men are not wise' nor are 'all women stupid' and the 'only standard for the guidance of men and women in all the affairs of life – national, social or personal' – should be fitness and ability.

The article was indelibly linked to Millicent's maiden speech by the leader, 'The following article has been specially written for the *Sunday Times* by Miss Preston Stanley MLA, whose splendid speech in the NSW Parliament during the past week made a most favourable impression upon all political parties'. All political parties being favourably impressed is blatant hyperbole. Whether Hugh McIntosh, the owner of the *Sunday Times* and a life member of the Legislative Council suggested the publication of this article or Millicent prevailed upon him to publish it, it was a nifty move that ensured her ideas were widely aired and her identity as the first woman parliamentarian firmly entrenched in the public imaginary, well beyond the lens of parliament watchers. One week later that paper reported Millicent was 'not enjoying the warm welcome' she had expected from her party 'soreheads'.[29]

Although there were few avenues for an opposition backbencher to influence the parliamentary agenda, Millicent was eager to make a start. On Tuesday 1 September she submitted two notices of motion, one for a Royal Commission into maternal mortality and the other for legislation to provide for the care of mentally defective persons. The same day, she asked a question without notice of the Minister for Public Health, George Cann: 'Would the Minister obtain a copy of the prize-winning essay on Maternal Mortality and Infant Welfare by Dr Emmanuel Sydney Morris and make it widely available?'. Cann hedged.[30] Two weeks later on 16 September, Millicent put a further question to the Premier asking if he would make funds available for the implementation of Dr Morris's maternal mortality recommendations. Lang obfuscated.[31]

Then on Thursday 17 September she submitted a motion for leave to introduce her private members Guardianship of Infants Bill.

> That leave be given to bring in a Bill to amend the law relating to the guardianship, maintenance, and custody of infants; to remove certain disabilities of married women with respect to the guardianship of their infant children; to amend the Testator's Family Maintenance and Guardianship of Infants Act, 1916, the Infants Custody and Settlement Act, 1899, and certain other Acts; and for purposes connected therewith.[32]

The parliamentary notice papers for 29 September listed her motion for a Royal Commission into maternal mortality. At last she was making progress. However, before the Speaker called on her, James Arkins accused the Premier of improperly promising Millicent special consideration because she was a woman. Before Lang could respond Millicent leapt to her feet and declared she desired 'no privilege or preference of any kind' because of her sex. Lang launched into a denunciation of Arkins' 'tittle-tattle tactics' and reproached the Opposition's persistent interruptions which were delaying Millicent's motions. It was an accusation that ignored Labor's own delaying tactics.[33]

As a result of the toing and froing, time for general business expired.

The House then turned its attention to the Forty Hours bill, one of the initiatives Millicent had fulminated against in her maiden speech. Frustrated that her own party had thwarted her Royal Commission initiative, she sat in the back row making no contribution to the debate. At the end of that day, Lang told the House he wanted 'to give hon members a full day' to consider the Forty Hours bill so he would 'not allow any other business to interrupt' it.[34] That put paid to Millicent's Royal Commission motion for the next day.

The parliamentary orders for 6 October included Millicent's three motions. Questions without notice took only the first half hour leaving half an hour for Millicent's motions. But she was not in the Chamber that day. So, at 11.30 Nationalist, John Lee moved the second reading of another Private Members bill.[35] Lee was deputising for the mover of this bill, Harold Jaques, who was 'detained on some particular business' and therefore unable to 'be present this morning'. However, without Jaques to explain aspects of the bill, debate was adjourned to a future date.[36]

In Millicent's absence, her three motions lapsed.

Overlooking Jaques' absence from the House, journalists pointed only to Millicent's failure to attend. One journalist noted that the previous week she had been 'blocked from speaking by concerted action on the part of the mere males in the Chamber' but this week, when 'their chivalry prevailed' she was not there.[37] Another journalist, writing under the headline she 'Missed the 'Bus' said the matters which 'she has had on the business paper practically since the session began went by the board'.[38] However, another journalist commented that her absence was the result of the 'unavoidable circumstances' of 'sickness in the home'.[39]

On 13 October Millicent gave notice for two motions, one for the implementation of Dr Morris's recommendations to reduce maternal mortality and the other for leave to introduce the Guardianship of Infants Bill. There were few Members in the Chamber on 20 October when she rose to move suspension of standing orders so that the House could consider her motion that Dr Morris's recommendations 'should be put into effect immediately, owing to the alarming and preventable maternal mortality and morbidity in this State'. The state's high maternal mortality rates were a disgrace, she declared, because these deaths could be prevented by establishing better maternity hospital accommodation, improved midwifery teaching, ante-natal clinics and endowment for research, as Dr Morris recommended.

In his response, Minister Cann damned her with faint praise: 'But for her newness in Parliament,' he purred, 'she would not have put such propositions forward'.[40] Although he did not mention it, Cann had received a deputation from Labor women who were lobbying against 'costly, protracted and ineffective' measures and he had promised that maternity wards would be built in new hospitals.[41] He did not mention the deputation in his response, but simply told the House past governments had not implemented Millicent's suggestions, because of their excessive cost. He then despatched a barb at the spinster's barren state:

> I have had as much experience of children as any man in this House. I cannot include the lady because, naturally, I could not be expected to have the experiences a woman would have as far as children are concerned.[42]

Somewhat unusually, Cann's comment prompted the Nationalist Fitzpatrick to critique his sarcasm. The Speaker promptly terminated debate.

And so the year rolled on without any further action on Millicent's maternal mortality motion.

When Lang introduced Labor's promised Widows' Pension Bill on 26 November 1925, Theodore Hill, a Progressive Party member exploded in an incendiary indictment of this 'soul-destroying, poisonous bill'. It was communistic, arose from a 'diseased humanitarianism' and would create immorality by deterring widows from re-marrying, he declared. Hill's 'extraordinary and reactionary speech' prompted Millicent to seek the call. She had some reservations about the details of Lang's bill, she told the House, and would propose amendments in due course but she congratulated the government on the initiative and roundly denounced Hill's outburst.[43] According to the *Herald*, 'Mr Hill must have felt that the three Furies, with whips and scourges, were abroad' as Labor members cheered the 'fair Nationalist Member, who was saying exactly what she thought and exactly what she meant, not only about the bill but also about Mr Hill'.[44] Once again, Millicent had stirred a viper's nest.

In the second reading debate on 2 December, Lang emphasised that the bill's purpose was to 'give the benefit of home life and a mother's care to the children who have been bereft of their father'. Millicent again spoke in support of the bill but she also reiterated her criticisms of Labor's dishonest election campaign that implied it would benefit all widows. She told the House she had received hundreds of letters from women who had voted for Labor but who now felt cheated because this legislation only applied to widows with dependent children.

As a preface to another attack on Hill, she stated that she was 'quite prepared to take what is coming to me as long as I can hit back in return'. Hill's arguments about this bill causing immorality were 'wrongly based, economically unsound, and socially false'; it was 'want, misery, privation and insecurity', which degraded women, she declared. Not surprisingly, Hill refuted Millicent's statements and reiterated the bill was a 'damnable, humanitarian humbug' vote-buying exercise that would undermine women's 'spirit of self-reliance'. Although his reasoning differed, his position on the bill was in partial agreement with Millicent's; like her he considered the bill was not a Widow's Pension bill but one aimed only at widows with children.[45]

Millicent indicated she supported the bill but she would propose amendments to it. However, she did not do so and voted with her Party in all the divisions. After a turbulent debate, the Widows' Pension Bill passed and was assented to on 24 December 1925, a generous Christmas present for widows with children, which brought little relief to widows without children. This turbulent debate was captured in an anonymous verse published in *The Sun*.[46]

> Once again to bore us
> To lecture and to jaw us
> To bluff and overawe us
> The Nats and Labs make haste;
> With lungs and larynx rested
> And interjections tested
> Determined and deep-chested
> (at least below the waist).
> Jack Lang the great tactician
> Resumes his mighty mission
> Of stoush – or abolition
> To use no vulgar term;
> AND Tammy Bavin's there in
> The Rival ranks a'glarin'
> And censurin' and swearin'
> He'll make the foeman squirm,
> With eagle eyes now grandly
> Comes in Miss Preston Stanley
> To snub the brutes unmanly
> Who grudge the widows' mite.

> Fitz wears the jaunty flower
> But Theo Hill sinks lower
> Upon his bench to glower
> Till she renews the fight.
> High up sits Speaker Dooley
> To do his duty truly
> Should Jack and Tom unruly
> Each other seek to slay
> With anything but glances –
> While ready for what chances
> The Serjeant gamely prances
> To scent the coming fray.
> Heigho! Another Session
> For some to shout Oppression
> And some to yell Recession
> And some to crouch and snore …
> How will it end, this flurry?
> Some bills, a frantic hurry?
> And lots of gag? Why worry –
> You've seen it all before.

On 23 December, in the 'dying minutes of a dying session' Premier Lang sprang an unwelcome surprise on the Opposition. Despite having promised no further bills would be introduced in this session, he attempted to rush the Constitution (Amendment) Bill through in one day. As journalists later pointed out, Lang, who 'never misses any advantage', had seized the opportunity of Opposition members' absences to bolster 'his case for the appointment of additional Labor representatives to the Legislative Council'.[47]

Opposition members were livid. While Thomas Bavin repeated

Millicent's maiden speech assertion that the women were to be put there to abolish the Council other members indulged in an avalanche of misogynistic denunciations. Frank Chaffey called women 'cackling hens'; James Arkins spoke of the 'pitiful spectacle' of women 'unsexing' themselves and 'aping men'; David Drummond asserted 'the people of this State do not want women included in Parliament'; Tom Hoskins argued a woman has 'enough to do to carry out her duties as a mother', John Fitzpatrick said it had been a mistake to give women the franchise; and Thomas Keegan asked why the one woman member of this parliament was absent.

Keegan's question prompted Theo Hill to launch into another bellicose condemnation of women in general and Millicent in particular. Women who wanted to enter parliament were 'crowing hens' whose brains were 'much less' than men's, he sniped. Millicent was the worst example as she was 'practically absent the whole time' and did not even have a 'husband to look after'. Hill was probably unaware that Millicent's absences sometimes arose from her need 'to attend to her aged, invalid mother'.[48]

Keegan's vituperation, somewhat surprisingly, evoked a supportive response from Cecil Murphy. 'Intellectually, physically, morally and in every way,' Murphy told the House, Millicent 'stands head and shoulders above the rank and file of the male members of this Assembly' and no other member 'possesses higher intellectual attainments and qualifications'. Murphy asserted it was Millicent's own party that wanted her 'outside this Chamber' and Hill had only attacked her because of her 'candid criticisms' of him.

With Hill's 'wild outburst' widely reported in the press, Millicent responded with a letter to the editor published in both the *Daily Telegraph* and the *Sydney Morning Herald*. Denouncing his 'peculiarities and prejudices' she rejected his presumption to speak for women, refuted his statement of women's smaller brains and, although she did not mention her mother's health, justified her absences on two grounds; firstly, Opposition votes 'have no effect on the actions of Government' because of the 'system of guillotine and gags' and secondly, Opposition members have 'public service' obligations beyond 'mere mechanical vote-registers'.[49]

Not to be outdone, Hill responded with another letter to the Editor, decrying Millicent's 'vulgar abuse' of him and criticising her irregular attendance despite drawing her parliamentary salary. He claimed he did as much as Millicent outside the House without missing a single division. As one journalist noted, although Hill 'rarely missed a division', he was 'there' – but 'asleep'.[50] Hill also asserted Millicent's absence allowed Lang the large majorities to pass his bills.[51] This was a ridiculous accusation as evidenced by Session Attendances – several members missed many more divisions than Millicent who was 'well down the list' of opposition absentees.[52]

While most parliamentarians put aside party politics for the season of good will, the spat between Millicent and Hill continued to play out in the press. Hill wrote further letters to various newspapers and Millicent responded, point for point with criticisms of him as a 'political anachronism' with an overblown vanity. It was an undignified public display that illustrated her determination to stand her ground.

Millicent ended the year not on the high note she had hoped. Having locked horns with many members, her failure to navigate a course around the obstacles placed in her path did not bode well for success in the second year of her sojourn in the House.

6

A Trick and a Stratagem (1926)

... having placed my motion upon the business paper according to the form employed by the House, the Government, by stratagem, and Mr Cann by a trick, allowed Mr Tonge to move as a matter of public urgency, something that was not urgent, ... that was done simply to prevent me from bringing my bill before this House.

Millicent Preston Stanley, *Hansard*, 29 November 1926

On 22 January 1926, a journalist, incorrectly, reported that Millicent had just departed the Blue Mountains for Sydney after spending a month 'recuperating' in the 'restorative Mountains air'.[1] Millicent had, in fact, returned to Sydney ten days earlier for the resumption of parliament on 12 January. She attended every session during January, February and March, voting in divisions and even fulfilling the role of teller on eight occasions, six of them on 22 January.

To her frustration, on 15 March Lang prorogued parliament until 1 June. The recess proved to be a busy, but rewarding time. Her spat with Theo Hill had brought an unexpected bonus. In late January, *The Daily Telegraph* offered her the editorship of a newly established 'Women's Supplement' with a salary of £750. She embraced the role not only because of the remuneration but also because it permitted her to 'speak as a woman to women – an Australian woman to the women of Australia'.[2] Her aim was to highlight every 'branch of feminine activity' including 'women's movements, dress, and social life', the 'care of children, cooking, modern housekeeping, sport, and amusements, everything in fact, of interest in the women's world' including an 'exceptionally fine serial story, written by a Sydney authoress'.[3]

In addition to commissioning articles from respected women writers, Millicent wrote features on diverse subjects such as women in history, the evolution of women's legal position, and the international women's movement. She also penned columns titled 'My Daily Message', comprising short homilies on various pertinent issues. One proposed 'enthusiasm' as an 'antidote to fear' and a 'creative', 'dynamic force' for power,[4] while another advised, 'You can't control the little fellows who tell big lies about you' but 'you can control the influence which those lies shall have over you'.[5] In one column she used the metaphor of a dog that simultaneously barks and wags his tail to urge readers not to 'sit on the fence' – 'If you believe in a thing, fight for it. If you don't believe in it – fight against it'.[6]

Later that year, Cornstalk Publishing Co, an imprint of Angus & Robertson, published two volumes of Millicent's 'My Daily Message' columns. In a preface to one edition, Billy Hughes praised her 'simple yet sufficient philosophy of life' which spoke 'directly to our hearts' like 'a friend talking at our side' in words as 'clear as a voice on a frosty night'.[7] One reviewer likened the 'simple but trenchant language' to the work of the American philosopher Elbert Hibbard.[8]

Millicent had expected parliament to resume sitting on 1 June, but Lang extended the prorogation. His leadership was under threat from disgruntled Labor Party members and with a majority of one in the parliament, he was wary of defectors crossing the floor to bring down his government.

During the extended recess, like other parliamentarians, Millicent continued her work outside the House. In addition to her editorial duties, she retained her executive positions in various organisations including the Feminist Club[9] and the Temperance Alliance[10] and she attended many fundraising events for charity organisations.[11]

Parliament eventually sat again on 22 September and the Speaker announced that during the recess the Independent

Member for North Shore, Alick Kay had resigned. Kay, a vegetarian, had accepted the Premier's offer of a lucrative position on the Metropolitan Meat Board. The Premier nominated Labor stalwart, Arthur Tonge as Kay's replacement. Thomas Bavin immediately challenged the appointment but Lang defended it under the *Parliamentary Casual Vacancies Act*. Kay, he argued, had previously voted with the government on Confidence and Supply so he was justified in appointing a Labor party member to the seat.

Millicent, recalling Kay's assertion of keeping the government in office for three years, was indignant. She directed a question at Lang, although it was more of an accusation than a question. She pointed to the inadequate remuneration Dr Morris received for his 'vital and scientific' contributions to infant health compared with the very generous remuneration of £1500 paid to Kay for 'unskilled services' to the Meat Board. Needless to say, Lang brushed her intervention aside.[12]

As the weeks ticked over, Millicent kept up her strategy of using questions without notice to keep the spotlight on her issues. On 19 October, unwisely, she put a question to the Speaker himself. Prefacing her question with the statement that members were 'greatly interested in the business of this house', she asked if he would raise his voice or have 'a loud-speaker installed'. Her question clearly irritated him; the problem was not his voice, he snapped, but too many members speaking at the same time.[13]

Her next target that day was the Minister for Health, George Cann. She prefaced her question with a long preamble about inadequate staffing levels adversely affecting Dr Morris's work in infant and maternal health. The Speaker warned her 'to ask a question', not 'give information'. Injudiciously, she challenged him, but he cited Standing Order 77 and instructed her to reframe her question. Millicent obeyed: 'I ask the Minister whether it would not be advisable in the circumstances, and considering the important character of the services of Dr Morris, that a staff of persons necessary to carry out his work be appointed?'. Cann responded dismissively that the Government was taking all appropriate steps 'to provide the necessary officers'.[14]

Millicent then devised a strategy for ensuring her motions were placed on the Orders for the Day in positions that would ensure they were dealt with. Her two priorities were the care of the feebleminded and infant guardianship so she submitted two motions dealing with these issues and nominated two specific dates, Tuesday 26 October and Tuesday 2 November. On Tuesdays between 10 am and 12 noon, once questions and petitions were exhausted, General Business took precedence. She expected each motion would be the first on the Notice Papers for that day. Unfortunately, she had not anticipated the tricks the government could employ.

On Tuesday 26 October more than sixty questions occupied members until midday. Although her motion for a bill to care for the feebleminded was listed as No 1 for General Business, it was not dealt with on that day. At 12.01 the Speaker called on Government Business to proceed 'in pursuance of sessional order of 22nd September 1926'. Members turned their attention to Land Agents, Newcastle District Abattoir and Sale Yards, Fire Brigades and Coal Mines. Once again Millicent sat powerless as men's affairs took precedence over women's concerns. Surely, her infant guardianship motion, listed as No 1 for Tuesday 2 November would not meet the same fate?

In preparing her speech, perhaps Millicent pondered the infant guardianship campaign Caroline Norton had waged in England a century ago. Caroline had been fortunate to have the support of Sir Thomas Talfourd who steered the legislation that gave mothers equal rights in their children through the House of Commons.[15] She perhaps hoped for support from the NSW Attorney General David Hall who had assisted the earlier campaigns waged by Maybanke Anderson and Rose Scott. Their work had achieved many positive changes for women but the father-right principle, enshrined in common law by the 18th century English jurist William Blackstone, who declared the mother 'is entitled to no power, but only reverence and respect', remained.[16] Yes, the mother is entitled to reverence and respect, Millicent maintained, but she is also entitled to the power to make decisions for her child.

On Tuesday 2 November 1926 northerly winds and showers lashed Sydney. Millicent entered the Chamber expecting to move that leave be granted to bring in her bill, and once leave was granted, she would outline her bill's key provisions and answer any questions. Debate on the bill would come later.

At 11.33 am the Speaker gave her the call. She rose and moved 'that leave be given to bring in a bill to amend the law relating to the guardianship, maintenance, and custody of infants'. Surveying the men before her, she told them she was speaking on behalf of 20,000 women and men – this was no rhetorical figure but the actual number of people who signed the 1924 Polini petition. That case affronted women's sense of 'right and justice', she told the parliament, because it had done a 'great injustice' to the mother by depriving her of her child. But, she continued, the problem was not the judge or the judgement *per se*, but the law that permitted it. The salient point was the law did not require the judge to take into account the mother's wishes.[17]

Dr Herbert Vere Evatt, a barrister with a doctorate of laws, interjected. The courts did take account of mothers' wishes, he declared. Millicent rebutted his statement. He asserted it was a 'fact'. She refuted his fact. He accused her of objecting not to the law itself, but to the 'application of the law in one case'. Millicent responded that she had no objection to 'the application of the law by Mr Justice Harvey' in the Polini case, but her concern was with the law, and she quoted *verbatim* from Harvey's judgement: 'The law in this State has not put the wife's right to the custody of the children so high as the law in England has'. Or 'in other words', she explained, 'the law in New South Wales does not require the court to have regard to the wishes of the mother'. She apologised to Evatt for having had to 'cross swords with such a distinguished gentlemen'. Evatt admitted he was unaware of that passage in Harvey's judgement and she diplomatically thanked him.

However, fellow Nationalist James Arkins, a less distinguished gentleman, then interjected disdainfully, 'If you read the report you will see he said he was sorry for the mother!'. Any reasonable judge anywhere in the world, she quipped, would naturally feel sorry for the mother but the point remained, the judge was sorry the law required him to make that judgement.

Aware of the limited time available, Millicent explained the maternal preference clause included in her bill, which, like the English law, established the mother as the natural guardian of children of 'tender' years. Arkins again objected, throwing up a series of hypothetical scenarios that attributed the blame for marriage failure to the mother. Millicent countered each scenario until, in frustration, she finally riposted, 'Men have just as many faults and peculiarities, and are just as difficult to live with, as women' and men are 'responsible for just as many shipwrecks as women'. Her barbed response indicated she would no longer tolerate his constant needling. Finally, another Nationalist John Lee asked about any retrospectivity that could be applied to 'the case referred to'. The intent of his question was to test whether Millicent's bill would overthrow Harvey's judgement. The legislation was not retrospective, Millicent assured him, although Polini 'may make application under it'.

Millicent drew her remarks to a close by demonstrating how far advanced England was in recognising mothers' rights by comparison with this state. Unfortunately, she chose a problematic case to illustrate her point – a British mother who had given birth to an illegitimate child had not been denied the right to her other legitimate child. For the moral warriors in the Chamber this was a bridge too far! Millicent reassured them she was not endorsing immoral behaviour, but simply pointing out the differences in legal rights between married and unmarried mothers.

However, not content to stop there, she continued, 'If there is to be any differentiation in the status of parents towards their children, then let the inferior status be given to men and not to women'. Not surprisingly, this prompted a further eruption as members accused her of denying fathers their 'natural' rights. For Millicent this was the nub of the problem – no law court should be able to take from a mother 'the inalienable right' that she 'unquestionably has in her baby' she snapped. And with that, time had expired.

Attorney General Edward McTiernan declared he was 'not prepared to oppose the motion that leave be given to introduce the bill', and he was 'very anxious to see the content of the measure', a statement Millicent would come to see as duplicitous. With the bill read a first time, Millicent felt a surge of satisfaction; this was her first real success in the parliament.

Regrettably, that feeling soon deflated. Millicent's bill was listed for Second Reading on 16 November. The session began with printed questions and answers followed by more than sixty questions without notice, mostly Dorothy Dixers, on vital subjects such as Newcastle Racing Club, Corridor Tram Cars, Bricklayers' Wages and Parliament House Members' Private Entrance, all of which filled the time for General Business. At 12.02 pm members turned their attention to Government Business. Colonial Secretary Carlo Lazzarini moved that the Police Offences Amendment (Drugs) Bill be read a second time. Millicent's bill was not considered on that day.

The events of the previous week should have forewarned her. The Orders of the Day for Tuesday 9 November had listed two motions. The first was Millicent's motion for a bill to care for the feebleminded which had not been dealt with in October, and the second was Arthur Tonge's urgency motion for the suspension of standing orders so the House could debate the establishment of a 'select committee to inquire into and report upon the case of Nicholas versus Andrew, and the whole of Frank Quigg's interest under his father's will'. Millicent sat through the first eighteen minutes which were taken up with sixteen printed questions and answers and thirty seven questions without notice.

Then, without any advance warning, the Speaker ignored the listed order of motions and gave Arthur Tonge the call.[18] Tonge began to explain the situation behind his motion but the Speaker counselled him to address the argument for the urgency first before he dealt with his motion's substance. Tonge obliged; it was urgent because the matter had stood on the business papers for months, some aspects went back a decade and the situation stretched back fifty-nine years – questionable arguments for urgency to say the least, but the Speaker allowed them. The question was put, and the urgency motion passed.

Tonge then outlined the details of a long standing dispute about a fence and three and a half acres of land in the Canterbury district. Thomas Bavin promptly interjected, pointing out that Tonge's motion concerned a 'purely private matter' of no public importance, which should be dealt with in the courts and since the matter began in 1867 it could 'wait another week'. Moreover, he went on, the Government was permitting an 'electioneering stunt' for Tonge to 'advertise himself to his electorate'. The disputed land was not in Tonge's North Shore electorate, but in Canterbury which, Bavin presciently predicted, Tonge would contest at the next election.[19]

Furthermore, Bavin asserted Tonge's matter was not as important as Millicent's motion which 'really affects the welfare of the people of this country' and the 'result of taking this motion will be to interfere with Miss Preston-Stanley's chance of bringing before the House a matter of very great public interest'. Fellow Nationalist Frank Chaffey added that the 'House was being trifled with' since 'Miss Preston Stanley took the proper course of giving notice early in the session' while Mr Tonge 'gave notice of his motion only a few days ago'.

Millicent was probably grateful for this support but these arguments did not convince the Speaker. He permitted debate on the 'purely private matter' to continue. Vexed that the issue of the feebleminded was being pushed aside with such disdain, but powerless to do anything, Millicent voted against each motion in the divisions. When debate about the composition of the select committee became heated, Cann applied the gag. Some members attempted to move further amendments but the Speaker called for Order and ruled no further amendments could be put. Tonge's manoeuvre consumed the allocated time for General Business and at 12.14 pm the House moved on to consider the Police Offences Amendment (Drugs) Bill. That put paid, once again, to Millicent's motion for a bill to care for the feebleminded.

Millicent was perplexed by Cann's role in the manoeuvre that thwarted her motion, since he would have been the Minister responsible for introducing the mental health bill she was advocating. Perhaps she gained some insight into his motives when she read the press accounts. Under the headline 'Getting in First', one journalist reported that Cann intended to introduce a government bill to deal with mental defectives and hinted that this was the reason for his 'forestalling' Millicent's initiative.[20] Another paper reported that, as he gave notice, Cann 'glanced slyly' at Millicent but 'the lady member returned him a withering frown'.[21] Whether this was an accurate account or not, Cann's tactics were designed to shore up his own position and exert power over Millicent. She would lock horns with him again before the month passed.

At 4.39 pm on Monday 29 November Millicent entered the Supply Bill (No 2) debate.[22] In a fiery speech in which she initially appeared to be in support of the government's bill, she proffered a conditional proposition. 'If the Government could be trusted to keep its promises there would be very little objection to passing the proposal', she said. Then came the twist; she opposed the bill precisely because the Government could not be trusted. She pointed to the 'bitter experience' that had reinforced her belief in the Government's perfidy in its 'logrolling', 'engineering', and 'devious, tortuous and sinuous practices'. The worst instance of this deceit was the 'improper approach' Minister Cann made to her the previous Friday.

Millicent's account of Cann's proposition surprised many Members, perhaps less because of the nature of his proposal than her exposure of it. She claimed he asked her to cross the floor 'in order to nullify the influence' of the Labor members who had been threatening to defect. She quoted what she said were Cann's words:

> We understand you are not open to any material bribe. We understand that money cannot buy you, but we also believe you are a woman who puts legislation affecting the womanhood of the country before all party considerations.[23]

Cann told her he would be sorry if she, 'the first woman to come into this House' lost her seat after a mere sixteen months. If the Supply bill was not passed, he warned her, there would have to be an election and she would undoubtedly lose her seat. She had heard this as a threat, as Cann probably intended it to be heard. She succinctly summarised his proposition for the chamber:

> You can, if you are prepared, occupy a most important position in the political life of this country. You have only to cross the floor of the House and support the Labor party on Monday morning and this is the position you will be in.[24]

To ensure Members understood the implications of her disclosure, she then interpreted his proposal in her own words; 'If you cross the floor of the House the Government is prepared to allow you to dictate the terms on which the Budget will be passed'. Both sides of the chamber erupted in interjections.

Millicent initially assured the House she had rejected Cann's offer on moral and ethical grounds. Her letter to Cann, which she read to the Chamber to ensure her words were recorded *verbatim* in Hansard, said, *inter alia*, 'I could not think of casting my vote on the side of a Government in the manner suggested – even though it would place the fate of the Government in my hands and ensure the introduction and passage of legislation which I have so long advocated'.[25] These must have been some of the most difficult words this social justice warrior ever uttered.

Cann's offer, she declared, was irrefutable evidence the Government was not honourable because it was 'prepared to buy or to barter or to bribe or to purchase' its position. Despite being offered the chance to realise her ambitions, she 'could not buy it at such a price', certainly not 'at the price of my personal honour'. The events of the past month seemed to coalesce and clarify in her mind as she accused the Government and Cann of usurping her motion with a 'trick' and 'stratagem':

> It was an outrage upon this House that we were not allowed to discuss one of the most important motions invoking the physical and mental health of the people which had ever been placed on the business paper. That is why I say to every hon. Member here that when we know that this is the sort of thing that is happening, when we are not permitted to bring forward such important business, then we realise the whole thing is farcical and absurd in the extreme.[26]

In an explosion of emotion she accused Cann of warning her earlier that day not to expose him, to which she had responded; 'I am the arbiter of my own fate'. She had indeed become the arbiter of her own fate and it was now sealed.

The passionate intensity of her speech was a revelation to those who had previously witnessed her tightly controlled anger but not her emotional distress. But that did not prevent them from attacking her. Cann interjected with denials and retorts, hurling *ad hominem* abuse; 'You are a squib', 'You are not sincere', 'You are misleading the women'. Other government members also launched their verbal missiles. 'Why should you have precedence over Mr Tonge?' barked John Tully; 'You deserve all you get' snarled Christopher Kelly and 'Do you honestly believe that for the sake of a problematical two months you have the right to sacrifice those women and children' bayed Mark Gosling. Millicent was bereft of her usual defences, and for the first time in the parliament she struggled for words.

The Speaker permitted Cann to respond at length to Millicent's statement. He declared he was not surprised at her seething overflow of passion, her 'ebullition', although he absolved himself of blame. He denied being involved in Tonge's motion but admitted phoning Millicent. Contrary to her account, he asserted she was eager to meet him, a statement she refuted. Cann conceded he offered to introduce his Mental Defectives bill and Hospitals bill but claimed Millicent demanded the Guardianship of Infants bill be included in the deal. He admitted he told her she would 'have to come over and vote' with the government. He then asked the members, 'Is there anything wrong with that? Did I offer anything? Did I offer her the Speakership or anything else?'.[27]

Insisting he had 'no authority from anybody' to make the offer he then counter-attacked. Millicent was 'a fraud of a member', the 'most callous representative of women', who was 'sailing under false colours' because she did not properly represent 'the womanhood' of the state and she had lost women's 'confidence'. Incredulously, he added that Millicent had not drafted the letter she had sent him; he did not know who drafted it, he asserted, but 'Miss Preston Stanley did not'.

Millicent refuted each of his statements; 'It is not true' and 'I did not' she repeatedly cried, but government members amplified his hostility. The Speaker assisted the onslaught using points of order to prevent Millicent offering personal explanations, ruling she was 'not entitled to reply to the statements made by the Minister so far as their general accuracy is concerned', although he would permit her to make a statement if the Minister misquoted or misrepresented her. She became flustered and only managed to splutter one feeble correction to Cann's accusations; she never used the slang word, 'kidding'.

Deflated and isolated, she was thankful that one Nationalist, Tom Hoskins rose to condemn Cann's treatment of her. 'I want to tell the hon. Member', Hoskins said, 'that the unkind and unmannerly remarks he made this afternoon were not deserved'. At that the Speaker shut down debate and the House adjourned.

These interchanges were fodder for the press. The scene was reported under headlines such as 'Rowdy Scenes in Parliament' and 'Uproar in Legislative Assembly' while the bribe was highlighted in headlines such as 'The Temptation', 'Miss Stanley's Disclosure', 'Inducements to Cross Floor' and 'Told She Could be Dictator'. One reporter commented on the level of emotion Millicent displayed, noting her 'dangerously red' face, her voice rising 'a tone' and the 'glance of splendid scorn' she cast on the 'unrepentant Mr Cann'.[28]

One of the most colourful accounts was published under the headline, 'The Triumph of Virtue'. It described the 'Machiavellian diplomacy' of the 'political Don Giovanni', Minister Cann, who attempted to lead astray a woman of 'courage and political acumen'. Knowing he could not tempt her with gold or high office, he offered her the legislation she had set her heart on. Millicent had been given a lesson in politics by a man who, under his 'kind countenance and genial manner', was nothing more than a 'ravening wolf'. However, the journalist continued, Cann chose his victim badly and showed himself naïve in the psychology of the fair sex, as she remained 'steadfast and true'. By exposing Cann in the parliament, she gave the opposition 'a splendid opportunity for that display of virtue which dazzled the House'.[29]

However, another journalist writing under the pseudonym 'Vignette' captured their *contretemps* as a boxing match and suggested that Millicent had only won by landing 'a smart punch below Mr Cann's belt'.[30] This was not the kind of press she wanted to attract.

Millicent's performance left her despondent. By refusing to compromise her values she had effectively undermined her own agenda. She attended the last sitting days of 1926 without speaking, although she voted with her Party on each division. Neither of her motions appeared on the notice papers. Nor did Cann's supposed Mental Defectives bill make an appearance.

The Supply Bill passed; the Government retained power; Lang remained Premier. On 24 December, the final sitting day of 1926, Members exchanged the customary expressions of seasonal good wishes. Lang, overlooking the presence of a woman in the House, opined that politics was 'a very contentious business' because it involved 'men holding sincere views and opinions', but each member is working for the good of the country 'as it appears to him' and despite the turbulence, parliament exhibits a 'brotherly feeling'.

Millicent was probably perplexed that parliamentary language elided the woman's presence. Despite her own statement to the house about the inclusivity of the word 'man', she did not feel the word 'brotherly' embraced her in the same way it included the male members.

As members left the Chamber for the Christmas break Millicent perhaps considered she had been naïve in refusing Cann's bribe and then exposing it to the House. Nevertheless, she reassured herself, she had stood true to her principles.

And so she set off for her brief respite in the Blue Mountains, probably pondering how she might be able to achieve her goals when she returned in January for the last year of her parliamentary term.

7

Pass that Bill
(1927-1930)

Millicent Preston Stanley MLA. Parliamentary Champion of a mother's right to have care of her children.

Sun, 7 August 1927[1]

When parliament resumed on Tuesday 11 January 1927, Millicent was frustrated to see her motions were again competing for a place on the parliamentary agenda. Labor intended to push through a plethora of bills before the end of its term. However, as an opposition backbencher she had few avenues to ensure her bills were included. Moreover, she had experienced the government's nifty footwork in blocking her attempts to do so.

On Friday, 14 January, Millicent submitted a motion that her Guardianship of Infants bill,

> ... which was introduced in the Assembly during a previous session of the present Parliament, but was interrupted before its completion by the close of the session, be now re-introduced at the stage it had reached at the time of such interruption.[2]

In other words, she did not want to go back to square one and reintroduce the bill but proceed from the Second Reading stage her bill had reached when it lapsed the previous year. Her motion was listed, albeit at No 6 on the Orders of the Day for Tuesday 18 January. But once again she was destined for disappointment. Questions without notice and debate on the Transport bill, the Crown Lands Amendment bill, the Closer Settlement and Returned Soldiers Settlement Amendment bill and the Parliamentary Electorates and Elections bill consumed the morning session. No time remained for her motion.

Millicent was irritated but she had no intention of remaining mute. The next day, when Lang moved that 'leave be given to bring in a bill to make provision against the discharge or escape of oil into navigable waters', Millicent rose to speak, but not to oppose his bill. Rather, she applauded his initiative to prevent pollution in Sydney Harbour but asked Lang to extend the bill to sewage pollution at Sydney's ocean beaches. Her concern was the public health risk for people using ocean beaches, particularly Bondi Beach in her electorate. Once again she encountered Lang's condescension; the 'eternal and ever-present consideration of finance', he advised her, would be an insurmountable obstacle.[3]

The following week, when the Minister of Justice, William McKell sought leave to introduce the Liquor Amendment bill, which aimed to ease restrictions on the sale of alcohol, she was not so easily silenced. This bill opened up a chasm in the Chamber, not along party lines but on attitudes to temperance. Millicent was quickly on her feet declaring

> ... when we come to think of what is actually involved, when we come to think that most of the misery, most of the crime, most of the debauchery, and most of the sorrow of the human family is caused by the liquor business which we are now asked to protect, it ill becomes us to be so spiritually dead that we cannot show feeling over a matter of this character.[4]

She spoke with passion, and while the members were aware of her commitment to temperance, they were oblivious to her personal experience of the destructive effects alcohol had on families.

There were two main grounds for opposing the bill, Millicent told the House; firstly, it infringed the integrity of 6 o'clock closing approved by the 1916 referendum and secondly, it discontinued payments by the liquor industry into a compensation fund designed to recompense affected industries should prohibition be introduced, as it had been in America, and as Millicent hoped it would be in Australia. She was not alone in her opposition to the bill – many members on both sides of the House were temperance advocates but she was irritated by Nationalist Party members who supported the bill, particularly the leader, Thomas Bavin.

A majority of people voted for 6 o'clock closing in 1916, and a majority of people still wanted early closing, Millicent asserted, although this was a dubious declaration. Unwisely, she supported her case by citing the former Justice Minister, Thomas Ley, whose 'unctuous manner' and 'virulently sectarian' support for temperance had earned him the nickname, 'Lemonade Ley'.[5]

Multiple members were quick to point out that whatever Ley, who was no longer a member of parliament, may have said then, or whatever he may say now, was irrelevant. The current Act was no longer fit for purpose, they declared, and in particular, 6 o'clock closing created insurmountable difficulties for policing hotel dining rooms where it was legal to serve liquor to hotel residents after 6 o'clock but not to hotel residents' guests. As one Member reminded Millicent, she had been present at the Empire Parliamentary Delegation banquet at the Australia Hotel and had witnessed this law infringement when alcohol was served to guests after 6 o'clock.

Undeterred by their counter-arguments, Millicent attacked the Minister who, she asserted, had 'tricked and fooled' the Temperance Alliance by denying the government was planning any amendments to liquor laws in this term. To prove her point she read his incriminating letter to the Chamber.

> I have to inform you that no alterations of the liquor laws in any direction are at present in contemplation. In the event of any necessity arising to amend these laws, every facility will be afforded your Alliance to fully place any representations it is desired to make in the matter before me for consideration.[6]

As the level of passion escalated, debate descended into something resembling theatre of the absurd. Members indulged in convoluted dissertations about whether clubs and wine bars, which

Millicent asserted 'degraded' Australian womanhood, should, or should not, fall under the bill's provisions and debate revolved around what constituted a *'bona-fide* meal'. Was a 'sandwich' or 'a bit of cheese and a biscuit' a *bona-fide* meal? Must a person eating a *bona-fide* meal sit at a table? Did a person have to consume the food or only order it? Members tossed their claims and counter-claims around the Chamber sharpened by *ad hominem* barbs. 'You are a wowser', 'That is absurd', 'That is only a lawyer's subterfuge', they snarled. The Speaker frequently called for order but they challenged his rulings – 'I cannot see I am out of order' and 'I wish to dissent from your ruling'.

Some taunts were aimed directly at Millicent – 'You are only a novice', to which she snapped, 'If it is a sign of my novitiate in the public life of this country that I am not absolutely dead to things of this character, then may I long remain a novice', until eventually she exploded, 'I am not a child'. Albert Lane, who had been a councillor on the NSW Prohibition Alliance summed it up; 'The whole question has been fought with so much personal abuse', although that insight did not prevent him from engaging in fisticuffs with Carlo Lazzarini on the floor of the House. Both Members were escorted from the Chamber by the Sergeant-at-arms. Despite the turbulence and turmoil, the bill passed.

Millicent's next opportunity to speak about issues of concern for women came when Minister John Baddeley introduced the Family Endowment bill on 8 February.[7] This bill provided for child endowment to be paid to mothers – a policy in line with Millicent's values although not one applauded by Theo Hill who, to Millicent's disgust, labelled it 'advanced communistic legislation' and a 'vote-catching exercise' that would have a detrimental effect on the 'character of the people' of the state.

Millicent 'supported the principle of family endowment as warmly as any member', she assured the House, because children were the nation's 'greatest asset' and the family was the 'one indispensable base upon which the whole social structure is reared'. Mothers performed the most important social function for the state because they bore and reared the nation's greatest asset – children. She acknowledged that the inadequate basic wage caused lower living standards for large families and child endowment would help to alleviate this problem. But, she warned, the cost of endowment should not fall solely on industry as Labor's bill provided, but should be shared with the general taxpayer.

Millicent then turned her attack on the government. Labor was hypocritical in asserting this was their initiative, she carped, because family endowment was Nationalist Party policy and Labor had not supported it when a previous Nationalist government attempted to introduce it. Not content to leave it there, she launched into criticism of fellow Nationalist, Thomas Henley. She was appalled by comments that Henley had previously made about the hardships his mother endured. How could he 'gloat and glory over the difficulties his mother' endured, she quipped, but not see any need for her 'to be released from her labours'. Once again she picked the wrong target. Henley demanded she withdraw her comments but Millicent read her refutation to the parliament, accusing Henley of sending her a 'bellicose' letter. Needless to say, the Speaker called her to order, she challenged his ruling, but he cut her off. The bill passed and the House moved on to other matters.

Time to introduce her motions was slipping away. There was an election due this year and Millicent became concerned that Labor was not focussed on women's concerns. Even the Metropolitan Milk Bill which William Dunn introduced on 9 March was concerned with the establishment of an authority to develop and regulate the milk industry, rather than with health issues associated with supplying fresh milk for children in the metropolitan region. On 23 March, Millicent spoke against the composition of the bill's proposed authority – the Milk Board, because of its weighting towards men who were advocating pasteurised rather than fresh milk and she succeeded in having an amendment passed that ensured the availability of 'both fresh dairy milk and pasteurised milk' for children.

As time moved on, Millicent sensed opportunities to debate her Guardianship of Infants bill were fading. After three months of intense sittings, on 24 March, Lang moved the adjournment. Country Party leader, Ernest Buttenshaw commented he had not 'experienced a session as strenuous as the one which is just closing' and the Speaker wished members a 'well-earned rest'. The House adjourned until 5 April. Then unexpectedly, on 4 April parliament was prorogued. Millicent was aghast; her bill was now at real risk of lapsing, again.

Nevertheless, not one to waste a moment and with parliament in recess, she poured her energies into her political work in the community, particularly generating support for her bill.

Public interest in infant custody legislation was revived in July with news of Emélie Polini's death. Under the headlines, 'EMELIE POLINI NOW FINDS REST IN DEATH. Mother's Broken Heart. Beautiful Actress's Vain Fight for her Baby Girl Recalled by Sympathisers', the journalist reprised the narrative of the 'brilliant actress, adoring mother, and splendid wife' whose tragic life was ruined by an unjust law. The journalist outlined the attempts 'Millicent Preston Stanley. M.L.A., Parliamentary Champion of a mother's right to have care of her children', was making to amend the legislation and explained that Labor blocked them because it did not want the Nationalists to 'reap the credit of enacting a law so popular with women voters'. According to Ruby Rich, 'when Miss Preston Stanley's Bill becomes law, it will be a monument to Emelie [sic] Polini' because Polini was speaking to them from the grave, 'Pass that bill'.[8] Millicent was determined that when parliament resumed it would pass that bill.

But, parliament did not resume.

On 7 September the Legislative Assembly, which had not sat since March, was dissolved and the election set for 8 October. Millicent turned her mind to her third election campaign. It was complicated by Lang's successful amendments to the Parliamentary

Electorates and Elections Act which abolished multi-member seats and altered electoral boundaries.

Millicent was endorsed as the Nationalist Party candidate for the Bondi electorate and she threw herself into her campaign with her customary energy and determination as women's organisations rallied to support her re-election. She would raise women's issues in the parliament – children's health, maternal mortality, supporting deserted wives, raising the age of consent and – she would pass that bill, she promised her audiences.[9]

Although Millicent did not expect her campaign would be glitch-free she did not anticipate Harold Jaques' subterfuge. Jaques, who had resigned from the party after Millicent defeated him as the endorsed candidate for Bondi, cunningly presented himself as the Independent Nationalist candidate for that electorate. He even claimed, falsely, that there were two Nationalist candidates and since he was the preferred one, Millicent should direct her supporters to allocate their first preferences to him, to ensure the seat was won by the Nationalist Party.[10] The 'How to Vote' card issued by his campaign placed the numeral 1 against Jaques, 2 against Millicent and 3 against the Labor candidate, Susan Francis. One journalist suggested Jaques was extracting the 'wages of loyalty'[11] from the woman who had usurped what he considered his rightful place. Even if that was not his motivation, it was an effective manoeuvre; Jaques defeated Millicent with a clear majority, gaining more than 7,000 votes to her 3,000. He then rejoined the Nationalist Party and returned to parliament as the member for Bondi in the Nationalist government.

Millicent had hoped to make 'saner laws' and establish 'more just conditions' for women but now that women had no representation in the parliament, she quipped, they had only themselves to blame.[12] She remained angry and despondent that her attempt to amend custody legislation had been thwarted by Labor government tactics and her re-election obstructed by the machinations of a fellow Nationalist, who, as an unmarried man, could have little understanding of the plight of mothers and children. If only she had been elected, she was sure the Nationalist government would have passed that bill.

But there was light at the end of the tunnel. Francis Boyce KC, a temperance advocate with progressive social views about women and children was appointed Attorney General. At the 1928 Premiers' Conference Boyce successfully moved 'That the law relating to guardianship of infants should be uniform in all states and should be based upon English law of 1925'.[13] A bill for equal rights for mothers now seemed within reach but, with no woman in parliament, it was not a time for women's organisations to rest on their laurels. 'It is easy enough to give up – at the 'giving up point' but it is 'holding on that takes pluck', Millicent declared. While the 'weak give up and fail', she opined, 'the strong hold on – and win'. She was determined to hold on and win this vital legislation while the Nationalist government was in power.[14] As a student of the parliament, she also knew there had been a change of government at each election since 1920, and it was all the more urgent that the Nationalist government pass that bill before the next election.

Women's organisations were alert to the moment and they revitalised their campaigns. In August 1929, the National Council of Women (NSW) arranged a deputation to Attorney General Boyce of three hundred representatives from more than seventy organisations. Millicent's bill, they told Boyce, should be the model for a new bill,[15] and Nationalist Reginald Weaver would be the women's ambassador in the Cabinet.[16] Elegantly clad in coats, gloves and cloche hats, these middle-class women posed for the cameras on the steps as they left parliament house.[17] The newspaper accounts don't mention Millicent's participation but her influence is evident in their reference to her bill as the basis for the new bill and Weaver as their ambassador.

The campaign gained further traction when an article in the

Sydney Morning Herald argued it was time 'archaic laws' dealing with child custody were amended and replaced with more enlightened and equitable ones.[18] The writer was a prominent Sydney businessman, A E Norden, Manager of the Union Trustee Company of Australia, which dealt with wills and deceased estates. He frequently published articles on issues such as 'Intestate Estates' and 'Double Probate Duty' and his interest in child custody legislation may have stemmed from following the protracted hearings in the Polini will case.

Four days later, Justice Long Innes KC handed down his decision in that case ruling against the conditions in Polini's will, which he determined were an attempt to interfere with the court's discretion in regards to custody and which would deter the father from performing his parental duties.[19] Whatever prompted Norden's interest, his intervention was timely; four days later, Premier Bavin announced the laws would be amended to bring them 'into conformity' with those of England.[20] To the delight of women's organisations, the following month, in opening the new session of parliament Governor Dudley de Chair announced:

> In response to the representations made by representative deputations of women it is proposed to introduce bills amending the law relating to the age of marriage and dealing with the question of guardianship of infants.

Boyce introduced the government's bill into the Legislative Council on 17 December 1929. In the Second Reading in February 1930, he paid tribute to the large delegation of 'womenfolk of the community' who were demanding this bill. The Polini case had caused a 'great outcry amongst the womenfolk of the community' and, he assured Members, 'this bill does what his Honour the Chief Judge in Equity then hinted should be done'. The bill was, he said, a long-overdue measure that would put NSW law on an equal footing with English law and bring it in line with Victoria.

Millicent was encouraged that there was little initial resistance to the bill. Nationalist William Robson queried whether it would overthrow Justice Harvey's judgement while Labor member Joseph Coates noted that the Polini case had drawn the 'attention of the public to a wrong that might be done to a mother' which this bill would now rectify. Boyce's bill passed through the Council without amendment and was despatched to the Legislative Assembly. This seemed to be an auspicious introduction and some journalists predicted its ultimate success since it had passed the usually conservative Legislative Council without any disagreement.

Despite the optimism, Millicent was perturbed that Boyce's bill did not include the maternal preference clause.[21] Having returned to the Presidency of the Feminist Club after a split that saw some members resign and establish a rival organisation, the United Associations of Women, Millicent took the lead in lobbying for the bill. Her first foray was a deputation of Feminist Club members to Boyce. The women argued for the inclusion of the maternal preference clause for children of tender years. A mother had an 'inalienable right to her child', she told Boyce and it was vital that this bill included that maternal preference clause just as English law did. Without committing to including the clause, Boyce reassured the deputation they 'had a friend in him' – an assurance that Millicent would later come to doubt.[22]

On 12 February 1930 Premier Thomas Bavin moved the First Reading in the Assembly without any adverse commentary from members. In the Second Reading in March, Minister for Justice, John Lee acknowledged wide community support for the bill which Millicent had first brought before the House. Labor member William Davies asked him what the situation would be if both mother and father were found to be of good character, to which Lee responded that the mother was better fitted than the father to bring up a child, a view in accord with Millicent's perspective.

Not all Members agreed. Nevertheless, some members indicated they would not oppose the bill but during the Committee stage, they would contest features such as the centralisation of court procedures in Sydney and the court jurisdiction clause. Harold Jaques unsuccessfully sought an adjournment because, in his opinion, the bill was a 'very great alteration' to the existing legislation since it removed the father right principle.

The following day arguments erupted around issues relating to the Polini judgement, the women's campaigns and the powers of the courts. Some members voiced a spirited defence of Justice Harvey's judgement in the Polini case; some accused the government of using the bill as a 'sop' to women; others focussed on procedural aspects relating to the operation of the courts. Amidst the disputations, three amendments passed: the court's jurisdiction was widened to allow Magistrates in lower courts presiding under the District Courts Act and the Justices Act to hear custody cases; the payment of child maintenance by the father was limited to children under sixteen years; and a mother or father would be permitted to leave the Court's jurisdiction without *ipso facto* being disqualified from gaining custody – an issue that had played a part in the Polini decision. It was a lively but civilised debate and as Jack Lang commented, it was carried out in a 'non-party atmosphere'. On 13 March the amended bill was returned to the Legislative Council, where it sat idle for two months.

From her own experience in the House, Millicent doubted whether this parliament would pass that bill, or indeed any bill designed to improve the lives of women and children. She determined that women's organisations must maintain pressure on the government. As one journalist reported, with 'Miss Preston Stanley, ex-MLA' as President, the Feminist Club established a Legislative Committee to monitor all parliamentary bills affecting women and children and a Lobbying Committee 'to influence the trend of political thought towards the reforms required' so as to ensure women's issues were included in all bills.[23] To support this work, the Club outlined a Charter of Goals that included making democracy safe for motherhood, making equality real for womanhood, and ensuring the maximum chance for childhood.[24] In her keynote address to the Club, Millicent assured members that women did 'not want to take the privileges from the men', but they wanted the barriers to equality removed.[25] Lady Game, the Governor's wife praised the Feminist Club Charter expressing her pleasure that 'there is no spirit of competition with men, as the longer one lives the more firmly one believes in the spirit of co-operation'.[26]

Millicent certainly hoped that co-operation would prevail as Boyce reintroduced the amended bill into the Council. Alas, that was not to be. He moved that some of the Legislative Assembly's amendments should be rejected. Nationalist lawyer Broughton O'Conor supported the Assembly's amendment to allow District Court judges to hear custody cases but in a Chamber dominated by lawyers his view was in the minority. The Council rejected that amendment on the basis of the lack of 'machinery' in either the District Courts Act or the Justices Act to deal with custody issues.

The Legislative Council returned the amended bill to the Assembly on 21 May where it encountered turbulence. Members were irate that mothers, particularly those from regional areas, would be forced to make application to the most expensive court in the land, the Equity Court in Sydney. Lang fulminated that there was to be one law for rich mothers and one for poor. Others were concerned about the relationship between the two Chambers. Labor member Andrew Lysaght summed up the situation – the 'Legislative Council should not attempt to control the actions of the Legislative Assembly, as the will of the elective House should take effect.' When it became obvious that members would not accept the Council's advice, Minister Lee adjourned debate.

On 4 June, Lee presented the Assembly with advice from Attorney General Boyce that the extension of the court's jurisdiction inserted by the Council should stand until the District Courts Act was amended. The opposition rejected this advice, leaving Lee in an irresolvable situation. The parliamentary session ended on 20 June without the bill receiving any further consideration.

Women's organisations were irate. In an article in the *Herald*, Joyce Cocks from the National Council of Women fulminated at the bill's sad situation – 'unacceptable to the Assembly in one form, and rejected by the Council in another'. She warned that women would no longer 'suffer a thwarting of their wishes by a handful of politicians without emphatic and effective protest'.[27]

A deputation from the United Associations of Women comprising Linda Littlejohn, Marie Byles and Emily Bennett met with both Attorney General Boyce and Minister Lee. They argued that work on the bill should continue and suggested that if the present parliament passed the bill it would be 'one of the best pieces of work' this Government could accomplish. Diplomatically, Boyce told them he was looking for a 'suitable compromise'.[28]

Millicent revived the Polini petition and lodged it with the Majestic Theatre, Newtown where more women and men added their signatures to the original petition.[29] A letter to the editor by M C Videon bemoaned the fact that 'this much needed reform has been shelved when the goal for which many of us have been striving seemed to have been reached'.[30]

The shelved bill was not salvaged before the October 1930 elections. The Bavin government was defeated and the incoming Lang government dashed Millicent's hopes that the parliament would pass that bill. Nevertheless, the United Associations and the Feminist Club continued their lobbying campaigns with the newly installed Labor government. Although ideologically opposed on some issues these two women's organisations were of one mind on this matter, despite their reluctance to engage in collaborative strategies. In December 1930 a Feminist Club deputation led by Millicent to the Minister for Justice, Joseph Lamaro, was rebuffed with a non-committal response.[31] The United Associations deputation to Premier Lang, led by Jessie Street, was assured the bill would shortly be brought forward.[32] But no bill appeared.

The frustrations spilled over into 1931. In January, the United Associations held a mock parliament to debate the guardianship bill.[33] In February Marie Byles addressed the Women Justices Association and organised a further deputation to Minister Lamaro.[34] In March, with no action forthcoming, Jessie Street took another deputation to the Minister who said the government had to deal with other matters of much greater importance. Street commented this illustrated the 'iron hand behind the velvet glove of courtesy'.[35] The women's campaigns were further hampered by the deepening Depression which was pushing social issues to one side as all governments turned their attention to economic problems.

The 1930 state election result had been particularly abhorrent to Millicent. Not only did it thwart Boyce's bill, but she believed Premier Lang's agendas would bring disaster upon the state. Lang had immediately set about introducing what *The Australian Worker* called 'legislative measures calculated to benefit the social, industrial and economic welfare of the masses',[36] but which Millicent saw as socialist policies. Moreover, Millicent was monitoring Lang's political ambitions to enter the federal arena, which, like state politics, was in a state of turbulence.

Australia's first Irish Catholic Prime Minister, James Scullin, had the misfortune to come to office on 22 October 1929, one week before the Wall Street Crash. When he appointed 'Red Ted' Theodore as treasurer, Millicent was amongst the most vocal critics, construing Theodore's appointment as a means of ushering in the 'non-moral and incredulously awful doctrines of Bolshevism'.[37] The instability reached a climax when Eddie Ward won the federal seat of East Sydney in a by-election and joined with other Labor defectors to move a confidence motion that brought down the Scullin government.

In the midst of this turbulence, a new political party, the United Australia Party (UAP), formed from a merger of Labor dissidents in the All for Australia League and the Australian Party and the Nationalists. Joseph Lyons was elected leader and John Latham deputy leader. The newly formed UAP won the December 1931 federal election with a solid majority. *The Australian Worker* attributed Labor's 'staggering defeat' to 'treachery',[38] while *The Sun* applauded the UAP win as the conquering of socialism in favour of 'plain democracy'.[39]

This fractious political situation at both federal and state levels created the very conditions Millicent needed to revitalise the infant guardianship campaign.

8

WHAT POLITICAL ACTION FAILED TO DO
(1931-1932)

... I wrote this play ... hoping that Drama might accomplish what human suffering and political action had failed to do.

Whose Child 1932[1]

As Prime Minister Joseph Lyons steadied the Australian federal ship, Premier Jack Lang rocked the NSW state boat. Determined to abolish the Legislative Council[2] because of its continued opposition to his legislation, Lang pressured Governor Philip Game to make Council appointments to support his legislation.

Lang's disregard for process extended to the official opening of the Sydney Harbour Bridge. In March 1932, he breached vice-regal protocols by sidelining Governor Game and Governor General Isaac Isaacs in order to cut the ribbon himself. Ironically, he was gazumped when a member of the New Guard, Francis de Groot, rode onto the bridge ahead of him and slashed the ribbon with his sword before being arrested and charged with offensive behaviour, using threatening words and maliciously damaging a ribbon.[3]

Two months later Game's patience with Lang expired. In contravention of the *Financial Agreement Enforcement Act* (Cth) 1932, which established the legal framework for financial agreements between the Commonwealth and the states, Lang refused to pay the interest owed by NSW on British Loans. Prime Minister Joseph Lyons made the NSW payments from federal funds, and then attempted to recoup the money from NSW, but Lang instructed public servants not to repay Federal Treasury. Problematically, Governor Game determined Lang's instruction was illegal[4] and, since Lang refused to retract it, on 13 May he withdrew Lang's commission. Parliament was dissolved and a state election called for 11 June 1932.

Millicent immediately threw herself into campaign mode to support UAP candidates. At one rally of 20,000 people in the Domain, in sight of her former office in Richmond Villa, she declared Lang had ushered in a 'reign of terror'.[5] He had allowed communist infiltration of the state and if he won this election, she warned her audience, it would be another step on the 'red road to Sovietism' and NSW would be 'plunged into revolution and civil war' with the other states dragged into the 'vortex'.[6] For some in her audience, this was not hysterical panicking.

The Labor Party had affirmed its commitment to socialist principles and the University Labour Club had formed a 'Socialisation Unit', to produce 'socialisation drama' that would actively propagate socialism in the university.[7] As infiltration fears increased, Catholic Archbishop Sheehan preached that socialism was 'economics raised to the level of a religion'[8] and a *Herald* correspondent warned it 'can only be finally suppressed by making it impossible to secure converts to its cause'.[9]

The Labor party was decimated at the state election. Labor's 20 seat majority vanished and the UAP was elected with an unassailable majority of 42. The UAP leader Bertram Stevens, the man Lang had dismissed from Treasury in 1925, became Premier.

The changed political landscape was a *carpe diem* moment for Millicent's infant guardianship campaign. But she would not use the old strategies of lobbying and petitions. She was 'thoroughly disgusted' with the process of 'deputations, agitations, intimidations, organisations' and with pushing 'the bill in Parliament and out of Parliament'.[10] Rather, she devised an innovative strategy to 'accomplish what politics could not do'.[11]

It is not clear when Millicent decided to write a political play. Writing was not new to her; in addition to her forays into journalism, she published several poems, some containing moral messages,[12] some expressing her romanticised responses to the natural world,[13] and others celebrating the newly constructed Sydney Harbour Bridge.[14] As President of the Feminist Club, she also participated in the Club's drama program, which was renowned for its 'great originality in the writing, production, and presentation of plays'.[15] However, the political play Millicent set about writing was far removed from her previous works.

Political plays were not new to Sydney. While the Depression had seen the demise of some of the city's commercial theatres, the people's theatre movement had gained traction. In early 1932, the Labor Movement founded the New Theatre with the express purpose of staging productions that would prompt political action. As President of the State Labor Party P J Keller said, 'By giving dramatic expression to the workers' aims and ideals ... we can combine the propaganda of the public platform with the powerfully moving appeal of the theatre'.[16] New Theatre productions were unashamedly propagandist – theatre was a weapon to right social wrongs.

It is unlikely Millicent patronised New Theatre productions but she understood the power of theatre and was intent on using it as a weapon in her fight against the injustices inflicted on mothers. One reviewer later noted her play, *Whose Child* was 'propagandist ... like some of the dramas of Mr Bernard Shaw or a medieval morality play'.[17]

Millicent wrote *Whose Child* to critique both the law that made possible the Polini judgement and the misogyny of the parliament, which had thwarted her attempts to amend this legislation. She fictionalised two true stories – the Polini case and the saga of her Private Members bill – interweaving them through her two main characters, the actress Margaret Windsor (née Charteris) and the female parliamentarian, Miss St John.

Margaret, an actress is estranged from her husband, John,

who is demanding custody of their infant daughter, Mab. In the opening scene, members of Margaret's extended family, discuss the 'eternal problem' of this 'little golden haired girl'. Margaret's father disapproves of her attempt to retain custody of her child since a 'father has claims to his child'. However, the Charteris women support Margaret and place the 'entire responsibility for Margaret's tragedy' on her estranged husband.

The family debate ends with a tableau scene, which mirrors the Madonna-like image of a 1922 photograph of Polini and her daughter, Patricia.[18] Mab, attired in her pink nightgown kneels at her mother's feet reciting her prayers. 'Look upon a little child', she intones and then asks her mother why she should ask God to 'bless daddy since he never comes'. Margaret soothes her with one of Anton Dvořák's melancholic songs –

> Songs my mother taught me,
> In the days long vanished;
> Seldom from her eyelids
> Were the teardrops banished.[19]

The child is taken to bed by her nurse as John erupts onto the stage demanding his child and threatening court action. 'No court in the country will give the child to you', he asserts and, as the curtain falls, Margaret responds,

> I can't believe that any Court in the world would give a baby girl of two years of age to a father in preference to a good mother when she can prove she has kept the baby and its father, herself and her home, also when she can give the child a better chance in life that it can ever hope to have from its father.

The first scene of act two opens with a moment of comic relief. The family servants gossip about Margaret's custody case and criticise men for having 'all the say when it comes to the law'. In a reference to the 1920 appointment of John McGirr as NSW Minister for Public Health and Motherhood one asks 'what can you expect from Parlyment when they're that silly that they make a man the Minister for Motherhood'. Family members enter and their lawyer advises that 'a father's powers are conferred by marriage not by fatherhood', to which Margaret despairingly responds that wives 'are property – the goods and chattels of marriage'.

The second scene takes place in the lawyer's chambers after the 'legally possible but morally wrong' judgement has been handed down. Margaret is despondent that 'the wishes of a mere mother are of no importance to the law in this country'. Her barrister, attempting to explain the decision, comments that the judge is 'crazy about children not leaving the jurisdiction' of the court and he poses a poignant question that is directed as much to the audience as to Margaret; 'If a mother can't earn her living within the jurisdiction, does that mean she's got to stay there and starve, in order to have a title to her child?'. This was Polini's dilemma – like Margaret, she had to go overseas to earn her living.

Millicent uses the barrister to trumpet her message. The women must 'rouse the mothers', he tells the family, 'educate' and 'enthuse' them to campaign to change the law. He goes on to dictate the wording of the two clauses that would be needed to amend the legislation – clauses that Millicent had included in her bill; the court must consider the 'wishes as well of the mother as of the father' and the fact a mother leaves the jurisdiction of the court should not be 'reason for denying such mother the custody of the child'.

The scene comes to a dramatic close, with two phone calls – the first from Miss St John, who proclaims she will lead the women's campaign for equality for mothers and the second caller announces John has taken the child. Margaret collapses – a dramatic premonition of what is to come for her in the final scene, and a reminder of Polini's death.

Act three opens with another comic moment as the parliamentary Ushers gossip. 'God gave children to women' says one, 'so why wasn't that good enough for politicians to set the Law by?'. Another criticises the Premier, the 'slippery', 'wily old sprinter' who has no intention of giving in to the women's campaign. The Premier enters, furious because this 'she-devil' female politician, Miss St John, has attracted so much press attention. He is determined to prevent her bill from passing and he tells his colleagues they must 'dodge it' or else they will have 'women in parliament for good' and then parliament will be 'pulled at the apron strings of women'.

As the bells ring, Members assemble and the two women, Miss St John and Margaret enter. Margaret has been permitted to stand at the bar and petition parliament for the law to be amended. She describes herself as 'one of that great army of sad women who have been robbed of their children by laws made in the Parliaments of the world'. The members listen in silence to her pleas and after she exits, Miss St John, makes a speech that resembles Millicent's first reading speech for her Private Members bill. This prompted one journalist to comment that it was 'a speech which Miss Preston Stanley actually delivered' in parliament.[20]

> The decision of the Court in the Windsor case has shocked the community. By this decision we find that the law in this State is such that a mother can be deprived of her child – not because she is inferior to her husband as a parent – not because she is unable or unwilling to keep her child as in this case she has done ever since it was born – but forsooth because she might be forced to go abroad to earn her living owing to the fact that her husband is unable to keep her.

The parliamentarians' caustic interjections echo Millicent's parliamentary experiences. One interaction, for instance, alludes to George Cann's snide remark about her spinsterhood;

> Miss St John: ... It will be generally conceded that a good mother is the natural guardian of her child of tender years.
> Member: How do you know – you're not a mother.
> Miss St John: Neither are you, but that does not prevent you wanting to assume all of a mother's prerogatives.

The scene builds to a climax with the Premier using the gag to block Miss St John's bill, as Cann had blocked Millicent's;

> Premier: Mr Speaker I move that the debate be now adjourned.
>
> Miss St John: Which being interpreted means THAT THE BILL WILL NOW BE SHELVED.

The final Act is set in a theatre eight years after Margaret's court case. It is a pastiche of Victorian melodrama and Shakespearean-style play-within-a-play with an on-stage audience of women who have been given complimentary tickets to the performance of this 'woman's play'. The on-stage audience, which includes Miss St John watches the mystery play, comments on the action and on the actress, who has been billed as Olive Olivier, making clear the connections between this 'play' and the Polini story. Olive, the actress playing the role of the nurse, is unknown to them although she seems familiar and her performance suggests 'she's rather living something over'.

The plot centres on the nurse, Olive, who has been employed by Mrs Brook to care for her ailing child, Diana, supposedly the offspring of her previous marriage. Mr Brook, Olive's former husband, is initially away on business so he is unaware that his current wife has, inadvertently, employed his former wife to nurse the child. As the child's condition deteriorates, Olive becomes convinced that Diana is actually her own daughter, Pamela, who supposedly died as an infant in Mr Brook's custody. She persuades the doctor to use 'science to ascertain truth'.

Under hypnosis, (the 'science'), Diana reveals a childhood experience of near drowning and a house fire which only Pamela could have known about. In a *deus ex machina* moment, another character produces Diana's death certificate. The truth is revealed; the child is not Diana but Pamela. Olive is vindicated. Mr Brook returns, furious to find his deception exposed. Olive reclaims her child, who is now recovered as the doctor declares, 'Mother love is better than all our pills and potions'. The scene closes with a mother/daughter tableau of Olive/Diana which recalls that of the first Margaret/Mab scene.

But one mystery remains – who is this unknown but familiar-looking actress? In an epilogue, the Theatre Manager announces that the actress Olive is also the author of the play and she is actually the gravely ill, Margaret Windsor. Margaret enters and confesses she was 'stabbed by eternal longing – tortured by the memory of the little girl that life had carried further away from me than Death'. She wrote this play, she tells the audience, 'hoping that drama might accomplish what human suffering and political action had failed to do'. The curtain falls as Margaret collapses on the stage, a stark reminder that Polini died without ever seeing her child again.

Millicent's choice of venue for the production was inspired. The elegant Criterion Theatre, 'The Cri' as it was then popularly known, in central Sydney was built in 1886 by entrepreneur, John Solomon and in 1932 leased by J C Williamsons. The Georgian interior seated around 1000 in stage boxes, stalls, lounge, and dress circle before a proscenium arch stage, bedecked with a ruby-velvet gilt-fringed curtain. Throughout its history opera, musical comedy, pantomime, Shakespeare, classical English dramas, and Sunday night sacred music had been staged at The Cri although, unlike the New Theatre, it was not home to political theatre.

Significantly, during her Sydney seasons, Emélie Polini had performed there in six plays, including in Henry Arthur Jones's mystery thriller *The Lie*. In 1923, *The Flaw*, a mystery play co-authored by Doris Egerton Jones and Emélie Polini had a season there with Polini playing the lead role.[21] However, Millicent's play was The Cri's first political production by a former parliamentarian and Australian woman playwright, as Millicent now promoted herself.

The prominent American-born director George D Parker, who had directed Polini in four plays at The Cri, directed *Whose Child*.

The cast included famous actors such as Nancye Stewart and Mayne Lynton who had also performed with Polini. Embedded in the cast list between Metta Bennett White and Benita Appleton was the name Preston Stanley. Millicent played the role of Miss St John, a role so closely based on her own parliamentary experience that one journalist commented she 'ought to be at home' in it.[22]

Millicent's publicity campaign for the production was strategically targeted. Newspaper advertisements proclaimed the play's political purpose, trumpeting it as 'An Australian Play ... with a Message to Australian Mothers' and a 'tense, throbbing drama of real life of heart interest to women' based on the 'Celebrated Emilie [sic] Polini case and many others'. Millicent admitted that propaganda was her 'principal intention',[23] and to reinforce her point, and to promote the production in the weeks prior to opening night she gave author talks at Women's Luncheons at upmarket retail venues such as Farmers and David Jones[24], and was accompanied by actors Molly Raynor and Meta Bennett White.[25]

Ensuring the most receptive audience was also essential to her strategy, particularly for the opening night. Millicent admitted she had invited the people 'whose sympathy was most needed',[26] including women from the various organisations that had campaigned for the legislative amendments over the past decades. However, she was not simply intent on preaching to the converted. Her purpose was to attract those who had not yet been drawn into the fold and to prompt those with power to take action. She made sure these people were included on her opening night guest list.

Theatre opening nights were important events in Sydney's social calendar. In addition to the opening night of Millicent's play, there were two other opening nights on 26 November 1932 and both those productions were overseas imports, not uncommon at the time. At the Theatre Royal, the renowned German-born stage and film actor, Theo Shall, who was billed as the 'Idol of Vienna' and the distinguished English actress, Dorothy Peters were starring in the play, *Autumn Crocus*. This romantic comedy written by English novelist and playwright Dodie Smith under the pseudonym C L Anthony, tells the story of an unmarried school teacher who falls in love with the married owner of the hotel where she is staying during her holiday. At Her Majesty's Theatre, 'Australia's Queen of Song', Gladys Moncrieff, was singing the part of Nadina in Oscar Straus's 1908 popular comedy operetta, *The Chocolate Soldier*, a story of romantic love set against the backdrop of war, which is based on George Bernard Shaw's play *Arms and the Man*. Such top-billed productions with world-famous stars performing for Sydney audiences would normally boast vice-regal opening nights.

Vice-regal opening nights were invitation only events attended by the upper echelons of society. It is remarkable that Millicent was able to announce the opening night of *Whose Child* would be 'under the distinguished Patronage and in the presence of' an impressive list of guests. The list included the NSW Governor His Excellency Sir Philip Game and Lady Game,[27] the Prime Minister the Hon Joseph Lyons and his wife Enid, the NSW Premier the Hon Bertram Stevens and his wife, and the Lord Mayor the Hon S Walder MLC and his wife.

Although not mentioned in the pre-production notices also in the official party, were Lady Game's private secretary, Miss Isabel Crowdy OBE who was accompanied by Lieutenant General Sir Harry Chauvel GCMG, a distinguished soldier who had served in Gallipoli,[28] and the Minister of Justice, Lewis Ormsby Martin and his wife. Martin's presence was crucial to Millicent's propaganda strategy. Despite opposing aspects of Boyce's 1929 bill, Martin would now be responsible for preparing the Infant Guardianship bill and ensuring its passage through the parliament should her strategy succeed. Conscious of the de-railings of previous bills, Millicent needed a public commitment from the Minister that could not be easily sabotaged. She admitted she had 'induced Mr

Martin to attend the performance', although she did not elaborate on the nature of her inducement.[29]

The fact that Millicent was able to secure the patronage and presence of so many dignitaries was testament to the extent of her networks and influence. But it was not enough to simply produce a play attended by such honoured guests. The real force would be located in the action that followed the final curtain. For some in the audience, the opening night seemed to be 'a deputation of a new kind',[30] an astute assessment of Millicent's political strategy. One Sydney newspaper headlined its story, 'Miss Preston Stanley Turns Politician Again in New Play'.[31] It was not only Millicent's appearance in the role of the female politician in her propaganda play, with its echoes of the tragic Polini story and the frustrations of her own campaigns that contributed to this appearance of political lobbying, but her overtly political performance during the curtain calls.

Theatre productions commonly concluded with curtain calls, floral presentations and sometimes impromptu speeches from the director and/or the playwright. When Millicent, playwright and actor took her bow, the audience called for a speech. Millicent obliged, not with an impromptu talk but a prepared script. Holding up a piece of paper, she told the audience it was a letter to her from the Minister of Justice which, she said, 'Mr Martin had written at the theatre that night'.[32]

> I congratulate you sincerely as the author of *Whose Child*, and also you and all others associated with you in its splendid production. It will help to achieve a great purpose. On Monday I will give instructions that the bill which I will very shortly introduce in Parliament shall provide for the mother's rights as so eloquently depicted in your play.[33]

The audience applauded. Millicent's production had achieved what political action had failed to do.

Despite her claim that Martin had been moved by the play to

make his decision, this may have been stretching the truth. Lady Game later told the Feminist Club she was sitting next to the Premier that night and 'she could see that he was moved and was giving the matter great thought'.[34] Perhaps the play had challenged the Premier and the Minister to review their position on child custody but the purported spontaneity of the Minister's letter does raise doubts about this supposedly impromptu decision, the more so in Martin's permitting Millicent to make a government announcement from the stage.

There are some anomalies in the reported events leading up to the production that suggest other political initiatives may have been at play. In late September, under persistent lobbying from women's organisations, Martin announced the law 'in respect of guardianship, custody and marriage of infants' would be amended.[35] From 16 November advertisements for Millicent's production did not indicate the length of the season. Then, on 19 November it was announced the play 'will be definitely limited to one week's run'.[36] It is impossible to know if this decision was Millicent's marketing strategy to stimulate full houses, or to reduce her financial commitment from poorly booked houses. However, it is possible to read the announcement in conjunction with some other contingent events.

The day before the announcement of the limited season, Martin informed a deputation from the United Associations that he was preparing a bill for the next session of parliament.[37] Some reports of this deputation suggested Martin claimed his decision was a consequence of Millicent's intensive agitation. That afternoon another newspaper reported Mildred Muscio's criticisms of the Minister's announcement because it implied his decision was based solely on the work of one individual when so many other women were involved in campaigning. Two days prior to the opening night, another news item quoted Martin as saying he had taken the action as a consequence of Millicent's 'intensive agitation' about amending child custody legislation.³⁸ By throwing the spotlight onto Millicent's role as the most influential campaigner, Martin raised the shackles of those women who felt their contributions had been overlooked.

Fortuitously, a truce of a kind between the rival women's organisations was prompted by opposition from another woman, Adela Pankhurst Walsh. In a letter to the *Herald*, Pankhurst Walsh argued, implausibly, that infant guardianship had been given 'little public attention'. Proposing that first consideration must be given to the welfare of the child, she set out the conditions under which that welfare should be achieved. The father was under the obligation to provide a home and maintain the family, an obligation that gave him the right to custody. 'If the law is altered to make both parents equal, can this obligation of the father to maintain his family still continue?' she asked. Since providing for children was beyond the capacity of mothers, women must be 'willing to abide by the conditions' that maintain the family. Equal custody would deter the next generation of men from marriage and cause the 'downfall of home life and morals'.³⁹

The responses to Pankhurst Walsh's letter were so numerous the *Herald* published a column of selected quotations from readers' letters. At the head of the column, Millicent refuted Pankhurst Walsh's claim that little public attention had been given to the issue and she cited the 'ceaseless struggle' of the 20,000 people who had signed the Feminist Club Polini petition. Mrs Emily Bennett, industrial organiser for the Australian Women's Guild of Empire founded by Pankhurst Walsh, asserted every woman's organisation had 'striven to secure' this measure. Mrs Arthur Onslow, secretary of the United Associations declared equality was necessary in a capitalist society to maintain the 'standard of right and justice'. Mrs Mildred Muscio, President of the National Council of Women stated that Pankhurst Walsh's 'opposition to the claim of the mother for a right of guardianship equal to the right of the father, is in complete contradiction to the expressed policy of women's organisations'.[40]

Pankhurst Walsh's opposition alerted the women's organisations to the need to maintain a united front as the Guardianship of Infants bill began its perilous passage through a parliament of men, many of whom were less than sympathetic to their cause. The question remained, would they be able to do so?

9

The Final Factor
(1933-1934)

'Whose Child', which was part of the campaign, and indeed the final factor .... was really a part of her.

Sydney Morning Herald, 15 November 1934[1]

On 21 August 1933 the *Sydney Morning Herald* announced the Governor would open parliament the following day and would provide information about the twenty bills the government would bring down during the session. Amongst bills for City Council Elections, State Taxation and Company Law was a bill for the Guardianship of Infants that would 'provide equal rights to the mother and father in the custody of children'.[2] After parliament opened, Minister Martin commented that this bill was the 'result of protracted efforts on the part of a number of prominent Sydney feminists, including Miss Preston Stanley'.[3] By singling out Millicent, he unfortunately re-ignited rivalries amongst members of various women's organisations.

When Martin introduced the bill in the Legislative Assembly on 6 September he amended his previous public statement about Millicent's role. Mindful of the criticisms he had received,[4] he now refrained from mentioning Millicent, her play or her Private Members bill. It would be 'invidious', he told Members, to single out any individual organisation or any particular person. He reassured the House this draft was substantially the same bill that Attorney General Boyce had introduced in 1929, following the 1928 Premiers Conference resolution that all Australian states should bring their laws into line with English law. He pointed to salient features of the bill; the 'wishes' of the mother, as well as the father would be taken into account in awarding custody, a parent could leave the court's jurisdiction without automatically forfeiting custody, and cases could be heard in lower courts.

Millicent was encouraged when the former Minister for Justice, William McKell, on behalf of the Opposition, responded positively. Mothers should have the same rights as fathers, he said, since women were no longer considered their husbands' 'chattels'. However, memories of her 1926 bill were fresh in her mind. She recalled former Attorney General McTiernan's statement of support for her bill that proved to be duplicitous and she remembered the devious ways members thwarted Boyce's 1929 bill. She was determined to keep public attention focused on this bill. Four days later, *The Sun*, carried an article about the Guardianship of Infants bill under the headline, 'Hats off to Sydney's Public Women'. The article acknowledged the many women who had 'urged' this bill and proudly proclaimed:

> If there is one woman in Australia to whom all mothers should take off their proverbial hats, that woman is Miss Millicent Preston Stanley, whose agitations over years have at last borne fruit in the form of the Guardianship of Children [sic] Bill now before parliament.

The article recounted the custody campaign from the Polini petition to Millicent's Private Members bill and praised her play. It quoted from Minister Martin's note promising the bill and lauded Millicent's 'skilful riding which led the hobby horse finally to victory.'[5] This compliment re-established Millicent as the pivotal figure responsible for the successful outcome of the custody campaign. The publication of this article two days before the bill's Second Reading may have been coincidental although it was possibly initiated by Millicent through her journalist networks. The accolades heaped on her did not endear her to those women who resented the limelight she continued to attract to herself.

The bill's Second Reading began on 12 September. Minister Martin, beguiled by the supposed support from the Labor

Opposition, emphasised the bill was a 'non-party' measure. Millicent was probably not surprised when McKell criticised the women's persistent lobbying and declared he was no longer in favour of the bill. Former Minister Joseph Lamaro waded in with condemnation of the women's 'propaganda' which, he declared, was aimed at overthrowing Justice Harvey's decision in the Polini case. Other members leapt into the fray, criticising the way that judgement was being used to justify the bill. Basing legislation on such a complex case, one member declared, would result in bad law.

Fortunately, not all members of the Labor Opposition opposed the bill. Robert Heffron, who described himself as a 'proselytising rationalist' supported the long-overdue innovation. The time had passed, he told the House, when a 'husband had the right to thrash his wife with a stick no thicker than his thumb'. He was referring to the ancient common law principle that permitted a husband to chastise his wife with an implement of a thickness equal to, but no thicker than, the husband's thumb. Some members assured him that common law principle still stood, but Heffron, who was not a lawyer, asserted that, fortunately, it had fallen into 'desuetude'. His use of that legal term was shrewd, as Members were well aware the legal term established that a law ceased to have any legal force when it had not been used for a long period of time.

While some Members focused on the issue of equal rights, others were more concerned with various issues relating to court jurisdiction, particularly the provision for lower courts to hear custody cases. Some of the lawyers believed country magistrates were not as capable as Supreme Court justices to hear custody cases. For Country Party member Alfred Henry this was an absurd view, which moreover, ignored the additional costs imposed on country people who were forced to take their cases to the Supreme Court in Sydney.

For Opposition Leader Jack Lang the most invidious clause was the one that allowed a parent to remove a child from the court's jurisdiction. It would make it impossible, he asserted, for the court to retrieve a child that was no longer in the court's jurisdiction. Lang also took issue with 'judicial proceedings being held in camera', a legal provision that enabled a court to hear a case behind closed doors should the court determine it was in the parties' best interests. His view did not prevail and the clause remained in the bill.

Once the members of the Legislative Assembly were finished with their wrangling over the bill's clauses, on 10 October it moved to the Legislative Council. Attorney General Henry Manning introduced the bill late in the evening but the few members present grumbled about it being considered at such a late hour. Manning then adjourned debate to 1 November. Perhaps unsurprisingly when debate resumed, the Members of the Legislative Council proved even more reluctant to support the legislation than the members of the Legislative Assembly had been. To Millicent's disappointment, Ellen Webster, the sole remaining woman whom Jack Lang had appointed to that Chamber, remained silent throughout the debate.

For solicitor Hugh Wragge, the bill permitting women's equality would do 'more harm than good' and would cause 'social disturbance'. He repeatedly asserted that 'natural leadership must remain with the husband'. Manning adjourned debate without pushing for a vote. The various women's organisations began to fear this bill, like the two previous bills, would be stalled.

Stalled it was, although not by the machinations of Members but to accommodate the provisions of the *Constitution Amendment Act (Legislative Council Elections)* 1933. This legislation changed the constitution of the Legislative Council to allow for the election of a proportion of members every three years by a joint sitting of both Chambers. Debate on the Guardianship of Infants bill was, of necessity, suspended while the election took place. Ellen Webster was not elected; no female Member sat in either the Legislative

Assembly or the Legislative Council for the remainder of the bill's journey through the parliament.

On 9 May 1934 Minister Martin introduced the bill *de novo* into the Legislative Assembly. Once again, he referred to the Polini case and the 'persistent and sustained agitation' of women's organisations over many years but avoided mentioning Millicent. He assured members that the women's organisations supported it in its present form, despite the concerns some women's organisations had expressed about this draft.

The Second Reading took place on 15 and 16 May 1934. Women hoped there would be no further obstacles, but they had not reckoned on Joseph Lamaro who argued (problematically) that this bill would not change the judgement in the Polini case, since the Judge had not accorded the father any special privilege. He then set his sights on the court jurisdiction clause. It had been inserted, inappropriately, he bellowed, because of an *obiter dictum* in Justice Harvey's judgement about Polini taking her child to England. Justice Harvey's comment was merely an expression of opinion, he asserted, and such opinions or *obiter dicta* should never be taken into consideration when formulating legislation. Debate now descended into 'lawyers at ten paces' as Alfred Henry contradicted Joseph Lamaro and William McKell contradicted Alfred Henry.

After much batting back and forth, Robert Heffron suggested it was impossible to ignore the fact that the rights of women in the existing law are 'a relic of the dark ages' and are incompatible with the laws of a modern democratic country. Heffron attempted to anchor the debate in the children, rather than in the technicalities of legal interpretations and re-interpretations of what various speakers had just said, or what The Hon Harold Nicholas MLC had said in the Legislative Council during the debate on a previous version of the bill.

The debate slipped into farce as Lamaro suggested they should establish a court of domestic relations free from the technicalities and intricacies of the law. But, he commented, presumably sarcastically, even that court would inevitably be presided over by 'one's mother-in-law'!

Underpinning many of the comments was the belief in women's second class status – a view that irritated women, who were hoping that, at last, their rights as mothers would be legislated in this state, as it had been in other states. The press, picking up on the level of legal wrangling reported that the bill had become a 'bill for lawyers',[6] although one journalist optimistically suggested that, despite having been 'buffeted about' for years it might yet survive this onslaught.[7]

During the Committee stage of debate, Lang once again raised his *cause célèbre* – the court jurisdiction clause. There is no legal mechanism to return a child who has been removed from the court's jurisdiction, he complained, as he proposed an amendment to compel the court to reject any custody application from a parent who intended to leave the court's jurisdiction. Martin was reluctant to accept Lang's amendment despite considerable support from other lawyers. Fortunately, he was saved from doing so by John Ness who opposed the amendment arguing convincingly that it would make the child a state 'prisoner'.

Lang was determined to have the final word and it was another swipe at Millicent. Parliament, he quipped, should not be 'stampeded' by the recommendations of an 'organisation of spinsters'. Even after the bill was read a third time, Lang did not desist. The Opposition, he declared, was in accord with the general principles of the bill but not in agreement with the 'portion of the bill' that has been criticised.

The bill once again attracted press coverage. *The Sun* quoted Martin's statement that the bill put women on exactly the same level of equality as men in relation to guardianship and custody of children.[8] The *Herald* reported the legislation 'destroyed' the common law principle that gave the father paramount guardianship rights and quoted Alfred Henry, who approved of the bill because it would bring 'archaic laws into line with modern ideas',[9] and *Truth* devoted a column to answering readers' questions.[10] These accounts made no reference to Millicent – an omission that was remedied the following week.

On 17 May, the *Herald* published a long article that highlighted Millicent's role in the campaign accompanied by a large photograph of her. The journalist, identified only as 'V.H.' recounted the Polini story, her custody case, her death and the overruling of her will, describing it as a 'tragic example of the helplessness of women to obtain their natural rights in the face of the law'. V.H. then turned the spotlight on Millicent, describing her as the 'prime agitator' who had 'relentlessly pursued' the custody campaign for over a decade and, quoting directly from an interview with her the previous day, recounted the story of her bill and her play and included a verbatim copy of Martin's note. The journalist concluded that, for women, this bill constituted 'an epoch towards the attainment of their proper status'.[11]

It is highly likely Millicent had instigated this article, and perhaps another one published three days later in *Truth*. Under the headline, 'Custody Bill Must Become Law: Parliament Has Chance to Remedy Long Standing Injustice' the story focused on the Polini case, the 'leading part' Millicent had played in the campaign and how her bill had been 'stonewalled'.[12] The appearance of these articles suggests Millicent was determined to remain centre stage in the legislative drama as she had done in her play.

Meanwhile, the bill continued on its stormy passage through the newly constituted Legislative Council. Attorney General Manning again outlined the bill's principles and features, which had been rehearsed multiple times. Hugh Wragge gave a lengthy, lawyerly dissertation arguing the Polini case did not justify the public outcry that had been whipped up and warned there were dangers in trying to accommodate English laws when the laws of this State worked so well.

For other Legislative Council members the central problem with the bill was that it gave women rights. This was venturing into 'dangerous spheres' William Robson asserted, because 'When a woman gets rights in these days she generally begins to exercise them'. Thomas Holden opined that 'wherever a wife can take advantage of the law to embarrass her husband it is taken'.

The most vociferous criticism came from Alfred Hemsley. A St John's College Oxford graduate in law, Hemsley was a partner in Allen, Allen & Hemsley and like Justice Harvey a parishioner at St Marks Church, Darling Point. Unlike other lawyers, who quoted statute or case law, Hemsley quoted at length from the Bible. Laws should be 'framed more in accordance with the Divine Plan', he pontificated, than in contradiction of it; to give a mother equality with a father was 'in direct opposition to, and in defiance of, the Divine Plan'. While he supported the principle that the child's best interests should be paramount, removing the father as the natural guardian of the child was not in the child's best interests.

The press had a field day with Hemsley's speech. *The Canberra Times* announced it under the headline, 'Alleged Violation in New Bill',[13] while the *Evening News* headlined its article, 'Man is Master by Divine Law'. The journalist described the 'stir among women in the gallery' when Hemsley maintained women should be 'in subjection to men'.[14] The *Herald* noted Hemsley 'deprecated provisions in the bill' which would enable the wife to have equal rights with her husband',[15] while *Voice*, a Hobart newspaper reported the 'archaic' Hemsley's alarm that a Christian nation could support such a statute.[16] Another Tasmanian newspaper, *The Mercury* responded that most people consider it 'a grave reflection on human nature that legislation giving a mother at least equal rights with the father' had not occurred until the twentieth century.[17]

The lawyers in the Council continued to debate the bill's intricacies, much of their argument revolving around the operation of the courts, the orders each court could make and appeal processes. Country Members referred to the effects the decisions might have on mothers or fathers living in country areas, who would be forced to travel to Sydney to access the Supreme Court. One member argued the Council needed to bring all the legislation relating to infant guardianship under one single measure and urged the government to dispense with this bill and draft a totally new one, although Attorney General Manning argued against such a move. As the bill limped its way through the Council, amendments were moved and withdrawn and moved and passed.

Debate in August was dominated by amendments that were 'designed to improve the text grammatically'. These related to the workings of the courts and the practice of law – 'highly technical matters of procedure'. Words and phrases were the chief focus as the lawyers strove to 'make certainty more certain'. On 10 October, with all amendments agreed to, the bill was finally reported, read a third time the following day and returned to the Legislative Assembly where the Council's amendments must be considered for concurrence before the bill could be passed.

Like Millicent and the many women campaigners, Minister Martin hoped that Tuesday 23 October would be an auspicious day. He announced to the Assembly:

> This I hope, brings to a conclusion a very long agitation by the women of New South Wales to have the law with regard to the guardianship of infants brought into more modern form and into conformity to a large extent with the law as we find it in England.

The bill had been sent back from the Legislative Council with a series of 'drafting amendments', Martin told the members, and there was nothing in them that members would object to. 'Some clarify the position', he explained, while 'None takes away anything to which the Committee has agreed, nor will any one of them create difficulties in the administration of the measure'. The purpose of the Council's amendments, he reiterated, was to ensure the bill was clear and simple and able to be understood by lawyers and laymen alike.

Martin then marked out particular amendments that were of a 'machinery nature', and those that involved changes to wording such as the substitution of the word 'State' for the word 'jurisdiction', the addition of the phrase 'of petty sessions' after the word 'court' and the inclusion of 'religious instruction' to the word, 'upbringing'. When one member queried whether this was necessary, Martin reassured the Assembly that keeping these 'additional two or three words' would prevent a later legal fight in an Appeals Court. Martin was conscious of the need to placate all those who might be likely to delay the process any further after the bill's long, torturous, frequently interrupted journey over the last eight years. He certainly wanted to avoid having to send it back to the Legislative Council for further consideration and agreement.

Despite his assurances, the bill was not to be so swiftly dispensed with. At the last moment William McKell, who admitted he had not been in the Chamber during part of the debate, expressed his concerns about two clauses. The first related to the issue of the competing operations of the various courts – from District Court to Supreme Court, but Martin reassured him that issue was settled. McKell then expressed concerns at the alteration to the amount of the penalty that would be imposed on a father under a maintenance order, who failed to report his change of address. Martin again, seeking to avoid further detours requested that the Assembly accept the Council's amendment 'so as to prevent any wrangling with the Legislative Council'. The Members were indeed weary of the wrangling between the two Houses that delayed and disrupted so much legislation. They acquiesced to his request. With the Council's amendments agreed to, the Guardianship of Infants bill quietly passed into law. It was given Royal Assent on 31 October 1934, placed on the statute books and came into operation the following day.

After the long agitation it passed with a whimper rather than a bang. It became a mere footnote in some newspaper accounts.

The *Herald* simply stated at the end of a lengthy article detailing parliament's deliberations on various other bills that 'the Guardianship of Infants bill was passed',[18] a note repeated in syndicated papers throughout the state without further comment. In one article, headlined 'No Bells But Many Bills' *The Sun* described the scene as a 'Day of Peace'; the sitting that finally passed the bill had been 'so tranquil' after the 'rough and tumble' of recent sessions.[19]

Some journalists reported women were jubilant and several quoted Minister Martin's comments about the bill marking the end of their long struggle. Martin acknowledged the Polini case as the instigator of the campaign and said the campaigners now 'had the satisfaction of knowing that there was on the statute books' a measure that gave equal rights to mothers and fathers.[20] Also referring obliquely to the Polini case, the *Catholic Freeman's Journal* noted that judges do make mistakes but mothers will now be 'spared the very sad experience of the lady whose plight began the movement' for the legislation.[21] In the general jubilation there were scant references to Millicent's role in the campaign other than in *The Australasian*, which acknowledged her as the 'earnest worker' for the bill for fourteen years.[22]

For feminist journalist Linda Littlejohn, a prominent member of the United Association of Women, the *Guardianship of Infants Act, 1934* warranted an extensive account. In an article in the recently established *Australian Women's Weekly* under the headline 'A Great Triumph ... for the Woman's Cause' the leader poetically proclaimed:

> At long last, the Guardianship of Infants Act has arrived in port. Its passage has been a stormy one. It set sail many years ago, but met so many storms on the way that time and again it was wrecked; its constant reconditioning and the inefficiency of the crew that steered it occasioned many delays, but the little barque, cram full of justice, has at last found a haven on our shores.[23]

The Act would bring 'relief to many a storm tossed and terror-stricken mother's heart', Littlejohn assured her readers.

Noting that NSW was the slowest Australian state to 'wake up to the restrictions' of the existing custody Act, Littlejohn outlined the aspects that gave a woman rights she had previously been deprived of, the most important of which was equal custody and she noted custody cases could now be heard in lower courts. This amendment, she asserted somewhat problematically, had been inserted by the Labor Party and by implication, initiated by the United Associations of Women. She pointed out a mother could also apply for custody and maintenance while she was still residing in the father's home enabling her to feel secure about being able to support her child when she did leave an abusive husband. Finally, she highlighted a clause, which she named the Polini clause, which made provision for a mother to move out of the court's jurisdiction without that fact disqualifying her from custody.

However, Littlejohn did not mention that the Act retained the clause requiring courts to give paramount consideration to the child's best interest in determining custody. Neither did she point out the Act did not define the child's best interests but left it to the Court's discretion, a determination to be made by male justices. While the legislation was a leap forward, it still left men making these decisions, and as had been the case with Polini's daughter Patricia, they did not always make the most judicious decisions about the child's best interests.[24]

Littlejohn's only reference to Millicent was a dismissive statement that a petition 'organised by Miss Preston Stanley' was signed by thousands of people. Millicent was effectively airbrushed out of Littlejohn's account of the campaign victory. Like Jessie Street and other women involved in the 1929 Feminist Club split, Littlejohn was reluctant to allow Millicent any credit for a campaign that had involved many women's organisations.

Millicent was not included in the celebration organised by

the United Associations of Women at Hordern Bros where Jessie Street presented Minister Martin with a gold pen to mark the passing of the bill. Littlejohn congratulated him on the safe passage of the bill and proclaimed, problematically, that 'women were now united' and 'spoke with one voice'.

The UAP Women's Education Circle organised its celebration at the more upmarket venue of David Jones to honour both Minister Martin and Millicent. In reporting this event under the headline 'A TRIBUTE', the *Herald* listed the many influential women in attendance and recounted the Chair of the Housewives Association, Eleanor Glencross's speech. Glencross indelibly linked Millicent with Minister Martin as being 'largely responsible' for the Act and praised Millicent as the one who had 'blazed the track to overcome the injustice' and Martin as one of the 'greatest champions of women'.

In their responses both Martin and Millicent adopted deferential positions. Martin commented he felt a 'sort of thief' accepting all the credit for the passing of the bill and he acknowledged the work of Attorney General Boyce in introducing the 1929 bill and Premier Stevens for supporting the current bill. However, even in that forum he did not publicly acknowledge the first bill Millicent had introduced in 1926.

In her turn, Millicent moralised on the importance of not indulging in pride but admitted to 'tremendous satisfaction' that her work over all these years had not been 'in vain'. She expressed her appreciation of Martin's contribution and despite her professions of modesty, trumpeted the story of her campaign and emphasised the role of her play and Martin's note in the outcome. The play, she confessed had become 'a part of her', and, despite her protestations of humility, she declared it was, in fact, the 'final factor' in the campaign's success. To reinforce this impression, her niece, elocutionist Joan Preston Stanley recited 'two scenes of the play'.[25] Once again, Millicent was ensuring her contribution to the campaign's success was acknowledged and remained in the public gaze.

In late December 1934, a long article under the headline, 'Victory for Women' appeared in the *Dubbo Liberal and Macquarie Advocate*, a newspaper that generally focussed on stories about events in this north western NSW country area. The article, which included quotes from Millicent, recounted her custody campaign story from the initial Polini petition to the passing of the bill. It was, in effect, a paean to Millicent. The women of NSW, it declared, owe 'a great debt of gratitude' to her for her 'ceaseless, untiring work over a period of fourteen years'.[26] Why this newspaper chose to publish this story at this time is something of a mystery. However, it was a fitting tribute at the end of a momentous year which had set Millicent on a new path in her life.

10

A Citizen's Life

(1934)

Miss Millicent Preston Stanley ... will not give up her public life after her marriage to Mr Crawford Vaughan. ... 'I shall certainly continue to lead what I feel may be called a citizen's life'.

The Argus, 19 May 1934[1]

While the Guardianship of Infants bill was wending its way through the parliamentary maze, Millicent slipped out of Sydney with her nephew Lieutenant Harold Preston Stanley on Saturday 26 May 1934. She was taking a motoring holiday to Melbourne – or so she said. That same day Crawford Vaughan, a former Premier of South Australia, left Adelaide bound for Melbourne. Rumours soon circulated that this Sydney feminist was engaged to the Adelaide-born former South Australian Premier Crawford Vaughan.

Millicent and Crawford were married on Tuesday 29 May at St Johns Anglican Church in Toorak. It is not clear why they chose to marry in Melbourne although it may have been to maintain privacy. The Parish Rector Dr Archibald Law, who was a Temperance advocate, officiated at the ceremony. Millicent's nephew gave her away and Crawford's political ally and friend, Frederic William Eggelston was best man. Millicent's seventy-five year old mother was not well enough to travel to Melbourne for her daughter's wedding and there are no records to indicate whether other family members attended.

Journalists reported the wedding under headlines such as, 'Love Wins with Feminist Leader',[2] 'Sydney's Feminist Leader: Cupid Captures Her'[3] and 'Romantic Coalition: Ex Politicians Wed'.[4] Some of the stories highlighted the bride's honey coloured chiffon gown, velvet coat trimmed with fur and matching velvet hat although not surprisingly, they paid no attention to Crawford's attire.[5] Some accounts suggest the journalists were not actually present at the ceremony. The *Sun* reported Emélie Polini's daughter Patricia Ellis greeted Millicent at the church, although the following day it published a correction, stating Patricia was not known to Millicent and was not at her wedding.[6] Others variously reported the bride arrived late and kept the groom waiting at the altar, or the newly-married couple slipped out the back door to avoid the press. The *Argus*, however, published a clearly posed photo (by an unidentified photographer) of the newly-weds at the Church entrance, captioned 'Leaving the church after the ceremony'.[7]

The wedding guests gathered for luncheon at Menzies, one of Melbourne's grand hotels, which boasted British royalty and celebrated authors Mark Twain and Anthony Trollope amongst its previous visitors. After luncheon, the newly-weds set off on their motoring honeymoon to South Australia. At the time, Crawford was Chairman of the South Australian Bird in Hand goldmine and he also had other business interests there which required his attention.[8]

The *Australian Women's Weekly* reported that Millicent used this trip to 'bury herself' in the Adelaide hills and escape from public life.[9] Millicent was not, of course, contemplating any permanent escape from public life. She had every intention of returning to Sydney and resuming her positions in those organisations that worked to improve women's lives. As another journalist reported, 'her friends do not think that she will allow matrimony to interfere with her career' but rather they believe her marriage to Crawford 'will open up wider spheres in which her pronounced political ability will find a scope denied to her in Australia'.[10]

Despite the press hype around her wedding, Millicent was no naïve romantic. At fifty one years of age, she did not see herself as a Cinderella marrying her Prince Charming. She was realistic enough to know her happily-ever-after years with the sixty year old widower would be limited. Her marriage may have changed her marital status but it would not change her *modus operandi*. She would not sacrifice her independence and autonomy and unlike married women who accepted their *femme covert* status, Millicent would not adopt her husband's first name. Although newspapers referred to her as Mrs Crawford Vaughan, sometimes appending her earlier identity in words such as, 'formerly Miss Preston Stanley',[11] she usually identified herself as Mrs Millicent Preston Stanley Vaughan or Mrs Preston Stanley Vaughan.

Despite their different beginnings, different careers and different life paths, they had much in common. Millicent had always been a committed liberal while Crawford left the ALP and embraced liberalism. Both supported conscription, temperance, imperialist nationalism, and feminism. Both were brilliant speakers and had experience in business, and journalism, Millicent writing for the Sydney *Daily Telegraph* and Crawford for Adelaide's *The News*.

It is not clear when or where Millicent and Crawford met. He had relocated from Adelaide to Sydney in 1920 with his wife, the novelist Evelyn Maria Vaughan OBE[12] and pursued various business interests, including his managerial role in the British-Australian Cotton Growing Association. Crawford and Millicent may have first met through the temperance movement when he was Campaign Director of the NSW Prohibition Alliance. Their paths almost certainly crossed during the 1925 NSW election campaign; Crawford stood, unsuccessfully, as the Progressive Party (later renamed the Country Party) candidate for Ryde and Millicent won the Eastern Suburbs seat for the Nationalist Party. They were probably acquainted by the October 1927 NSW State election when both stood, unsuccessfully, as Nationalist Party candidates, she in Bondi and he in Hartley.

Crawford's wife died one month after the 1927 election. It is not surprising that following his wife's death, Crawford found

Millicent compatible company; their interests and activities were closely aligned. In February 1930 Millicent, as President of the Feminist Club, invited him to give a talk to the club members on the Cotton Industry of Australia.[13] Later that year, she invited him as her guest at a Feminist Club 'At home', which featured a viewing of Royal Art Society paintings, the presentation of a musical program with 'elocutionary items' and afternoon tea in the gallery of the Education Department building in Bridge Street, Sydney.[14] They established a friendship based on their shared political and cultural interests.

Crawford returned to South Australia in 1931 to offer himself as a Lyons-Latham candidate for the seat of Adelaide in the forthcoming federal election. He invited Millicent to travel to South Australia and support his campaign. To those who expressed surprise at her decision to support a male candidate, she replied that Crawford was one of the best feminists; sometimes a man was a better feminist than a woman and not all women were feminists, so supporting a man who was a feminist was preferable to supporting a woman simply because she was a woman.[15] Because of her 'remarkable gifts of oratory and repartee' her campaign speeches for Crawford were a 'wonderful success', or so the press reported.[16] Nevertheless, Crawford was not elected.

Millicent had also offered herself to the Nationalist Party as a NSW Senate candidate for that election. As she sought support from women in the party, she emphasised the 'necessity for co-operation among women' and the importance of women's representation in the parliament.[17] However, she was not selected by the Nationalist Party. Along with two other women, Elizabeth Laverty and Eleanor Mackinnon, Millicent was also nominated for a casual vacancy in the Legislative Council caused by the death of Dan Rees. None of the women was selected.[18] Millicent was frustrated with these rejections and when a journalist asked her about her future political intentions she responded that she would now simply lead 'a citizen's life'.[19]

What did she mean by a citizen's life? A glossy black and white four-page A4 document in her papers in the NLA perhaps provides some clues. The front page contains a large framed photo of Millicent in a stylish beret with a lapin fur draped around her shoulders. Her customary *pince nez* spectacles are absent and there is no visible jewellery. The photo caption, somewhat unusually, omits her first name – 'Mrs Preston Stanley Vaughan'. She describes herself as 'PLAYWRIGHT DISTINGUISHED FEMINIST JOURNALIST AUTHOR' and 'First woman elected to the Parliament of New South Wales'. She also declares herself to have been 'Acclaimed by the Press and her country as one of the greatest speakers of the day'.

Millicent listed among her careers 'author', 'playwright' and 'journalist'. Her claim to authorship was based primarily on her play, the editing of *The Daily Telegraph*'s women's pages and other oped pieces, three minor books and her published poems. She did, indeed, continue an authorial career by writing, scripts, novels and poems, few of which were published or performed.

Her boast to be 'one of the greatest speakers of the day' reflects the many commendatory comments she received throughout her life about her public speaking skills. She later explained that she first learned public speaking when she joined the School of Arts Debating Society at the age of thirteen and she gave her inaugural public address two years later – an address, she said, that startled the 'greybeards'.[20]

On the back page of her document Millicent provides a long list of lecture titles that indicate her political interests – 'Organising for World Peace', 'Australian Legislation for Women and Children', 'Woman's Place in the Future'. Also underpinning these topics is her commitment to feminism – to women's equality. She had certainly established herself as a leading feminist not only with her Presidency of the Feminist Club but also in her positions in other organisations.

Millicent's document also indicates her reluctance to expose her personal life to public gaze. While it mentions her marriage to a former state Premier, it reveals only the barest facts of her family. The emphasis is firmly on her public persona and her assumed social class status. It promotes her as playing a 'leading part in the public life of her country' through her work for justice for women and cites her two most innovative and successful campaigns at that stage – 'horses' rights for women' and infant guardianship.

Millicent's document includes an extensive array of testimonials including from former Premier Sir George Fuller, who admires her 'capacity to electrify audiences' and former Prime Minister Billy Hughes, who venerates her approach to 'every question from the standpoint of the earnest inquirer after truth'. These 'referees' indicate Millicent's capacity for networking with powerful men in politics. Other adulations include her 'independence of thought' and her 'courage, hope and optimism' as well as her 'magnetic personality', 'impressive manner' and 'fine voice' and recognise her as having a 'genius for public affairs', being 'superior to most men' and always providing 'orderly marshalled facts'. It is not clear how Millicent used this document but what is clear is she was affirming her past achievements and redefining herself in her new citizen's life.

This new life did not preclude her continued involvement in politics. In September 1934 Australia was facing another federal election and she was convinced the policies of UAP Prime Minister Joseph Lyons had begun to steer Australia on the path to recovery from the Great Depression. Both Millicent and Crawford were determined to work for the re-election of the Lyons government. The Labor opposition was still bedevilled by the rifts and divisions that had crippled it over the past few years. Opposition leader, James Scullin, was under constant challenge from former NSW Premier Jack Lang and his supporters, now labelled 'Langites'. Millicent had no admiration for Lang and she feared he was manoeuvring himself to supplant Scullin as the federal Labor leader – an intolerable situation in her view which, if Labor was elected, would bring the Australian nation to its knees.

In her position as Vice-President of the UAP NSW branch she assumed a prominent role in the election campaign. Moreover, she now had the pleasure of sharing the platform with her husband, who remained an active UAP member. At one campaign rally in Goulburn, Millicent and Crawford spoke in tandem although the press relegated her to a secondary role, reporting that Crawford was 'supported by his wife'.

Crawford mounted a 'vigorous attack' on the policies of both Scullin and Lang, particularly Lang's proposal to socialise credit. He argued that the crux of the current problems of political economics was the easy abundance of credit and the evil of inflation. The Labor Party was not qualified to deal with the current situation because it lacked members with the necessary expertise to handle the economy. Moreover, he continued, the Labor Party was bedevilled by the leadership tensions between Scullin and Lang. 'The Labor horse', he told his audience, 'was being ridden by two men', but he warned, the most dangerous aspect was that 'the man riding behind was not Lang but Scullin'. In other words, Jack Lang, not the Labor leader James Scullin was pulling Labor's reins. Crawford's equestrian image probably delighted his country town audience.

When Millicent took the podium, she picked up the theme of the UAP government's superior skills compared with Labor's rabble. It was the Lyons Government that had put Australia back on the path to recovery from the Depression, she told her audience. Attuned to the pastoralists in this oldest of Australian country towns, she emphasised the value of international trade to their local economy as well as to the wider Australian economy. Lang's tariff walls and protections, she warned them, would destroy their chances of recovery. And, recalling Lang's policy positions when they were both in the NSW parliament, she was not above drawing on the Red Scare trope; don't experiment with the Red element, she warned the electors, because it would bring ruin to them and to the nation. Millicent, who was adept at embroidering scare tactics, contrasted the 'dark track to red ruin' that would follow if Labor was elected with the 'long, broad, sun-lit highway' to recovery that was assured under a UAP government.

Edmund Manfred, a prominent Goulburn architect gave the Vote of Thanks to which Crawford responded on behalf of Millicent. He reiterated Millicent's red scare warning and told the audience that 'they had to determine whether they are going to march with Mr Lyons along the long, broad sun-lit highway to recovery, or vote with Mr Lang, Mr Scullin & Co. along the dark track to red ruin'.[21] The newly married couple were politically perfectly in sync.

After months of campaigning, Millicent and Crawford were reassured when the Lyons government was returned to power. However, since the UAP won only 33 of the 74 seats in the House of Representatives, they were concerned that it would now be crippled by its situation of minority government. This changed a couple of months later when the UAP entered into a formal agreement with the Country Party under Earle Page, which returned the Lyons/Page coalition to majority government.

Unfortunately for Millicent, personal sorrow shrouded her jubilation at the election victory. During her public campaigning, she had carried the burden of caring for her ailing, aged mother. Five years earlier, in Darling Point Road where she and Millicent were then living, a car had knocked Fanny down, causing 'severe internal injuries' and she was admitted to St Luke's Private Hospital.[22] Although she was not permanently incapacitated, Fanny never fully recovered from that event. She was a stoic and Millicent admired her mother's willpower and fortitude in the face of her weakened state. Millicent had nicknamed her mother 'Tige', short for 'Tiger', because of her strength and determination.[23]

In the final stages of the election campaign, Fanny's strength and determination waned. On 9 September 1934, at the age of seventy-five, she died at their flat in Cremorne. Her death certificate, signed by the Mosman general practitioner Dr Theodore Delprat, records two causes of death; Chronic Interstitial Nephritis or kidney injury from which she had been suffering for at least six months, and Uremia or kidney failure from which she had been suffering for three days.

The last weeks of Fanny's life were stressful for both Millicent and Crawford. Since their return from South Australia, they had been actively involved in the election campaign and Millicent had been monitoring the progress of the Guardianship of Infants bill through the NSW parliament. On the day before her mother's death, Millicent made an election broadcast on the radio station 2UE and also gave an address alongside the Prime Minister at a UAP meeting in the southern Sydney suburb of Hurstville.[24]

On the day of Fanny's death, Crawford was campaigning at McGowan's Corner near Bathurst west of Sydney. This electorate had been held by Ben Chifley from 1925 to 1931 when UAP candidate John Lawson defeated him. It should have been a comfortable campaign rally for Crawford with a generally supportive audience. However, standing on the platform that day, he found his audience was less than receptive to his message and, somewhat unusually, he became rattled by their interjections.[25] Perhaps he was worried by Fanny's deteriorating health and concerned for the pressure it was placing on Millicent.

On the day of her mother's death, Millicent had been advertised to speak at 3.00pm at a Mosman Town Hall campaign rally alongside the Post Master General Mr Parkhill.[26] But she withdrew from this and all her campaign commitments and four days later published an appeal in the *Sydney Morning Herald*. In her absence, she urged women to vote for the UAP and to lend their assistance 'with finance or with work' for the campaign.[27]

It fell to Millicent, as her mother's oldest surviving descendant, to place Fanny's death notice in the *Sydney Morning Herald* and organise the funeral arrangements. The death notice identified her mother as Frances, the 'widow of the late Charles Stanley'. This lie maintained the fiction she had created about her deceased father, Augustine Gregory Stanley. Intriguingly, the fictional name Charles, which Millicent inserted for Fanny's 'husband', was the middle name of Millicent's deceased brothers, Frederick and Victor. The notice airbrushed Fanny's first born son Frederick out of the family although it identified Fanny as the mother of the 'late Victor Charles Preston Stanley' and 'Mrs Preston Stanley Vaughan', as well as 'grandmother of Harold, Joan and Betty Preston Stanley'.[28]

Another notice published in the *Herald* the same day invited 'Relatives and Friends' of the late Frances Ellen Preston Stanley to attend her funeral, although there are no records to indicate if any did so. The funeral cortege left the Wood Coffill Chapel, 810 George Street at 1.30pm for the Church of England section of Rookwood cemetery where Fanny was interred on top of Victor.[29]

Fanny's death left a considerable hole in Millicent's life. She revered her mother who had been the inspiration for her life-long mission to improve the lot of women and children. Sometime after her mother's death, Millicent compiled a document she described as her exploration of 'the past and present of my mother's family history as a tribute to her memory'. In the 'Preface' she asserted her mother had told her many stories about her father, and his family, the 'proud Prestons', and the 'not ungallant part played by them throughout the centuries'. No wonder she chose to add her mother's name to her own after her father deserted the family!

In this document, Millicent claimed a 'disastrous fire' had destroyed the family papers so there was no documentary evidence for the stories she was telling in her history. There also appears to be no written evidence for the Ballarat house fire despite her protestations that she wrote her 'book' to retrieve that burnt history.

Her 'book' exists only in manuscript form. Her brown leather suitcase contains her research notes – multiple loose pages of handwritten slabs of text copied from books of dubious provenance. It is, in truth, a fabulous fiction in which she constructs a heritage that positions her family in the upper social echelons. Apart from her attempt to connect the Preston family's noble lineage to the ancient Lancasters she also tries to link the Stanley side of the family to another line of ancient English nobility although she ends that thread with William Stanley of Astle who died in 1732, neatly avoiding any mention of the convict origins of her paternal grandfather. Significantly, in the final paragraph she appends a 'Note' pointing out that William Stanley was reputedly descended from an illegitimate son of one of the Stanleys of Alderlay. But, she counsels, 'in the absence of any proof, I think the statement doubtful'. Doubt is probably the most appropriate response to the claims of aristocratic lineage in her 'book'.

However, the fact that Millicent 'researched' (albeit from dubious sources) and wrote it does indicate both her determination to maintain the fiction of her aristocratic forebears and the great admiration and devotion she felt for her mother. Despite her situation as a deserted and divorced working class mother, Fanny had managed to raise her two children under what must have been very difficult circumstances. For Millicent, who never became a mother herself, Fanny provided the supreme model of motherhood. She captured her feelings about the value of motherhood in her play, *Whose Child*, and in her other writings. In one of her *Daily Telegraph* columns, 'Motherhood', Millicent proclaims 'the mother is the priestess of humanity – she is the great altruist – she is the great teacher – she is the great creative artist'.[30] This column was also a personal paean to her mother.

Millicent so revered her mother that throughout her career she had ensured Fanny was included amongst the official guests at her public appearances wherever possible. In 1915 Fanny attended the party hosted by Mrs Edmund Playfair to farewell Millicent as she set sail for America.[31] As President of the Feminist Club,

Millicent frequently acknowledged her mother's value, as she did at a December 1920 luncheon to inaugurate a 'Women's Millions Club' where she praised women such as her mother and her distinguished guests who work to shape a better society.[32] The following year, at a Feminist Club luncheon to honour Rose Scott, Millicent included her mother amongst the official party. She praised Scott's many successful campaigns for women's freedom and justice and urged the next generation of women to develop 'a virile and unfettered womanhood to take our place in the world' and to take up Scott's baton and carry on her work, as she had taken up her mother's baton.[33] In September 1924, when Millicent spoke at the Great White Fair in the Town Hall, a fund raising event for the Prohibition campaign hosted by the Lady Mayoress Mrs David Gilpin, she ensured Fanny was included amongst the official guests.[34] This campaign was not only close to Millicent's heart but also very significant for her mother who had suffered so much at the hands of her own drunkard husband.

It was not only in women's organisations that she made space for her mother. As a newly elected member of parliament, Millicent was able to engineer some invitations for Fanny to attend formal government events. Fanny was present for the opening of parliament in June 1925 when Millicent took her seat for the first time in the Legislative Assembly. In July 1925, Fanny joined Millicent at the official government reception in honour of the American Admiral S S Robinson. This was a lavish affair attended by the American Consul, the Speaker of the Legislative Assembly and other parliamentarians and their wives, and included a police band recital and an afternoon tea hosted by the President of the Legislative Council, his wife and daughter.[35]

As one journalist opined after witnessing Fanny's attendances at so many official events, 'Mrs Preston Stanley is sharing in the triumphs of her daughter'.[36] Fanny was indeed sharing in Millicent's triumphs and Millicent was delighted to be able to share them with the mother she so admired.

Fanny's death, although not unexpected, was a moment of deep sadness for Millicent – perhaps the more so as Fanny did not live to see the Guardianship of Infants Act placed on the statute books in November that year and was not able to join in the celebrations that acknowledged Millicent as the initiator of the custody campaign.

The year 1934 marked a year of endings for Millicent. Fanny's death brought an end to her long years of sharing her life's achievements with her mother. And the passing of the Guardianship of Infants Act brought to a close her long campaign to ensure equal custody rights for mothers.

But 1934 also marked a year of beginnings. The Housewives Progressive Association nominated Millicent as 'associate delegate to the League of Nations' in Geneva – a nomination that signalled the expansion of her political horizons.[37] Her marriage opened up a range of new possibilities which she would embrace with her customary enthusiasm. In an oped piece in *The Daily Telegraph*, Millicent rehearsed her new role. 'Is Marriage a Handicap to Women's Ambitions?' she asked. 'If we are handicapped', she answered, the fault 'lies not so much in marriage as in ourselves'.[38] She would not allow marriage to handicap her ambitions – on the contrary, Millicent positioned herself with those to whom marriage brings 'a flowering of the capacities, an irresistible impetus for expression'. The years to come would indeed witness the blossoming of Mrs Millicent Preston Stanley Vaughan's capacities.

11
PEACE AND WAR
(1935-1945)

Her main objective during her visit is to promote interest in the co-operation of England and America as being the greatest factor in world peace.

The Advertiser, 30 September 1936

With the momentous year of 1934 behind her, Millicent turned her attention from the national arena to the 'inflammable world conditions' kindled by the rise of fascism and the spread of communism across Europe.[1] In September 1935 she published an article in *Truth* about the Abyssinian crisis. This diplomatic stoush over borders between the Kingdom of Italy and Abyssinia (Ethiopia) ignited the Wal Wal skirmish that resulted in the deaths of more than 150 soldiers and precipitated Italy's withdrawal from the League of Nations. Millicent argued that since the Italian 'fascist leopard' Benito Mussolini was shaking the 'mailed fist of Italy' at a 'peaceful world', Australia must stand firm with the League of Nations because that was the 'only practical possibility of averting the tragedy of war'. To reinforce her message she told her readers 'the Great War' demonstrated that 'the victor in war pays equally with the vanquished'.[2] Preventing another war and maintaining world peace became her mission.

Millicent set about harnessing women's political energies and expertise in an attempt to prevent the world from spiralling into war. In 1935, she persuaded women UAP members to collaborate with her in establishing the Women's Co-ordinating Council, an autonomous body that would bring together intelligent women from the organisations connected with the Party.[3] Elected President, she promptly convened the Council's inaugural conference to discuss the need to ensure the efficacy of the League of Nations. The conference resolved to commend the Government for its support of the British Government and urged it to assist the League of Nations to provide 'the best safeguard for the preservation of world peace'.[4]

However, instabilities in Europe – Germany's 1933 withdrawal from the Treaty of Versailles, the 1936 onset of the Spanish Civil War, and the 1937 attempted assassination of the Italian Viceroy Graziani – began to shake Millicent's faith in the League. Like others, she feared the League was hamstrung in its capacity to preserve peace because the most powerful nation, the United States of America, was not a member. President Woodrow Wilson had been one of the key architects of the League of Nations at the Paris Peace talks in 1919 and its central mission of disarmament and the prevention of another war. He had won the Nobel Peace Prize for his role in its creation. However, once the League was established in Geneva, Wilson was unable to convince Congress that America should become a member.

As her confidence in the League wavered, Millicent cast her gaze across the Pacific, just as Prime Minister John Curtin would do in his New Year's Message after the Japanese bombing of Pearl Harbour on 7 December 1941 – 'Australia looks to America, free from any pangs as our traditional links or kinship with the United Kingdom', he would tell Australians who had hitherto considered themselves welded to the British Empire. Millicent was not alone in coming to the view that neither the League nor the Empire would be able to maintain peace without co-operation between the two great powers – the British Empire and the United States of America.

In 1936, when Crawford became Secretary of the British American Co-operation Movement, Millicent willingly joined him as an ambassador to promote the Movement's work. The Movement was not intended to be a substitute for the League but rather a parallel organisation which not only sought to strengthen business ties between Australia and America but to actively engage these nations in the project of maintaining world peace. Her status as a former parliamentarian and her skills as a persuasive orator enhanced the Movement's profile as she argued co-operation was vital to the future of the world.

Millicent's role as ambassador involved giving speeches at public meetings and making radio broadcasts. At a meeting in the Adelaide Town Hall in 1936, she declared British-American Co-operation was 'a radio-active force' that would close the 'seas against warring influences'[5] – a metaphor that would become rather too vivid after America dropped atomic bombs on Hiroshima and Nagasaki in 1945 and the British conducted atomic tests at Montebello Islands in 1952 and Maralinga in 1956.

In January 1937 on Sydney radio station 2GB she discussed the geographical situation of Australia and the USA to illustrate the importance of British American Co-operation for both nations and the following month she explained how 'Pacific Problems' could be resolved through such co-operation. On 24 May 1937, following the fracas of King Edward VIII's abdication the previous year, Sydney was bedecked with flags to celebrate the centenary of Victoria's ascension to the throne, and at the official Empire Day celebration at the Martin Place Cenotaph, attended by Premier Bertram Stevens, Archbishop Howard Mowll and Lord Mayor Archibald Howie, the NSW Governor Lord Wakehurst acknowledged growing divisions amongst Empire nations and appealed for 'closer unity in the Empire'. Millicent, the only female speaker at this event echoed his call.[6]

For the next few years, preserving Empire unity and securing Pacific co-operation and world peace pre-occupied Millicent. She took advantage of every opportunity to promote these concerns in Australia as well as in the Pacific region. In July 1937 she sailed from Sydney on the *HMNZS Monowai* bound for a Peace Conference in Canada. Ironically, on her arrival in Vancouver, she was detained 'on suspicion of being a communist', although 'the authorities soon released her'.[7] Crawford was highly amused when he learned of his wife's arrest, breaking out in 'a loud laugh' and 'chuckles' and commenting that 'when they found out who she was they practically offered the country by way of compensation'.[8]

Millicent was one of fifteen Australian delegates attending the fourth Pan Pacific Women's Conference, titled 'Practical Ways and Means of Promoting Peace', which attracted more than 400 delegates. It aimed to support inter-cultural exchange and inter-racial friendship amongst Pacific nations and promote peace amongst all nations.[9] In one of her reports on the Conference, Millicent wrote there was such 'keen interest' in the disarmament topic that 'three round-table' sessions were arranged, one of which she was invited to lead. The 'well balanced distribution of commodities and purchasing power', she argued optimistically and rather too simplistically, 'would to a great extent solve the problem of starvation and therefore lessen the causes of war'.[10]

Millicent saw her mission as a 'Pilgrimage of Peace' at this 'miniature League of Nations' and the outstanding feature, she declared, was 'the amazing development of public interest' in the issue and 'the growth of a will towards peace'.[11] This, she thought, suggested there was real hope for a peaceful future. Despite Millicent's upbeat Conference reports the *Workers' Weekly* alleged, without citing evidence, she provided the 'only jarring note' and 'got a very bad reception' at the Conference.[12] This newspaper, the official organ of the Communist Party of Australia, was a constant critic of Millicent.

Following the Conference, Millicent spent several months touring the United States in her role as ambassador for the British American Co-operation Movement carrying with her what she described as a 'Magna Carta of World Peace'. Her task was to persuade American audiences that transnational co-operation was essential because the Pacific Ocean was the 'back door' to England and the 'front gate' to America.[13] During her tour, she spoke to women's associations, men's clubs and conventions from the west to the east coast, in numerous towns and cities from San Diego to New York.

She addressed organisations such as the Federation of Women's Clubs and the Hollywood Chamber of Commerce, attended functions such as the World Affairs Institute Dinner, met with influential people and even anticipated an invitation to call on Mrs Roosevelt at the White House although there are no records to suggest she received it. Reflecting on her American tour, she later concluded it demonstrated that women's organisations were capable of exerting a significant influence on legislatures – at least in America.[14]

Crawford was justifiably proud of Millicent's performance on this transnational stage. Not only was she supporting his project but doing so with skill and panache.[15] In a press article he expanded on her achievements, commenting on the 'outstanding response given by immense audiences' and asserting his confidence that 'Americans are already responding to the appeal to defend Anglo Saxon civilization in the Pacific'. He concluded by quoting the proverb, 'Blood is thicker than water' to reinforce the connectedness of the British race regardless of geographical location.[16]

The Australian press generally lauded Millicent's performance. One journalist praised her mission to 'bring the power of British and American women to bear upon National Legislatures in 'the cause of world peace';[17] another noted she 'secured an overwhelming vote in favour of co-operation' at a large dinner meeting;[18] while another reported that the 1000 professional and business men who attended a breakfast meeting she addressed in Hollywood had voted her 'some Australian'.[19] High praise indeed!

Millicent returned to Sydney on the MV Aorangi on 21 October 1938, just two weeks before the Kristallnacht pogrom that would come to be seen as one of the early sallies of World War II. Her tour had been personally nourishing as she revealed in her poem, 'To the Brown Hills of California'[20] as well as politically triumphant. As a correspondent in the New York Office of the *Australian Women's Weekly* commented, 'it is seldom that an Australian woman is entrusted with an international mission' but this woman proved herself worthy of that trust. She put America under a 'magic spell of words' with her oratorical gifts that brought a 'paean of praise' from her audiences. Grace Lockhart, a correspondent for a Vancouver newspaper, commented Millicent not only knew all the questions but also all the answers, a feat that caused that journalist to wonder why she had not been blessed with a 'brain like that'.[21]

Once back on Australian soil, Millicent was eager to share her diplomatic experiences with women's organisations and to offer her advice about improving pan-Pacific co-operation. At a Women's Co-ordinating Council Meeting in November 1938 she outlined significant initiatives that would assist this co-operation. Britain, she said, should make the Singapore military base available to America, and America should extend the Monroe Doctrine to the Pacific.[22] Great Britain maintained the island of Singapore, nicknamed the 'Gibraltar of the East', as its gateway to the Pacific and America's 1823 Monroe Doctrine was a policy of non-interference by the USA in the affairs of European nations except in situations of external threat to America itself. With growing unrest in what was then referred to as the 'Far East' she argued these policies must change – communication and co-operation across the Pacific was needed.

Speaking at the annual UAP Convention the following week, Millicent alerted her audience to the 'seriousness of Australia's geographic isolation'; Australians needed to understand this isolation and view it within a broader transnational perspective.[23] In a letter to the editor of the *Herald* in December, she admonished Australians for their 'blindness ... at their own immediate peril', arguing that since America had 'stepped out of her isolationist shell' the Australian government must facilitate parallel action between the American and Australian wing of the British fleet in the Pacific.[24] As it seemed inevitable another war would not be avoided, Millicent's impatience with Australians' political insularity escalated.

Part of the problem, as she had outlined in her 1925 maiden speech, was politicians' disregard for women's views. She told a meeting in Rockhampton Queensland in 1939, that American women asserted political influence in Washington because women 'count in America', unlike Australian women who only 'think they count'.[25] The lack of women in the nation's legislatures was proof positive of Australian women's lack of influence. It was twelve years since Millicent's departure from the NSW parliament and only one woman had since been elected to the NSW Legislative Assembly (Mary Quirk)[26] and Australia had women in only three of its state legislatures – one in NSW, two in Victoria and two in Western Australia.[27] Four decades after federation, no woman had yet been elected to federal parliament or to the state parliaments of Tasmania or South Australia – the state that had first enfranchised women. Australian politics and policy development were the poorer for the lack of input from women, she lamented.

Millicent was particularly troubled that the UAP remained so reluctant to value women's contributions to the party or the parliament. Describing herself as the 'stone the builders rejected',[28] she told women they needed to 'realise that women can be useful in Parliament' – their service complemented that of men. Women in other countries and in other professions had demonstrated this; Florence Taylor, Australia's first woman architect was even awarded an OBE at the 1939 King's Birthday Honours, and as guest speaker, Millicent had praised the service Taylor rendered the nation, describing 'service' as 'the rent we pay for the room we occupy in the world'.[29] Women, who occupied half the world's room were certainly capable of giving valuable service in all areas but all too often their service was not valued. Throughout her life, she had not wavered from the view she had expressed in her maiden speech – 'women have a contribution to make to the life of the nation which is essential to the completion of men's work'.

Like many women, Millicent was shocked when the Australian Prime Minister Robert Menzies announced in a September 1939 Fathers' Day broadcast that it was his 'melancholy duty' to inform the Australian people that Great Britain had declared war upon Germany and 'as a result, Australia is also at war'. The Australian nation once again came face to face with the reality of war, which would, all too soon, come to their own shores.[30]

Now that war was here, Millicent channelled her energies into supporting the war effort on the home front. The welfare of soldiers was her first priority. She organised visits to sick and wounded soldiers in the Ingleburn camp hospital south of Sydney,[31] and in collaboration with Miss Anne Marsh, a 2GB radio announcer, she established a Women War Workers depot in the Rural Bank building in Martin Place in Sydney. The depot organised billets in Sydney homes for interstate soldiers who would otherwise be confined to barracks over Christmas. So successful was this initiative it was expanded to cover the New Year holiday period so as to provide home comforts for the soldiers who had volunteered to protect the nation.[32]

It was not only the plight of soldiers that concerned her. The war that brought American soldiers to Australian shores also left behind war brides who had married American soldiers in a romantic war-time whirl. Although some of these wives were eventually able to join their husbands in America, those who were deserted by their spouses, were not able to obtain divorces under the existing legislation. Drawing on her theatrical expertise, Millicent persuaded UAP women to organise a spectacular rally in the Sydney Town Hall. She wrote a protest song demanding change to divorce legislation, and invited the Premier. The women chorused it to the tune of 'John Brown's Body'.

Tell us, Mr Premier, why a woman's domicile
Is where a husband likes to live not where she stays the while.
She may for the best of reasons reside where he is not
So it does not make sense.
Chorus:
Who wouldn't be a Premier
Who wouldn't be a Premier
To bring tardy justice to ten thousand
With the stroke of a Premier's pen.

Millicent's strategy was a deliberate provocation to the UAP Premier, Alexander Mair. He was first elected to the NSW parliament in June 1932, the year she staged *Whose Child* to secure the Guardianship of Infants legislation. One journalist suggested it would be a brave Premier who ignored her plea.[33] However, like the Guardianship of Infants bill, the issue of domicile in divorce for deserted wives would simmer for some time before the amending legislation was passed.

After the strangely still months of the 1939-1940 'Phony War' exploded into military action, Millicent increased her commitment to her war work on the home front. She collaborated with Lady Wakehurst, wife of the NSW Governor and several Sydney women to establish the Women's Australian National Service (WANS) with the aim of uniting women in a common patriotic cause and mobilising their war efforts into areas where there was a shortage of men.[34]

Once again Millicent took an executive role – Honorary WANS Director-Secretary. In an initiative that resembled the WWI Women's Loyal Service Bureau, she organised WANS to train the 'woman power of Australia' in case war should come to Australia's shores.[35] In collaboration with Australia's first woman electrical engineer, Violet McKenzie,[36] the WANS trained young women in signalling, wireless operation and morse code, as well as in areas such as first aid, transport and clerical services. They also provided entertainment for soldiers and encouraged country women to make their homes available for evacuated metropolitan children. One group of WANS joined Air Force reservists at a National Fitness Camp at Patonga on the Hawkesbury River, north of Sydney where they completed daily drills with the reservists while carrying out duties as canteen cooks. In reporting this story, the *Daily Telegraph* published a photograph of Millicent, clad in coat, hat and high heel shoes being carried ashore by one of the reservists when she arrived by boat to inspect the camp.[37]

Millicent was determined to defend the status of the WANS as the 'only recognised co-ordinating authority for women required for Navy, Army, Air Force or "quasi-defence work".'[38] The WANS wore a basic uniform which, as Millicent explained, was because of its 'unifying influence', and she was critical of other women's organisations that arrayed themselves in showy uniforms. Millicent captured the WANS ideals of service, sincerity and steadfastness in another propaganda verse in which she appropriated Rudyard Kipling's poem, 'If'.

> If at Australia's call you joined us, seeing
> The need to serve in place of men away;
> If you regard your uniform as being
> A badge of service, not a vain display;
> If you can play the part you've undertaken
> As though upon "your" faith depended all;
> If you can face whatever comes unshaken,
> Until at length the forts of folly fall;
> If you can put the team above the players;
> If you can count the game above the team;
> If you can hold your rank amongst the slayers;
> If you can put foundations 'neath your dream;
> If you can win or lose and yet be steadfast;
> Striving 'till stars of peace the skies impearl,

Never retreating nay, and never downcast,
You'll be a "WAN," my girl!³⁹

Embedded in the words was a subtle barb that expressed her disapproval of women in other organisations who forgot they were 'engaged in a war' and instead adopted a 'mannequin parade' mentality making 'women's war work a fashion display – with gold braid, peaked caps, and swagger canes'.⁴⁰ The sole purpose of women's war work, Millicent proclaimed, was to support the nation during this time of war.

In November 1940, at a massed display of WANS in the Exhibition Building, Lady Wakehurst took the salute as 2500 WANS marched past – some in 'gym garb', canteen women in 'stiffly starched white' and others in WANS uniform,⁴¹ while the Hurstville Choral Society sang Millicent's verse.

Despite her busy war-work schedule, Millicent had not abandoned her writing life. In the years after her marriage she had penned several lyrical poems which she published under her maiden name⁴² and had written three novels and several unpublished dramatic, literary and musical works.⁴³ Gladys Moncrieff even sang 'A Little Brown House', one of thirty-five light-hearted songs from Millicent's musical, 'Husbands on Parade' on radio station 2BL,⁴⁴ although the musical itself does not appear to have had a production.

As the war accelerated, Millicent's writing became more infused with patriotic and propaganda messages. She dedicated one of her unpublished novels, 'Return to Carthage' to 'Field Marshal, Lord Montgomery of Alamein and all who fought for freedom along the road from El Alamein to Carthage' and in 1942 she published, again under her maiden name, a collection of short philosophical essays and verse. *Pulse of Victory* denounced Nazism, celebrated loyalty and lauded the valour of those defending the British Empire. In one verse titled, 'The Pulse of England' she wrote;

> Your greatness Mother England lies not in History's power,
> But in the children you have bred, to meet 'Your Finest Hour',
> Heroes of distant flaming goals, and epics of the seas;
> But your unromantic children, oft termed prosaic stuff,
> Millions who know you must survive, and find in that enough
> To face the terrible Unknown, and greet it with a cheer;
> Their gallant hearts great strongholds inaccessible to fear.
> These are your strength, oh England, to meet 'Your Finest Hour';
> These are your living Battlements, the pulse of all your power.[45]

Millicent's verse echoed British Prime Minister Winston Churchill's 'Finest Hour' speech to the House of Commons on 18 June 1940; 'Let us therefore brace ourselves to our duty and so bear ourselves that if the British Empire and Commonwealth lasts a thousand years, men will still say, 'This was their finest hour'.[46] Billy Hughes endorsed her book as indeed meeting 'our supreme need in this hour'.[47]

Millicent shared her passion for writing with Crawford who produced journalism and fiction. It is possible to imagine them in the evening in their flat at Elizabeth Bay, Millicent at one end of the table and Crawford at the other, both working industriously on their manuscripts, perhaps reading passages aloud to each other. Crawford's fictional biography of the poet Adam Lindsay Gordon, *Golden Wattle Time* was first published in 1939 as a serial in the *Sydney Morning Herald*. The editor introduced it as a 'lively and engrossing story' told by a 'skilled and sympathetic pen',[48] although in his brief biographical note, he mistakenly claimed Crawford previously had published *Days that Speak*, a work of fiction that was actually written by Crawford's first wife.[49] While some readers, including Mary Gilmore, challenged the historical accuracy of Crawford's story,[50] *Golden Wattle Time* was later published as a novel.[51]

As the war spread to the Pacific, in March 1942 President Franklin Roosevelt ordered General Douglas Macarthur to Australia to take command of the South West Pacific Area.

Millicent immediately despatched a cable to Ruth Bryan Owen, the first Florida woman to become a US Senator and the first woman to hold a diplomatic post as Ambassador to Denmark, whom she had met on her USA tour. Her cable, sent on behalf of two hundred women's organisations, asked Owen to pass on to the President and First Lady the gratitude of these organisations for this appointment which, she believed, must bring an end to the war.

Millicent's optimism dissipated as the Australian political home front erupted like a battle ground. In August 1939 the NSW UAP Premier Bertram Stevens had lost a vote of confidence in the House and had been replaced by Alexander Mair, after the Country Party leader, Michael Bruxner refused to remain in coalition if Eric Spooner became UAP leader. At the 1941 state election, much to Millicent's anguish, Labor lead by William McKell, who had helped to thwart her Guardianship of Infants bill, roundly defeated the Mair government. This prompted the Acting Labor Prime Minister Frank Forde to boast, 'the verdict of the people' augured well for the forthcoming federal election.[52]

The federal political battle front became even more turbulent. When Prime Minister Joseph Lyons died suddenly of a heart attack on 7 April 1939, Country Party leader Earle Page became caretaker Prime Minister until the UAP elected Lyons' successor. Robert Gordon Menzies assumed office on 26 April. Further disruption followed as Page withdrew his Party from the federal coalition leaving Menzies to govern in minority until Page himself was deposed. Menzies then negotiated a new coalition agreement. If Millicent felt confident the new Prime Minister could mend the fractured coalition and maintain stable government her confidence was misplaced.

In the 1940 federal election, the Menzies government lost its majority and was forced to depend on two independent members to remain in power. Menzies struggled to maintain stability and resigned in August 1941. Millicent was pleased when her long-time champion, Billy Hughes, was elected UAP leader, but her despondency returned as the coalition partner, Country Party leader Arthur Fadden, who had been Acting Prime Minister during Menzies' long absence in Britain was commissioned as Prime Minister. Fadden's government ruled for a fabled 'forty days and forty nights' before it fell when the two independents crossed the floor and voted with the Opposition. Governor General Lord Gowrie, sought to avoid a federal election during the war and on 7 October 1941 swore in Labor leader John Curtin as Prime Minister.

Millicent had abandoned any parliamentary ambitions of her own. The UAP Women's Co-ordinating Council had petitioned her in 1940 to put her name forward as a candidate for that election but she had considered mobilising support for a woman candidate was too risky when 'winning the war' must be everyone's first priority.[53] Nevertheless, in these darkest of days, after a term of Labor government she relented, offering herself as a UAP Senate candidate for the August 1943 election – an offer that was not accepted by the Party.

The 1943 election was another disaster for the UAP with Labor under Curtin returned to government in a landslide, although one bright spot was the election to the federal parliament of two women – Enid Lyons and Dorothy Tangney – four decades after the female franchise legislation was passed. The coalition won only 19 of the 74 seats in the House of Representatives and 14 of the 36 Senate seats.

Millicent, realising the UAP was in its death throes was faced with a dilemma – where to position herself politically amidst this turbulence. In November that year the UAP Council resolved to dissolve the party and join with smaller parties to form a new political organisation, to be named the Democratic Party. Millicent accepted appointment to the management committee tasked with setting up this new party. The committee elected her former campaign manager, Reginald Weaver as NSW Party president, but he died shortly after his election. Millicent was elected to the

Council of the new party but not to the Executive where the real decisions were made.[54] Although the Party was to be a 'party of the centre' offering a 'new and vigorous spirit in Australian politics' cynics dismissed it as old wine in new bottles.[55] Millicent also became lukewarm about its prospects of success.

For the ambitious Robert Menzies, on the other hand, this was a *carpe diem* moment. He had been positioning himself for a political comeback for some time, with speeches such as his May 1942 'Forgotten People' radio broadcast in which he projected himself as a kind of saviour of the 'middle class' – the 'backbone of this country'.[56] In October 1944, he convened a Unity Conference in Canberra, at which he argued that 'If non-Labour parties organised efficiently on an Australia-wide basis they would defeat the present Federal Government at the next election'.[57] The following week, a profile of Menzies in *The Australasian* predicted, 'Whether Curtin, Menzies, Evatt or someone else is the Prime Minister in 1946-49, it seems likely that Menzies will be prominent in the picture'.[58] Menzies did not become Prime Minister in 1946, but he did position himself centre stage in the national picture for years to come.

In December 1944 Menzies gave the opening address at a further conference in Albury, NSW, which he convened to unite the non-Labor parties. He spoke of the 'rapidly growing Communist movement' and cautioned that it was 'carefully concealing its revolutionary objectives'. Menzies set out the liberal principles that would underpin the new party and argued it must fight the communist menace.[59] Although the term 'Cold War' post-dated this movement, ideas about the communist menace were fomenting. This meeting drafted the constitution and nine months later, in August 1945 the Liberal Party of Australia (LPA) was officially launched at the Sydney Town Hall.

While Millicent's ideas about liberalism and communism were in line with those of Menzies' new party, she does not appear to have played any active part in its inauguration. Perhaps she remembered some of the dilemmas and difficulties she encountered with the previous manifestations of anti-Labor parties, or recalled the frustrations of her own career in the Bear Pit. Or, perhaps she now appreciated the advice Hilma Molyneux Parkes gave her when she joined the Women's Liberal League – women who join men's organisations sacrifice their autonomy and independence.

Whatever her reflections, Millicent determined she would chart an entirely new political course to win this cold war.

12

COLD WAR AND CAMELS
(1946-1949)

... by uniting the efforts of the women of Australia, ... this organisation can launch a women's crusade for liberty, the effect of which will be felt throughout the Commonwealth.

Daily Advertiser, 4 May 1948[1]

Four decades had passed since Millicent joined the Women's Liberal League, where she first encountered warnings about socialism, which now took on a new urgency in the post-war cold war milieu. Perhaps she read George Orwell's 1947 essay, 'You and the Atomic Bomb' in which he predicted that the ashes of World War II would give rise to a permanent state of 'cold war' between two or three powerful super states.[2] However, Millicent did not conceive of the approaching cold war as a conflict between nation states but rather as an ideological battle between democracy and socialism. Socialism, she opined, was a 'system of nationalised activity' in which the state determined 'forms of economic effort' to suit its own purposes, instead of allowing citizens the freedom to choose their own economic enterprises.[3] Socialism underpinned the United Soviet Socialist Republic (USSR) communist regime, and it was expanding across Europe in its quest for world domination and the destruction of democracy.

As the Federal Labor Government set out to take control of the monetary system Millicent became convinced it had become infected with this dangerous ideology. To manage post war reconstruction, Ben Chifley, who became Prime Minister in July 1945 following Curtin's death, had adopted a centralist model for administering national projects such as the Snowy Mountains Scheme. In 1945 the Chifley government passed legislation that required state governments to move their accounts from private banks to the Commonwealth Bank so as to secure the supply of money and credit, but the High Court declared the legislation unconstitutional. In response in August 1947, Chifley announced a more potent measure; the government would nationalise private banks.

Opposition leader, Robert Menzies attacked Chifley's proposal in language that provided vivid headlines for the press – 'bank grab', 'mandate for slavery', 'challenge to individual freedom', 'step towards servile state', 'tyranny and dictatorship' and so on. In an instant, bank nationalisation became a party political issue. Millicent was incensed but she had no intention of becoming embroiled in party politics. The issue was simple; any proposal to nationalise banks was a step on the road to socialism. The Prime Minister must 'first consult the people before he takes steps to nationalise the banks', she declared and women needed to throw their support behind campaigns to ensure this consultation occurred.[4]

One month later, Millicent launched the first sally in her own crusade against what she called 'socialisation' – the process of establishing a socialist state. Bank nationalisation was, in Millicent's view, the first step in this process. Somewhat flippantly, she stated that, with nothing more than 'a pencil, a phone and a brain', she contacted seventy influential women and invited them to join her in a Sydney Town Hall rally. 'Make this the BIGGEST WOMEN'S MEETING ever seen in SYDNEY. Let CHIFLEY know what you think of this threat to your individual freedom', the promotional flier declared.[5]

Federal parliamentarians, Enid Lyons and Annabelle Rankin joined Millicent to explain the dire implications of bank nationalisation to the 3000 women who attended the first of what would become many sallies in this cold war.[6] That rally in September 1947 resolved to establish a formal organisation of women to combat this threat to democracy.[7]

The women who joined the Australian Women's Movement Against Socialisation (AWMAS) included prominent members of community organisations such as President of the Country Women's Association Grace Munro OBE, and Life Member of the Red Cross Persia Porter; professional women such as architect and engineer Florence Taylor OBE, obstetrician Dr Katie Louisa Ardill OBE and gynaecologist Dame Constance D'Arcy; and women in the arts such as opera singer Evelyn Gardiner, theatre director Doris Fitton and visual artist Portia Geach. Once again Millicent took a leadership role, as Honorary Campaign Director responsible for co-ordinating events, addressing meetings and recruiting members. Despite her 'honorary' title, she was paid a 'salary' of £12 per week plus expenses. Members paid a membership fee of two shillings per annum, and additional funds possibly came from banks that stood to benefit from the campaign.

AWMAS was not formally aligned with any political party or any religious organisation. With its anti-socialisation stance, it was not likely to appeal to diehard Labor or Communist Party women. Eleanor Glencross, the Chairman of Directors of the non-aligned Housewives Association of NSW, pointed out the bank nationalisation policy was, in essence, a party political issue but, because it would lay the foundation for a 'stronghold for a Communistic coup', members from her association joined AWMAS precisely because the organisation was avowedly non-party.[8] Unfortunately, AWMAS also drew women away from the Liberal Party Women's Auxiliary, which caused some tensions in that quarter.[9] For Millicent, the rationale for this women-only organisation was to accord women the agency denied them in other political organisations, particularly the Liberal Party Women's Auxiliary.

Within a month of its establishment, Millicent organised a rally in the nation's capital which she promoted as a 'crusade for liberty'. This metaphor, with its evocations of medieval 'holy wars' to reclaim the Holy Land from the infidels had the desired effect. Several hundred women flocked to the Albert Hall in Commonwealth Avenue, Canberra to listen to Millicent, Enid Lyons, Annabelle Rankin, and Lady Mabel Brookes, Commandant of the Australian Women's Training Corps. This rally pledged to fight socialism, work for stronger ties with Britain and ensure the future of democracy. It also resolved to send a deputation to Prime Minister Ben Chifley to demand a referendum on bank nationalisation. That deputation, comprising Mrs Groom, Lady Mabel Brookes, Dame Enid Lyons, Mrs Eva Southcombe, Mrs Nelly Stewart and Millicent arrived at Parliament House, dressed smartly, in dark-coloured suits, wearing hats and clutching handbags – the image of middle-aged, middle-class respectability.[10]

The women 'had tea and a courteous talk' with the Prime Minister but were unable to extract any assurances from him that he would consult the Australian people by implementing a referendum on bank nationalisation.[11] As one journalist reported, 'He lit his pipe and told them bluntly that he could not agree to a referendum'.[12] According to Millicent, Mr Chifley was 'very, very courteous but very, very negative'.[13] When the Minister for Transport, Eddie Ward dismissed the women's rally as a 'jaunt' attended by a few women enticed by free meals and transport, Millicent was incensed. She promptly riposted that 623 women attended as 'a grave patriotic duty', and they shared transport costs and provided their own meals.[14]

Following this rally, Millicent produced a series of propaganda pamphlets. One leaflet cautioned that no-one was 'beyond the scope of the influence of Bank Nationalisation' and since this policy emanated from Lenin it would bring 'Dictatorship', 'The Servile State', and 'Bureaucrats in Jackboots'. Another, addressed to 'Everywoman', warned about 'STEP BY STEP' socialisation. In the medieval morality play *Everyman*, the allegorical character's good deeds are judged on the day of reckoning. Millicent's pamphlet implied every woman would do her good deed for her day of reckoning – Election Day – by joining the 'Women's Crusade for Liberty'.

Another pamphlet captioned 'Chip, Evatt & Co Drapers' featured an image of a fashion dummy attired in full skirt, tightly belted waist, bar-jacket and high heeled shoes. The dummy was labelled, 'The New Look', a reference to Christian Dior's Paris collection of February that year, which heralded a return to pre-war feminine fashions. Millicent's pamphlet juxtaposed this image with references to military features – epaulets, cuffs and pockets – to signal what she believed would be the militarised socialist New Look for Australia if this policy was implemented. Furthermore, beneath the model's face, which was a mask of Ben Chifley replete with signature pipe, Joseph Stalin's face was visible. Once again, Millicent was asserting communist infiltration of Labor.

Her propaganda hit its mark as membership of AWMAS expanded to include 'housewives, religious workers, business persons, clerks, actresses, ex-service women' and women from various associations around the nation.[15] Millicent's propaganda had tapped into the fears of many women about the threat of communist expansion and infiltration of Australia by stealth.

In November, Millicent set off on a recruiting campaign across the nation,[16] travelling 5000 miles in seven weeks giving speeches at rallies and drafting women to AWMAS ranks.[17] She made a 'flying visit to Brisbane' to speak to a rally of 700 women, which promptly set up a branch,[18] and toured the Riverina in southern NSW, an area renowned for its anti-communist towns, educating her audience about 'the dangers of socialisation' and organising them for 'the battle'.[19] Her crusade and battle rhetoric was empowering, galvanising women to join as warriors in this fight for the soul of the nation.

In late 1947, upon her return to Sydney, Millicent encountered another personal bereavement. In the late afternoon of 15 December she returned to her flat at 23 Onslow Gardens, Greenknowe Avenue in Potts Point to find her 73 year old husband Crawford lying fully clothed on their bed. According to the doctor who attended, he had died about one hour prior to her return. As with the deaths of her brother and mother, Crawford's death occurred in the midst of her political campaign leaving her little space to grieve.

As a former Premier of South Australia, Crawford was honoured with a state funeral at Christ Church North Adelaide, and buried at Centennial Park Cemetery on 18 December. South Australian Premier Thomas Playford along with his Cabinet Ministers attended and Reverend A L Bulbeck, who conducted the service, praised Crawford's political career and 'his rich gifts of leadership'.[20] Crawford's obituaries focussed on his quietly-spoken mild-mannered nature, oratorical expertise and powerful pen. One noted that, despite 'indisposition' in the last two years of his life, he had written two books that 'may yet be reproduced on the stage or silver screen'.[21] Millicent negotiated the publication of his last novel *The Last of Captain Bligh* with Staples Press, London in 1950, although she was not successful in securing publication or production of his other works or of starting the Australian film production company, Quality Pictures Limited, which Crawford had hoped to found.[22]

After Crawford's funeral, Millicent resumed her AWMAS crusade. Not only was the holy land not yet secure, but she also needed to earn an income. Even with Crawford's estate sworn for probate at £860, she was not in a secure financial position – a not unfamiliar situation throughout her life. When Millicent had been stressed financially she had often sought help from friends such as Billy Hughes. In 1927 she was even sued by Mrs Rubina Constance Howie following her failure to repay a loan. With the case settled out of court it is difficult to discern the terms of settlement.[23]

By early 1948 Millicent was on the road again. Prime Minister Chifley had called for a Referendum on Rents and Prices to be held on 29 May. Chifley wanted to change the constitution to extend the government's powers to make laws that would allow the government to continue to control rents and prices as it had done during the war. For Millicent this was another step on the road to centralised control of the financial system which, like bank nationalisation, would lead to socialism, and ultimately to communism. For the present, the focus of her crusade for liberty shifted to that referendum.

During this phase, Millicent appeared at numerous referendum rallies in capital cities and regional towns to put the case for the 'No' vote. At a Wagga Wagga meeting, she launched into one of her oratorical flights declaring women had suffered the privations of rationing during the war but they had 'staggered on, human camels, the burden bearers of a nation'.[24] She then reproduced this verbal metaphor as a visual image in a pamphlet depicting a camel with a woman's face, burdened with bulging string bags of groceries, and in her final rally she used actual string bags of groceries as quiz prizes. The camel became a potent symbol of women's burdens and their capacity to bear the nation's troubles.

One week before the Rents and Prices referendum, Millicent gathered about 1000 women in the Sydney Town Hall for another rally.[25] They began by singing a popular 1935 song composed by Leslie Sarony, 'No! No! A thousand times no!'. The melodramatic lyrics tell of an 'innocent maid', abducted by the 'poisonous villain' who demands she marry him. When she refuses, he ties her to the railway tracks but she is rescued by the hero. The AWMAS women sang of their determination not to be seduced by the 'poisonous villain' of socialism:

> No! No! A thousand times no!
> You cannot buy my caress!
> No! No! A thousand times no!
> I'd rather die than say yes![26]

Millicent's canny choice of song not only bound the women in solidarity through their choral singing but also reinforced the image of good (capitalism) versus evil (socialism). She presented the women with pamphlets that referenced her New Look propaganda; 'Chif may not have the oomph of a Clark Gable or a Ronald Colman, but he certainly achieved the new look', her pamphlet stated.[27] The rally readily adopted resolutions condemning the federal government's proposals.[28]

Chifley's Rents and Prices referendum was defeated. Millicent boasted women were the 'dynamic influence' in this victory, a boast that, despite her exaggeration, was not without some merit. She went on to assert the defeat marked the 'first time in history' women were 'aroused' and 'thinking on non-party lines' about the 'welfare of the home and the influence of politics on family life'.[29] Whether the women were focused on non-party issues or merely persuaded by her extravagant propaganda is open to question.

However, Millicent was quick to warn, this was only the 'first big victory' in the 'crusade for liberty' in this Cold War.[30] Industrial unrest, she cautioned, showed that communism had infiltrated unions; Labor must be defeated at the 1949 election. At a meeting in Prime Minister Chifley's Lithgow electorate in July 1948 she expounded on the connections between socialism and communism; the only difference was communists used weapons while socialists worked through industry. But socialism inevitably led to communism and communism had brought down the 'iron curtain' on twelve European nations and was bent on world domination.[31] The AWMAS was not anti-Labor but anti-socialist, she assured her audience, but they must remember the Labor Party was pledged to socialism. Her rhetoric persuaded the women to form an AWMAS branch in the Labor Prime Minister's electorate.[32]

Over the next year, the AWMAS members took every opportunity to propagate the message that the Chifley government was a danger to the nation that must be removed at the election. On occasions their enthusiasm led to outrageous claims. In March 1949, Evelyn Gardiner asserted Marxism was taught in NSW schools. When Mr Norington, Teachers' Federation General

Secretary refuted her claim, Millicent defended these assertions, saying AWMAS was not accusing all teachers of doing so but the Teachers' Federation President was a communist and, she insinuated, subtle means were used to inculcate those socialist values in children.[33] Millicent was not averse to resorting to questionable propaganda particularly when she could implicate unions.

Proof positive of the Labor government's unwillingness to deal with communist infiltration of unions, she believed, was the 1949 coal strike. Despite both the Prime Minister and his Deputy opposing this strike, the AWMAS alleged the Communist Party had infiltrated the Miners' Federation and established the Cold War on Australia's shores. Miner's wives at one Newcastle AWMAS meeting 'interjected angrily' at her claims and two thirds walked out and held their own meeting in support of the strikers in the park opposite the hall.[34]

Undeterred by such opposition, Millicent continued to speak at meetings around the state, articulating her message that free enterprise was 'older than Karl Marx, older than Ben Chifley' and it would outlast him.[35] Democracy would be victorious over communism in this Cold War.

However, opposition to her message grew. The newly established New Housewives Association, a radical breakaway group from the Housewives Association, was far from sympathetic. Its membership comprised working class women as well as socialist activists such as Jessie Street, who was labelled 'Red' although she never joined the Communist Party and was later 'forced to resign' from the ALP over her membership of the New Housewives Association.[36] She had crossed swords with members of various women's organisations including with Millicent at the Feminist Club. With these two determined women so prominent in these ideologically opposed organisations, it is not surprising they came to blows.

At an AWMAS rally in the Sydney Town Hall in July 1949 the

New Housewives Association attempted to disrupt Millicent's meeting. One journalist reported, 'groups of young women strategically placed around the hall' interjected during Millicent's speech, challenging her statements and making it difficult for her to continue. The 'bosses' not the workers 'caused this trouble', they asserted. This was not a perspective that Millicent accepted[37] and she reportedly refused to let the 'well known socialist' Jessie Street speak.[38] A photo of Millicent kneeling indecorously on the platform, gesturing aggressively at Street captioned, 'Women Figure in Rowdy Scenes' vividly captures this moment.[39] It was not Millicent's finest hour.

Throughout her career, Millicent seldom resorted to unseemly behaviour. She prided herself on her decorum but she was growing weary of the fight. A letter to the *Herald* from Pat Grayson, a frequent correspondent to that paper, congratulated Millicent on her skill in ignoring her opponents' 'puerile utterances' but also criticised her for not adhering to her own democratic principles.[40] The communist newspaper, the *Tribune*, on the other hand, accused Millicent of physically restraining Street and alleged she stated that AWMAS was against the miners regardless of whether they were right or wrong.[41] The women's fracas was a gift to the press which revelled in headlines such as 'bedlam', 'punches and uproar' and 'women fight at wild meeting' all of which cast the AWMAS women as witches and harridans instead of depicting them as virtuous crusading warriors as Millicent intended.

Four days later *The Sun* featured an article on the meeting that profiled Millicent as 'A Fighter for Women'. The journalist noted that Millicent, the main speaker at the Wednesday meeting had described the AWMAS as an organisation of 'fighters' that was 'powerful, vital and strong numerically'. The journalist reported that the meeting passed motions condemning communism and socialism and the 'lawless and heartless strike' and depicted Millicent's background as a Member of Parliament who instigated 'reforms for women'.[42] The positive spin of this article appears to be another one of Millicent's interventions to dilute the negative publicity the meeting had generated and to control her public image.

As opposition to her campaign messages grew and the 1949 election loomed, Millicent began to doubt that her crusade to rescue the nation would be successful – a doubt that prompted her to cable an invitation to former British Prime Minister Winston Churchill.[43] 'Would you consider invitation to visit Australia before Federal election, December 10,' her cable asked, 'under the auspices of powerful non-party, non-sectarian women's organisation opposing socialisation through over 100 branches'.[44]

Did she really expect the former British Prime Minister to travel to the antipodes to campaign for the AWMAS? It was common knowledge she had met 'many well-known American women leaders',[45] but there is no evidence in her papers to suggest she had met Churchill. Although he had modified his earlier views about women after witnessing their contribution to the war, he still maintained 'Women ought not to be treated the same as men ... the sooner they are back at their homes the better'.[46] However, Churchill was renowned for his anti-communist rhetoric and might have been sympathetic to the cause. Had he accepted Millicent's invitation he would have been a major drawcard for the campaign. Not surprisingly, his diplomatic cabled response read, 'Thank you so much for your kind invitation. Regret obligations here prevent me from accepting it'.[47]

Millicent's tactic attracted publicity although not the kind she desired. The *Australian Worker* accused her of being non-party and non *'compos mentis'*; her invitation was a 'panic SOS message' that proved the conservatives were facing inevitable defeat in the election. The Liberal Party would be irretrievably shattered, the journalist declared. The Victorian Liberals and the Country Party were fighting each other 'like dogs and cats' and the NSW Branch was totally at odds with 'Mrs Crawford Vaughan (née Miss

Preston Stanley)' and her women's group. The December elections, the journalist predicted, would be the 'greatest landslide' for Labor in the political history of Australia.[48]

Despite this backlash, Millicent was determined not to give in. In preparation for her spectacular campaign finale, *The Sun* carried a plea to readers;

> Where are those camels? Has anyone got a camel to spare next Wednesday? The Women's Movement Against Socialisation is looking for a camel — any age, size or sex — for an advertising stunt. The camel, if obtainable, will be decked in a mask, a ladies' hat with a large feather, and a huge string-bag full of parcels, and paraded from Parliament House to the Town Hall to open a lunch-hour rally at noon on Wednesday.[49]

Despite her plea, no live camel was forthcoming. On 7 December, three days before the election, Millicent staged her finale without camels but with all the flourish of a theatrical spectacular.[50]

Hundreds of women flocked to the Sydney Town Hall many wearing pinafores emblazoned with a Union Jack and the question, 'What does this flag mean to you?'.[51] Her program included a 'Mum's Quiz' hosted by radio and television presenter Gordon Currie. 'Who owns a £25,000 mansion in Vaucluse?' asked Currie. 'Dan Mulcahy' shouted an excited housewife and Currie rewarded her with a string bag of groceries. 'What member of parliament has a bathroom costing £200?'. Currie handed another bag to the woman who had answered, 'Dr Evatt'.[52]

As part of the spectacle, Millicent programmed musical items, one of which was her own composition, a march, 'Daughters of Australia' and rousing speeches. Ex-WAF ferry pilot Jenny Broad warned the women that 'socialisation is the greatest swindle of the age' and sixteen year old Janice Christy told them:

> We were born during a depression, we grew up during a war and we have entered adolescence in a period of inflation. We have little to look back upon. We are hoping

that we may look forward with optimism to a happier and more contented future.⁵³

Her speech resonated with the women who were also hoping for a better future without a Labor government. Millicent had not lost her penchant for making the political theatrical. She told the women they had been waiting for this moment since Prime Minister Chifley first 'announced his intention to nationalise banks' in 1947. On Saturday, she warned, they must decide whether they wanted to have 'free parliaments and electorates in Australia' or to surrender to socialism.

When the polls were counted the Labor Party won only 47 seats while the Liberal-Country Party coalition won 74. However, despite the Liberal Party attracting 51% of the two-party vote, it did not gain a majority in the Senate. The mainstream press welcomed the outcome, declaring socialism was soundly defeated. One journalist poetically proclaimed that 'The spring tide of Socialism set in strongly after the war but now it is ebbing unmistakably'.⁵⁴ Another suggested, somewhat optimistically, that the results were 'accepted by all sides with an unusual absence of acrimony'⁵⁵, while another stated the 'coalition Government now has an opportunity of inspiring and leading the nation to better days and greater achievements'.⁵⁶ Millicent certainly hoped that would be the case.

On 19 December 1949, Robert Gordon Menzies returned as Prime Minister, a position he would hold until January 1966. Amidst the back-slapping and congratulations, the Director of the Institute of Public Affairs advised Menzies to write a note to Millicent acknowledging the AWMAS's contribution to the historic victory.⁵⁷ If he did so, she does not appear to have commented upon it.

Millicent was probably more gratified by the tributes she received from women. The journalist Joan Pilgrim, whose 'Women's Interests' columns commonly tackled significant social and political issues applauded the 'big part' AWMAS women had played in the election campaign as they 'went out into the highways and byways ... spreading the gospel of free enterprise and personal freedom'. 'Full credit', Pilgrim said, must go to Millicent and the AWMAS for taking on the 'arduous – thankless job' of providing the 'political education of every woman who can put a pencil mark on a ballot paper'.[58]

The AWMAS held a Christmas party at the Feminist Club where Mrs Lilla O'Malley Wood, who chaired the AWMAS finance committee,[59] presented Millicent with a broach with a diamond-studded bow attached to the Australian Coat of Arms and inscribed with the words, 'Australian Women's Movement Founder'.[60]

As 1949 drew to a close Australia was poised on the eve of its fiftieth year of federation. A prescient journalist proclaimed 1950 would begin 'a vital new era for the Commonwealth'.[61] For Millicent, well into her seventh decade, the New Year ushered in an era of tributes and tribulations.

13

THE FORGOTTEN SEX
(1950-1954)

Labor Members didn't like me because I was a Liberal, and the Liberals hated me because I was a woman.

Sydney Morning Herald, 20 December 1951

As the calendar clicked over into 1950 Australians embraced the new decade with optimism. With the war behind them, post war rationing coming to an end and the suburban dream becoming a reality, they looked forward to an era of prosperity and opportunity. Although they may not have foreseen it then, this decade would firmly entrench consumerism at the core of Australians' lives. Men purchased Victa lawnmowers and Holden cars while women, securely lodged back in their domestic domains, welcomed marriage, motherhood and their new role as customers. They procured Sunbeam Mixmasters and revelled in the fashion pages of magazines such as *Woman's Day*, *New Idea* and the *Australian Women's Weekly*. As Lyndall Ryan recalls;

> For women of all ages, reading the *Weekly* in the 1950s was like stepping into a glamorous new home filled with desirable and up-to-date products, familiar objects, interesting and romantic men, practical yet alluring women, and happy children.[1]

Millicent was not drawn into this glamorous domesticity. She had established herself firmly in the public sphere and she intended to remain there and hoped to be publicly acclaimed for her contributions in that realm.

In 1950, her aspiration was realised when her portrait, painted by Mary Edwards,[2] was chosen as a finalist in the Archibald Prize and hung in the NSW Art Gallery. Established in 1921 from a bequest of Jules François Archibald, the editor of *The Bulletin*, the Archibald Prize commemorates the achievements of Australians distinguished in 'art, letters, science or politics'.³ In 1950 Millicent's portrait was hung alongside illustrious women such as writer and journalist Dame Mary Gilmore, pioneering aviator Miss Nancy Bird and eminent men such as the Prime Minister, The Right Hon R G Menzies CH, KC, MP, politician, diplomat and judge The Hon Percy Spender KC, MP and founding Dean of the Faculty of Architecture at Sydney University Professor Leslie Wilkinson OBE.

Mary Edwards, a controversial artist in the national art scene was a curious choice of portraitist for Millicent.⁴ In addition to her 1943 court challenge to the judges' decision to award the Archibald Prize to William Dobell, Edwards' 1945 commissioned portrait of Enid Lyons, the first woman elected to the House of Representatives, was rejected by the Historic Memorials Committee as unsatisfactory to hang alongside the men's portraits in Kings Hall.⁵ The *Sydney Morning Herald* art critic applauded the Committee's decision, condemning the portrait as 'a creation in blue and pink, which rivals in allure the best that Hollywood can offer'.⁶ However, former Prime Minister Billy Hughes commented the committee had rejected it because it 'glamourised' Enid and was 'too etherealised'.⁷ Edwards acknowledged her portrait was 'a bit unusual' because its background was 'a nocturne of Canberra instead of the conventional chocolate box background of brown tones'.⁸

Edward's post-impressionist portrait of Millicent was similarly unusual. She presents Millicent as an affable, engaging, spirited woman in a collarless soft red suit, a long two-stringed pearl necklace framing the v-neck of her blue blouse, purple feather boa draped over her left arm, pale pink flowers in her lap and a plume of fluffy feathers adorning her tam-o-shanter. Her lips are drawn back in a smile and her white-gloved hands gesture as if she is engaged in amicable conversation with an interlocutor. Whether this portrait was intended to be hung in the parliament is unknown but in 1952 it was unveiled in the redecorated Feminist Club rooms as a tribute to Millicent who had resumed the Presidency of the Club that year.[9]

In 1951, another portrait of Millicent by Jerrold Nathan was also hung as a finalist in the Archibald. Nathan, a traditional portraitist captures a proud, stately Millicent seated ceremoniously on a throne-like chesterfield arm-chair. She is attired in a square-necked ruby-red full-skirted taffeta cocktail dress with appliqued shoulder panels. Her signature pinc nez glasses are perched on her nose, a three stringed pearl necklace clings to her neck, and a white lapin stole is draped over her shoulders like a royal robe as she casts her majestic gaze beyond the viewer.

A Committee of Citizens of Sydney led by Mrs Lilla O'Malley Wood commissioned this portrait with funds raised through subscription. It was unveiled at the Royal Empire Society's Sydney rooms by former Prime Minister Billy Hughes, who remarked that this portrait would be a 'lasting tribute' to Millicent's 'contribution to public life in the political field and in voluntary movements'.[10] At this ceremony Millicent 'recalled her early struggles against prejudice from the male members'[11] of parliament. Following the ceremony the portrait was presented to the NSW Parliament where it still hangs adjacent to one of Jack Lang, who once called Millicent the 'skirts and brains of the Nationalist Party'.[12]

In 1953 Millicent would turn 70. Perhaps the time had come for her to rest on her laurels? Not Millicent. Ever the warrior, age would not weary her while there were still battles to be won. It was 'not years that matter in a woman' she declared, because a woman is only old when 'the fires die down'.[13] The fires that had burned hot throughout Millicent's life were still aflame as she cast her gaze across the nation and to shores beyond.

Like many Australians, Millicent had watched with concern when, in October 1949, the Communist Party Leader Mao Zedong announced the creation of the People's Republic of China. She became more worried eight months later when North Korea, supported by communist China and the USSR, invaded South Korea. She was not alone in believing that communism was creeping closer, knocking down one nation after another on its pathway to Australia – a belief President Eisenhower would shortly name the 'domino theory'.

Despite opposition leader Ben Chifley warning these conspiracy theories were whipping up unnecessary anti-communist hysteria across the nation, in April 1950 Prime Minister Menzies introduced a bill to ban the Communist Party of Australia. It passed both Houses with the support of the Labor Opposition right wing. The *Communist Party Dissolution Act 1950* declared the Communist Party of Australia an unlawful association, enabling the government to dissolve it and seize all its assets. Millicent was amongst those who rejoiced at this legislation, which she believed would, at last, halt the communist long march towards Australia. However, her rejoicing was curtailed when the High Court ruled the Act unconstitutional because it was beyond the Federal Parliament's powers to suppress an organisation based on its own opinion of supposed national dangers.

That decision was not unanimous; Chief Justice Sir John Latham dissented, arguing that defence policy was a fundamental power of government.[14] Prime Minister Menzies was infuriated by the High Court's ruling, but as he did not have a majority of seats in the Senate he was hamstrung. He sought to remedy the situation through a double dissolution election. To trigger that, he introduced the Commonwealth banking bill expecting Labor to reject it. But the opposition leader Ben Chifley referred the government's bill to a committee in an attempt to thwart his strategy. Nevertheless, Menzies convinced the Governor-General, Prince Henry Duke of Gloucester that by sending the bill to committee Labor had, in effect, failed to pass it, an action that justified a double dissolution election.

Menzies won that election, regained control of the Senate and, on Latham's advice, swiftly announced a referendum on communism would be put to the people on 22 September 1951. The new opposition leader, Dr Herbert Vere Evatt, campaigned for the 'NO' vote arguing that if it passed it would contravene fundamental democratic freedoms and grant despotic powers to the government. Menzies unfortunately miscalculated Australians' reticence to changing the constitution and their level of support for the 'YES' vote. The referendum was defeated and bitter at the loss, Menzies accused the 'NO' advocates of 'misleading the public with a 'wicked and unscrupulous' campaign'.[15]

While the politicians were hurling missiles across the party divide, Millicent, impatient to see real action was waging her own war against communism. Fixing her focus on what she believed was the harm communist-controlled unions were inflicting on housewives, she reprised her camel motif. In August 1950 she arranged for an 'enormous cardboard cut-out of a camel', 'burdened with strikes and shopping bundles' and with a 'Mum' face to be placed at the entrance to the AWMAS conference venue, and she ceremoniously pinned camel badges to delegates' dresses as they arrived.[16] Her keynote address was poignantly titled 'Korea and You' and she organised other speakers to discuss the Indonesian National Revolution and the communist unrest in the Philippines. As was her custom, she included theatrical elements; stars of stage and screen Queenie Ashton and Muriel Steinbeck entertained the delegates by singing patriotic songs.[17]

The following year Millicent chose the Trocadero, a fashionable dance hall in George Street Sydney, as the site for another AWMAS rally. This one protested at politicians' tardiness in dealing with communist infiltration of unions. The communist-controlled Miners' Federation had 'declared war' on Australia, Millicent warned the meeting, so 'war should now be declared on the Federation'.[18] The women sang her satirical lyrics to the tune of the American civil war song, 'John Brown's Body', reinforcing their belief that they must be on the warpath because the men were not.

Millicent emphasised this message with her references to Joseph Stalin and to John Steinbeck's 1937 novella, *Of Mice and Men*;

> A thousand blackouts daily
> Now Uncle Joe's on top
> A hundred thousand out of work
> It's really got to stop.
> ***
> When there's no coal at all, they have us in a vice
> We wonder if our men are really men or mice.[19]

Furthermore, she appropriated the Greek drama *Lysistrata* and Menzies 'forgotten people' trope to exhort women – the 'forgotten sex' – to stage a 'Kissing and cooking strike'.[20] In Aristophanes' play set during the Peloponnesian Wars, Lysistrata urges Athenian women to deny their husbands sexual pleasures until they negotiate peace. Millicent transposed Lysistrata's bedroom plea to the kitchen, demanding women deny their husbands dinner and caresses until they took action against the communist unions. In a photo of Millicent at this meeting she appears a little weary although her energy and determination to defeat the 'Communist-organised strike menace' that was wreaking havoc on the forgotten sex had not subsided.[21]

As she continued to recruit her army of the forgotten sex to defeat this enemy she began to resort to more alarmist rhetoric. She headlined advertisements for three Central Coast meetings with provocative statements, 'WOMEN, AWAKE' and 'IT'S LATER THAN YOU THINK' and she challenged her audience with the question, 'DO YOU WANT A COMMUNIST-RULED AUSTRALIA?'.[22] Millicent's 'reds under the bed' propaganda was not out of sync with mainstream thinking and Menzies himself was a devotee of this conspiracy theory, which he milked to his advantage with the 1954 Petrov Affair. However, while Menzies' attention was focused on issues of espionage, Millicent's concerns were the adverse consequences that would prevail for women should communism conquer the Australian nation.

Invited to return as President of the Feminist Club in 1952, she set about revamping that association, recruiting new members, connecting it with AWMAS and positioning it in a global context. Recalling her earlier involvement in the British American Co-operation Movement, she determined that it was vital for women's voices to be heard in Britain and America, Australia's main allies.

When Republican Dwight D Eisenhower became the 34th President of the USA in January 1953, she despatched a congratulatory letter to him and First Lady, Mamie Eisenhower, on behalf of both the AWMAS and the Feminist Club. In her reply, Mrs Eisenhower applauded 'the fine achievement of women's organisations', thanking the Australian Women's Movement and the Feminist Club for their 'good wishes'.[23] Millicent also arranged a Coronation Luncheon to celebrate Princess Elizabeth's ascension to the throne and composed an Address of Loyalty signed by 250 members which she included with their coronation gift to the young Queen.[24] There does not appear to be any record of acknowledgment from Buckingham Palace for this gesture.

In May 1953, as she approached her 70th birthday, Millicent was again re-elected President of the Feminist Club.[25] While she did not appear to be showing signs of slowing down, photos published in the press in these latter years reveal a tired, wan woman.[26] Even if she was not wearying, she certainly began to show signs of intolerance and exasperation which reached boiling point when the parliamentary press gallery journalist, Alan Reid, nicknamed the Red Fox, brutally dismissed women parliamentarians. Women 'might as well have stayed home in the kitchen washing nappies', he quipped, for all they had achieved in parliament.[27] For Millicent and many other women, Reid's words 'exploded like a bombshell'. In an article headlined, 'Woman Prime Minister is Feminists' Ambition' and sub-headed 'Sydney's women are on the warpath', journalist Valda Marshall reported the responses of prominent women to Reid's misogynistic slur.

Not surprisingly, an irate Millicent led the pack; women did not want to be 'back among the saucepans and nappies', she snapped and somewhat unusually, identifying herself as a 'victim', she complained that her own experience in the Bear Pit had resembled a combat zone of '89 to one'. Moreover, those men, she declared, had 'no doubts of the supremacy of all males – furred, feathered or born of woman'. She continued her tirade asserting that her own party had dismissed her because she was a woman – a claim she had made on previous occasions – and declared that men must be disabused of their misconception that a woman's role was to 'make democracy easier for the males'. Her pie-in-the-sky answer to the problem of lack of women in parliament was a 'truly representative' voting system with 'one man and one woman elected for each district'.[28]

Moreover, it was not only male politicians she targeted. Women's organisations must also share the blame for the undervaluing of women's role in public life, she barked. Their 'greatest weaknesses' were their 'no politics' positions. Many women's organisations adopted a code of conduct that forbade discussion of politics at meetings and events. It was not politics *per se* that was the problem, Millicent snarled, but 'party politics'. Her statement was reprinted a week later in another article along with comments on the contemporary world from international luminaries such as India's first Prime Minister Pandit Nehru and US Supreme Court jurist, Justice William Douglas – a tribute to the esteem in which she was held internationally, despite the dismissive stance of some male parliamentarians and journalists at home.[29]

However, the vehemence of her tirade suggests her despondency was growing, as if she felt her time was running out and her life's work for women's equality was not yet done. Her despair began to lead her into paranoid territory. She not only saw reds under the beds and infiltrating unions, but now they were also insinuating themselves into women's organisations and flooding them with expensively produced 'Left Wing' literature.[30] More strangely still, she even opposed a policy designed to benefit women apparently because it came from the male-dominated Australian Council of Trade Unions (ACTU). Millicent argued against pay equality on the somewhat dubious grounds it would be a 'two edged sword' that would allow employers to sack women and employ men in their stead.[31]

Millicent's frustration with men, particularly those who were 'enwrapped in the moth-eaten trappings of an age that is gone', as she had described them in her maiden speech, now took on a bitter note as she focussed firmly on the lack of equality women suffered at men's hands in all spheres. Perhaps she was casting her mind back to her mother's precarious situation after her father deserted the family when she lobbied for the relief of the 'acute and unjust' consequences of divorce laws for women. A husband who was 'determined not to be traced had a good chance of evading divorce action', she declared, by simply deserting his family, disappearing interstate and leaving them destitute, as her own father had done.[32]

It was not only the predicament of deserted wives that preoccupied her but also the plight of physically and sexually abused women. Proposals to abolish the death sentence as the maximum penalty for sexual crimes prompted her to issue a plea to the judiciary to 'deal out full measure to those beasts who set out to ruin young women'.[33] Perhaps to assuage those concerned about her punitive pronouncement, she organised a Feminist Club deputation to the Minister for Justice, Robert Downing, to propose, somewhat unrealistically, that 'sex perverts' should be segregated or sterilized. In addition, she wanted the legal age for marriage raised from eleven to sixteen to prevent predatory men taking advantage of innocent, vulnerable girls. Needless to say, the Minister was unmoved by her arguments, and affirmed the Government had no plans to segregate or sterilize sex offenders or to change the marriage age.[34]

The government then proposed a reduction in the age girls could become bar maids. Millicent was irate at this initiative which, she believed, would render susceptible girls open to exploitation by male predators. Moreover, the menace of alcohol, a menace she had spent her whole life fighting against, would exacerbate this exploitation. Furious at this 'retrograde step' she penned a letter to the editor arguing that this would expose innocent girls to temptations that would inevitably lead to 'lower morals'. She proposed the age of barmaids should be raised or that barmen should replace barmaids[35] – both unlikely outcomes given the power of the hotel lobby and the attitudes of the men in parliament.

Protecting vulnerable girls had become something of an *idée fixe* for her. Frustrated by the road blocks she encountered in her mission to deal with predatory men, she convened a conference of women's organisations to consider ways of protecting young girls from 'attack by sexual maniacs'. The use of hatpins and pepper were discarded in favour of a 'shrill whistle', which the delegates somewhat naively thought would 'bring help and frighten off the attacker'. Millicent demonstrated two types of whistles – one a 'Tom Thumb' version and the other a 'Girl Guide' whistle – and she advised girls to wear them either at their waists or around their necks.[36] In her desire to protect girls and encourage them to secure their own safety, she seemed to have realised her attempt to bring to account the men – the 'sexual maniacs', who were responsible for attacking young girls – was not going to succeed.

The uneven power relationships between the sexes and women's subservience to men – something she had spent her life fighting against, now regularly occupied her public pronouncements. In an article on the wedding ring in antiquity, Millicent claimed 'the ring that made "her" his chattel' was placed on the lady's finger 'only after they had been coaxed, or clubbed, into the pre-historic wigwam'.[37] Women, imprisoned by this ring, were at the mercy of predatory men. The previous week, a journalist had interviewed her about married men wearing weddings rings – a practice that was growing in popularity.

She used that interview to segue into women's vulnerability to exploitation by men, telling the journalist, that when women married they were 'branded' with the pronominal, 'Mrs', but men avoided this branding. This, she declared, allowed married men to 'dupe young girls'. Men wearing wedding rings would not solve the problem of men's exploitation of young girls, she told the journalist, but finding some way to 'brand' married men might be a good idea, she suggested.

Perhaps she was reflecting on her own mother's situation, when she argued the nub of the problem was that since abortion was illegal, girls who fell pregnant to predatory men were either forced into a shotgun marriage or left to give birth to an illegitimate child, who was then adopted out, because an unmarried mother was 'unfit' to bring up any child.[38]

Sadly, it was this issue of unmarried mothers that brought her face to face with her final campaign, another child custody battle – the Mace-Murray case. The unmarried Joan Murray, a bus conductress, had given birth to an illegitimate son, Wayne on 12 November 1952. In this instance, the father of the child was not a sexual predator but a minor who wanted to marry Joan. However, his own father would not give permission for the marriage. At the birth Joan agreed to give up her son for adoption to Norman and Gloria Mace, but before the adoption papers were signed, the Maces took the child to their Central Coast farm and changed his name to Peter John.

Shortly thereafter, Joan withdrew her consent to the adoption and sought a court order to retrieve Wayne under the *Welfare Act 1939*. In April 1953, in the Supreme Court, Mr Justice Herron found for Joan and ordered the Maces to return the child to his natural mother. The Mace's immediately appealed and in September Mr

Justice McClelland granted the adoption on the grounds of Joan's 'low moral standards' that rendered her 'unfitted to have the custody and control of the child'.[39]

Millicent was incensed by a case that ignored the 'inalienable right' of a mother to her child but she acknowledged that during the earlier campaigns she had not 'thought that adopting parents would come into the picture at all'. As journalist Lou d' Alpuget noted, Millicent, who was 'a worthy opponent for any group of law-makers' led the fight although this time she was not 'contemplating another play' but seeking the 'overhaul of adoption laws'.[40] She led a Feminist Club deputation to the Minister for Education, Robert Heffron on 1 October 1953 demanding changes to the *Child Welfare Act, 1939* that would prevent an adopting parent from taking possession of a child 'until all the adoption papers are completed'.

Heffron was unmoved and Millicent was unimpressed, the more so given his previous support for the Guardianship of Infants bill. Since the Minister was obdurate, Millicent advised unmarried mothers to keep their babies but move to new districts where they would be able to avoid the opprobrium attached to illegitimacy. Furthermore she counselled other women to be more compassionate to these mothers and their babies because illegitimacy was not the fault of the child. She was no doubt unimpressed with Mrs Mace's cry that 'no one ... can imagine the heartbreak of losing a baby after he has become one of the family' – a cry that totally ignored the heartbreak of the baby's birth mother Joan who had lost her own baby.[41]

Watching the legal battle, Millicent felt frustrated by the blocks still placed in the way of a mother seeking the right to her own child. When the press dubbed the case *Whose Baby?* she was confronted with the echoes of her play, *Whose Child*. She had been successful in ensuring equal rights for mothers of legitimate children, but had not pursued the question of illegitimate children.

Perhaps she experienced some self-recrimination as she reflected on the moments when she had flagged the illegitimate child issue but had retreated in the face of vehement opposition. Upset at her powerlessness to influence the Minister and fearing the judgement in this case would mirror the Polini decision, she warned that unless changes were made to the Act, there would be repetitions of this tragedy, 'to the detriment not only of the natural and foster parents, but of the community at large'.[42] But no politicians were listening.

Despite no action on the legislative front, the Mace-Murray case continued to wend its torturous way through the legal system with appeals from both Joan and the Maces going to higher and higher courts and decisions ping-ponging between courts with one upholding Joan's appeal and the next finding in favour of the Maces. By March 1955, when Joan had exhausted all her options in Australian courts, she instructed her barrister John Wentworth Shand KC, an expert courtroom tactician with a reputation for taking on challenging cases, to prepare a petition to appeal to the Privy Council in London.[43] In October 1955, the Lord High Chancellor of Great Britain, Viscount Kilmuir, a conservative politician, lawyer and judge who was renowned for his persecution of homosexuals, announced he had determined this 'was not a case in which their Lordships could advise Her Majesty to grant special leave of appeal to the Privy Council'.[44] Joan Murray had lost her final appeal and like Emélie Polini, she lost her baby.

Mrs Mace was triumphant; 'It's all over now.' she crowed. 'He's ours'.[45] Only one newspaper recorded Joan Murray's response as she sobbed for the child she had barely seen since his birth – 'I only hope when he is old enough, and learns who his mother is, he will come back to me'.[46]

Perhaps fortuitously, Millicent did not live to witness this tragic finale.

14

A Sad retreat
(1955)

Age ... should be a gentle ending – not a sad retreat.

M Preston Stanley Vaughan[1]

Millicent, who had been endowed with rude health most of her life, had been reluctant for some time to admit, even to herself, that her physical condition was deteriorating. In her position as President of the Feminist Club, she was determined to continue her campaigns for the 'forgotten sex' and in December 1954 turned her attention to the 'social cancer in our midst – our mental hospitals'. She was particularly distressed by the case of a 'sane old lady' who suffered from rheumatoid arthritis and was confined to a wheelchair, and as a result was 'forced to spend her declining years surrounded by maniacs'. This, she declared, was 'no place to die' and her incarceration in Gladesville Hospital was an 'indictment against the rest of the community'. While we admire old homes, cathedrals and trees, she lamented, old age for 'Man' had become 'unromantic, inglorious and ignoble' – 'a sad retreat' instead of a 'gentle ending'.[2]

One month after her re-election as President of the Feminist Club in April 1955 Millicent was forced to face the stark reality of her own failing health. She was admitted to the Seventh Day Adventist Sanitarium, a convalescent hospital in the northern Sydney suburb of Wahroonga. However, it soon became evident she needed more than convalescence and was transferred to Kiora Private Hospital in Avoca Street Randwick. She died there on 23 June, three months before her 72nd birthday.

Her death certificate, authorised by solicitor Harrie R Mitchell, and signed by the resident doctor C Steinbach, records three contributing causes: exhaustion for 'days', cerebral haemorrhage for 'months' and arteriosclerosis for 'years'.

There was no state funeral to mark the passing of the first woman MP in NSW. On 24 June 1955 Rector Clive Andrew Goodwin,[3] who was known as a 'practical achiever', a man of 'vision and drive' with a 'flair for seeing what could be done',[4] a description that could be equally applied to Millicent, conducted the private funeral service at the historic St Marks Church, Darling Point. Millicent would have been pleased her service took place in the same venue where the English suffragist Maude Royden became the first woman to preach in an Australian Anglican Church in 1928.

Following the service, the funeral cortege left St Marks for the Northern Suburbs Memorial Gardens & Crematorium. The landscaped grounds of this heritage listed site in North Ryde feature art deco statues, traditional rose gardens, avenues of trees, and curved brick walls containing niches for the ashes of the deceased. On one of the eastern walls, looking across Lane Cove National Park towards Chatswood, one plaque bears an inscription; making no mention of birth date or family members, it simply states,

> Millicent Preston Stanley Vaughan. Died 23 June 1955.
>
> A Tribute of Memory from the Aust. Women's Movement Against Socialisation.[5]

Only two newspapers reported Millicent's death, both in muted tones. The Melbourne *Argus* headlined its brief obituary, 'Pioneer MP Dies' simply noting she had been the 'first woman member of the NSW Legislative Assembly'.[6] The *Canberra Times* reported her death under the headline 'First Woman MLA Dies'. This notice stated this 'well-known feminist' had held the presidencies of fourteen women's organisations 'at the same time' and, during WWII had collaborated with Lady Wakehurst in the Women's Australian National Service.[7]

Millicent's 1951 Christmas card message had highlighted how the 'great people of a community' are remembered – sometimes their service is 'referred to in obituary notices, but not always', she had written.[8] For some decades, she was all but forgotten, her service was barely mentioned. Her portrait by Mary Edwards was removed to the Mitchell Library archives after the Feminist Club closed, while her portrait by Jerrold Nathan was the only remaining sign of her presence in the Bear Pit.

Members of her family have only hazy memories of Millicent. One of her great-nephews recalls her as Aunt Millicent, reserved and distant, a little haughty like the Nathan portrait, while another great-nephew and a great-niece have fonder recollections of Auntie Millie coming for Sunday lunches, attired in hat and gloves, *pinc nez* perched on her nose, friendly and chatty, more like the Edwards portrait. As youngsters, they all knew she was important but they were not really aware of her trailblazing political career in or out of parliament.[9]

Preston Stanley family lore – those slippery stories passed down orally from one generation to the next, often embroidered along the way, whose veracity and authenticity are always open to question – remembers her as a bossy woman who put on airs and graces to impress people, her political achievements buried in the gossipy mists of her pretentiousness.

Historians frustrated that she left no diaries, journals or personal correspondence have constructed various impressions of this trailblazer. She was so 'guarded about her background' that '[o]nly the barest outline is known'[10] complains one, while another couches her statements in low modality verbs such as 'she may have ...'.[11] Nothing is certain – everything is guesswork, and sometimes the guesswork misses the mark.[12] But her 'passion for politics',[13] her 'forceful leadership' of the Feminist Club and her use of that Club as a 'bastion against communism'[14] provided clear targets for criticism. While some historians lauded her networking and organising abilities[15] and acknowledged she was a 'powerful public speaker' and 'articulate advocate',[16] others criticised her for dealing with interjectors 'mercilessly'.[17]

Her political play was deemed to be 'one of the rare examples in Australian literature of a play written in response to a legal judgement',[18] but also condemned as 'cloyingly sentimental',[19] and 'consistently verging on melodrama'.[20] Some have described the AWMAS, which she led for the last years of her life as an 'extreme right wing organisation'[21] and have accused her of engaging in hysterical, 'aggressive public rallies'.[22] In parliament she did not conform to the expectations of a woman,[23] flouted maiden speech conventions[24] and was extreme in her provocations,[25] others assert. However, she did call out the 'masculine ethos' of the parliament, acknowledges another historian who then poses the apposite question; 'Why does her first speech seem so relevant 80 years later?'.[26] Why indeed?

Nine decades after Millicent's skirts rustled on those sacred benches, the NSW Parliament acknowledged her service in an exhibition, 'A Fit Place for Women: NSW Parliament'. The title was appropriated from Millicent's maiden speech –

> ...we are told that Parliament is no fit place for women. I am not prepared to admit that such is the case, otherwise I would not be here; but if it is so it is the most serious indictment which can be lodged against men, because parliament up to date is an institution entirely of their own making.[27]

In conjunction with this exhibition, the Minister for the Arts unveiled the restored Edwards portrait of Millicent, prior to its hanging in the Exhibition Galleries at the State Library of NSW.[28] The parliament also renovated the former Members Bar as a conference room and named it in her honour – a tribute that would have delighted this life-long temperance advocate. The wall plaque acknowledges Millicent as 'a driven politician, advocating fiercely for child welfare reform and equal rights for women'.[29]

In the Preface to the Exhibition Catalogue the co-writers, the Speaker of the Legislative Assembly and the President of the

Legislative Council state that this exhibition pays homage to 'the past 100 years of our social, political and cultural history' and they identify those years as a 'time during which women have been campaigners, voters, protestors, advocates, activists and more recently parliamentarians and parliamentary officers'. Millicent was all of those.

More significantly, they reassure readers, that today 'women play a significant role' in the parliament.[30] If Millicent were to sit in the parliament today, she might be surprised by that claim. She might be concerned that some of the obstacles she encountered have not yet been removed, and that the highly confrontational political culture, which former Liberal MP Pru Goward describes as 'ruthlessly sexist'[31] and current Labor Minister for Regional Transport and Roads, Jenny Aitchison labels 'sexism ... on steroids' has not been extinguished.[32]

If Millicent could cast her gaze beyond NSW, she would be concerned at the pervasiveness of what former Foreign Minister Julie Bishop calls 'gender deafness'[33] in politics and aghast that the 'battle-axe' slur inflicted on her had morphed into the medieval 'ditch the witch' insult hurled at Australia's first female Prime Minister. She would be saddened at Senator Penny Wong's assessment that 'just as our great-grandmothers fought the battle for suffrage' so 'our daughters will continue to fight the battle for equal representation in our parliaments'.[34] She would undoubtedly join the chorus of applause for former Prime Minister Julia Gillard's misogyny speech – 'I will not be lectured about sexism and misogyny by this man. ... Not now, not ever'.[35] Millicent would probably add – 'or any man.'!

How then to write the epitaph for this Battle-axe in the Bear Pit?

Perhaps the words of the epigraph to her own unpublished manuscript, 'Resurgam' ('I shall rise again') should speak for her.

Every song should have its lyrics, sounds are not enough.
Words are the script of lost raptures; of desperate longings, calm renunciations; loves and hates; and unutterable sorrows.
Death leaves no more trace of them than the wild sea-spray tells of the sobbing waves beneath.
Truth and grief joining hands hold every man's dream and epitaph and with unerring fingers here, write my script:
an echo of the silence yet to come; where none shall trace me where hot pulses beat; nor my own voice wake me with its sound.[36]

NOTES

Introduction

1. *Sydney Mail*, 17 June 1925, 20. http://trove.nla.gov.au/newspaper/article/159722297
2. *The Argus*, 6 April 1922, 8. http://trove.nla.gov.au/newspaper/article/4671019
3. Heather Radi, 'Preston Stanley, Millicent Fanny (1883–1955)', *Australian Dictionary of Biography*, National Centre of Biography, Australian National University, http://adb.anu.edu.au/biography/preston-stanley-millicent-fanny-8107/text14153 , published first in hardcopy 1988, accessed online 21 January 2018.
4. *Australian Town and Country Journal*, 30 October 1886, 32.
5. *New South Wales Parliamentary Debates*, 19 August 1925, 205.
6. *Sydney Mail*, 17 June 1925, 20. http://trove.nla.gov.au/newspaper/article/159722297
7. *Sydney Morning Herald*, 13 January 1954, 2. http://trove.nla.gov.au/newspaper/article/18404283
8. Mitchell and Dixson Libraries Manuscripts Collection, State Library of New South Wales, Rose Scott Papers, MS 38/61 Item no. 2.

Chapter 1

1. Mary Liddell, 'An Impression. The Woman M.L.A.' *Evening News*, 1 June 1925, 6. http://trove.nla.gov.au/newspaper/article/113921462
2. *Evening News*, 1 June 1925, 1. https://trove.nla.gov.au/newspaper/page/12322240
3. *Sydney Mail*, 17 June 1925, 20. https://trove.nla.gov.au/newspaper/article/159722297
4. *Advocate* (Burnie Tasmania), 5 June 1925, 2. http://trove.nla.gov.au/newspaper/article/66960214
5. Mary Liddell, 'An Impression. The Woman M.L.A.' *Evening News*, 1 June 1925, 6. http://trove.nla.gov.au/newspaper/article/113921462
6. Mary Liddell, 'An Impression. The Woman M.L.A.' *Evening News*, 1 June 1925, 6. http://trove.nla.gov.au/newspaper/article/113921462
7. NSWPD, 26 August 1925.
8. Mary Liddell, 'An Impression. The Woman M.L.A.' *Evening News*, 1 June 1925, 6. http://trove.nla.gov.au/newspaper/article/113921462
9. Tony Smith, 'Perspective', ABC RN, 29 June 2007. https://www.abc.net.au/radionational/programs/archived/perspective/tony-smith/3232882
10. Ina Bertrand, 'Liddell, Mary Wherry (1877–1967)', *Australian Dictionary of Biography*, National Centre of Biography, Australian National University, http://adb.anu.edu.au/biography/liddell-mary-wherry-10827/text19209 , published first in hardcopy 2000, accessed online 2 March 2015.
11. Jeannine Baker, 'Australian Women Journalists and the "Pretence of Equality" ', *Labour History*, 108, 1-16, May 2015.
12. *The Star* (Ballarat), 8 July 1961, 4. http://trove.nla.gov.au/newspaper/article/66340456

13. *Sydney Morning Herald*, 22 February 1927, 10. http://trove.nla.gov.au/newspaper/article/16356706
14. *Kalgoorlie Miner*, 20 June 1906, 6. http://trove.nla.gov.au/newspaper/article/89356853
15. Millicent also enrolled in this course but did not complete it.
16. *Nepean Times* 5 July 1911, 3. http://trove.nla.gov.au/newspaper/article/50478570
17. *The Sun*, 13 April 1939, 23. https://trove.nla.gov.au/newspaper/article/231109089
18. *Examiner* (Tasmania), 9 June 1911, 6. http://trove.nla.gov.au/newspaper/article/50478570; *Evening News*, 31 December 1904, 10. http://trove.nla.gov.au/newspaper/article/113305204 ;*Sydney Morning Herald*, 1 March 1905, 6. http://trove.nla.gov.au/newspaper/article/14699101
19. The Spirit of Mothers' Day', address given at Lyceum Hall, 9 May 1926, published in *The Daily Telegraph*, 13 May 1926, 1. https://trove.nla.gov.au/newspaper/article/245757830
20. *Australian Women's Weekly*, 2 June 1934, 2. https://trove.nla.gov.au/newspaper/article/46467498
21. Mary Liddell, 'An Impression. The Woman M.L.A.' *Evening News*, 1 June 1925, 6. http://trove.nla.gov.au/newspaper/article/113921462

Chapter 2

1. *Leader* (Orange), 25 November 1913, 2. http://trove.nla.gov.au/newspaper/article/101294183
2. ²*The Age*, 1 September 1905, 2. https://trove.nla.gov.au/newspaper/article/31099589
3. Heather Radi, 'Parkes, Hilma Olivia Edla Johanna (1859–1909)', *Australian Dictionary of Biography, National Centre of Biography*, Australian National University, http://adb.anu.edu.au/biography/parkes-hilma-olivia-edla-johanna-7958/text13855 , accessed online 5 February 2018.
4. *Sydney Morning Herald*, 15 December 1903, 6. http://trove.nla.gov.au/newspaper/article/14586573
5. *Sydney Morning Herald*, 2 August 1904, 8. http://trove.nla.gov.au/newspaper/article/14646649
6. Women's Liberal League, *Monthly Record*, 31 July 1907, 4-5; *Evening News*, 9 April 1906, 6. http://trove.nla.gov.au/newspaper/article/114322002
7. *Gosford Times and Gosford and Wollombi Express*, 2 June 1905, 2. https://trove.nla.gov.au/newspaper/article/166607102
8. *Sydney Morning Herald*, 1 March 1905. http://trove.nla.gov.au/newspaper/article/14699101
9. https://adb.anu.edu.au/biography/parkes-hilma-olivia-edla-johanna-7958
10. The Latin origin of the name, Viavi meaning, 'the way to health' encapsulated the idea that the human body had a natural capacity to heal and Viavi's role was to assist Nature. Viavi products included a douche powder, laxative, and rectal suppository, contained an extract of the perennial herb, goldenseal (*Hydrastis Canadensis*), a member of the buttercup family (*Ranunculaceae*) that grew wild in the eastern states of America.

11. *Sydney Morning Herald*, 16 April 1910, 24. http://trove.nla.gov.au/newspaper/article/15145350
12. *The Sun*, 19 January 1911, 8. http://trove.nla.gov.au/newspaper/article/221569671
13. *Truth* (Perth), 31 October 1903, 3. http://trove.nla.gov.au/newspaper/article/207386047
14. *Daily Telegraph*, 27 November 1912, 14. https://trove.nla.gov.au/newspaper/article/238733954
15. *Daily Telegraph*, 2 July 1913, 15. https://trove.nla.gov.au/newspaper/article/238988975
16. *Sunday Times* 27 December 1914, 9. https://trove.nla.gov.au/newspaper/article/126761010
17. *Illawara Mercury*, 23 May 1913, 2. http://trove.nla.gov.au/newspaper/article/132313065
18. *The Border Morning Mail & Riverina Times*, 19 December 1913, 2. http://trove.nla.gov.au/newspaper/article/112142738
19. *Molong Express and Western District Advertiser*, 29 November 1913, 5. http://trove.nla.gov.au/newspaper/article/101041916
20. *Leader* (Orange), 25 November 1913, 2. http://trove.nla.gov.au/newspaper/article/101294183
21. *Cumberland Argus & Fruitgrowers Advocate*, 20 June 1914, 5. http://trove.nla.gov.au/newspaper/article/85957596
22. *Daily Telegraph* 25 May 1914, 14. https://trove.nla.gov.au/newspaper/article/238798501
23. *Sydney Morning Herald*, 1 August 1914, 21. https://trove.nla.gov.au/newspaper/article/15526835
24. *The Daily Telegraph*, 1 August 1914, 21. https://trove.nla.gov.au/newspaper/article/239070277
25. *Sunday Times*, 14 February 1915, 5. https://trove.nla.gov.au/newspaper/article/120797574
26. *Sydney Stock and Station Journal*, 14 June 1921, 3. http://trove.nla.gov.au/newspaper/article/123979544
27. *The Sun*, 27 February 1944, 2. http://trove.nla.gov.au/newspaper/article/231824395
28. The Eugenics Society of Victoria continued to operate until 1961. The legacy of Eugenics remains today in DNA studies.
29. Millicent Preston Stanley, *The Production of Human Degeneracy*, Sydney: H H Watson, 1917. Works she refers to include Richard Dugdale, *The Jukes: A Study in Crime, Pauperism, Disease and Heredity* (1877), Alfred Tredgold, *Mental Deficiency* (1908) and Henry Goddard, *The Kallikak Family: A Study in the Heredity of Feeblemindedness* (1912).
30. *Sunday Times*, 8 September 1918, 3. http://trove.nla.gov.au/newspaper/article/123129060
31. *Sydney Morning Herald* 9 June 1916, 11. https://trove.nla.gov.au/newspaper/article/28781607
32. *Sydney Morning Herald*, 12 June 1916, 11. http://trove.nla.gov.au/newspaper/article/28783591

33. *Sydney Morning Herald*, 13 June 1916. 3. http://trove.nla.gov.au/newspaper/article/15640407
34. *Sydney Morning Herald*, 14 June 1916, 12. http://trove.nla.gov.au/newspaper/article/15670010
35. Dianne Rutherford, 'The Adventurous Maud Butler', Australian War Memorial, https://www.awm.gov.au/articles/blog/adventurous-maud-butler
36. *Sunday Times*, 15 October 1916, 31. https://trove.nla.gov.au/newspaper/article/121346626
37. *Sydney Morning Herald*, 15 September 1916, 8. https://trove.nla.gov.au/newspaper/article/28101696
38. *Sydney Morning Herald*, 28 October 1916, 14. http://trove.nla.gov.au/newspaper/article/15683172
39. *Daily Telegraph* 14 December 1917, 5. https://trove.nla.gov.au/newspaper/article/239236596
40. *Sydney Morning Herald*, 14 December 1917, 8. http://trove.nla.gov.au/newspaper/page/1263212
41. *The Sun*, 12 December 1917, 7. http://trove.nla.gov.au/newspaper/article/221402758
42. *The Sun*, 23 February 1917, 5. http://trove.nla.gov.au/newspaper/article/15725296
43. Also on the podium were former Prime Minister John Watson, Labor Lord Mayor Richard Meagher and Nationalist MP George Fuller.
44. 780 guineas was the equivalent of more than Aus$100,000 today. *Sydney Morning Herald* 28 June 1917, 8. https://trove.nla.gov.au/newspaper/page/1263327
45. *The Australasian*, 7 July 1917, 46. http://trove.nla.gov.au/newspaper/article/140191786
46. *The Braidwood Review and District Advocate* 3 July 1917, 4. https://trove.nla.gov.au/newspaper/article/119239332
47. *Newcastle Morning Herald and Miners' Advocate*, 25 August 1917, 5. http://trove.nla.gov.au/newspaper/page/15196566
48. These women included a member of the State Recruiting Committee, Enid Macarthur-Onslow and her youngest daughter, Superintendent of the War Chest Depot, Mary Antill, founder of the Soldiers' Club, Dr Mary Booth, and journalist Mary Liddell, who took on the role of Bureau Secretary.
49. *Sydney Morning Herald*, 23 August 1917, 6. https://trove.nla.gov.au/newspaper/article/ 15762024
50. *Daily Telegraph*, 30 August 1917, 6; *Sydney Stock and Station Journal*, 31 August 1917, 13. http://trove.nla.gov.au/newspaper/article/124331152 *Sydney Morning Herald*, 6 September 1917, 6. http://trove.nla.gov.au/newspaper/article/15758313
51. *Sydney Morning Herald*, 24 August 1917, 6. http://trove.nla.gov.au/newspaper/article/15743720
52. *Sydney Morning Herald*, 7 September 1917, 8. https://trove.nla.gov.au/newspaper/article/15761541
53. Nairn Bede, 'Beeby, Sir George Stephenson (1869–1942)', Australian Dictionary of Biography, National Centre of Biography, Australian National University, http://adb.anu.edu.au/biography/beeby-sir-george-stephenson-5183/text8713 , published first in hardcopy 1979, accessed online 14 April 2020.

54. *Daily Telegraph*, 25 August 1917, 10. https://trove.nla.gov.au/newspaper/article/239373226
55. *Daily Telegraph*, 1 September 1917, 14. https://trove.nla.gov.au/newspaper/article/239376533
56. *Sydney Morning Herald*, 19 October 1917, 6. https://trove.nla.gov.au/newspaper/article/15736346
57. H V Evatt KC, *Australian Labour Leader: The Story of WA Holman and the Labour Movement*. Sydney; Angus and Robertson Ltd. 1945, 467.
58. J A Allen, *Rose Scott: Vision and Revision in Feminism*. Oxford University Press; Melbourne 1994, 213-214.
59. Tony Cuneen, 'One of the "Laws Women Need" – The Women's Legal Status Act of 1918', http://www.forbessociety.org.au/wordpress/wp-content/uploads/2013/03/tony9.pdf
60. Joan M. O'Brien, 'Evans, Ada Emily (1872–1947)', *Australian Dictionary of Biography*, National Centre of Biography, Australian National University, http://adb.anu.edu.au/biography/evans-ada-emily-6118/text10491, published first in hardcopy 1981, accessed online 16 April 2020.

Chapter 3

1. *Morning Bulletin*, 6 October 1919, 8. http://trove.nla.gov.au/newspaper/article/53874399
2. *Table Talk*, 29 May 1919, 2. https://trove.nla.gov.au/newspaper/article/148563456
3. *The Telegraph*, Brisbane, 21 June 1919, 10. https://trove.nla.gov.au/newspaper/article/176081582
4. Billy Hughes, Election Address Delivered at Bendigo, Victoria, 30 October 1919. https://electionspeeches.moadoph.gov.au/speeches/1919-billy-hughes
5. *Townsville Daily Bulletin*, 31 October 1919, 7. http://trove.nla.gov.au/newspaper/article/62655923
6. *Daily Mercury* (Mackay), 20 November 1919, 4. http://trove.nla.gov.au/newspaper/article/178640830
7. *Townsville Daily Bulletin*, 1 August 1919, 3. http://trove.nla.gov.au/newspaper/article/61753666
8. *Townsville Daily Bulletin*, 2 August 1919, 5. http://trove.nla.gov.au/newspaper/article/61763150
9. *The Northern Miner*, 27 September 1919, 2. http://trove.nla.gov.au/newspaper/article/82749202
10. *The Northern Herald*, 3 December 1919, 27. http://trove.nla.gov.au/newspaper/article/147965282
11. *The Northern Miner*, 18 September 1919, 3. http://trove.nla.gov.au/newspaper/article/82748721
12. *Sydney Morning Herald*, 27 February 1920, 4. https://trove.nla.gov.au/newspaper/article/28094499
13. *Sydney Morning Herald*, 6 June 1923, 7. http://trove.nla.gov.au/newspaper/article/224110573

14. *Goulburn Evening Penny Post*, 29 March 1921, 1. http://trove.nla.gov.au/newspaper/article/98932082
15. http://www.reasoninrevolt.net.au/objects/pdf/a000081.pdf
16. *News* (Adelaide), 4 December 1931, 5. http://trove.nla.gov.au/newspaper/article/129016092
17. *The Sun*, 16 May 1921, 6. http://trove.nla.gov.au/newspaper/article/221463448
18. *The Daily News*, 26 March 1923, 9. http://trove.nla.gov.au/newspaper/article/77894120
19. *Sydney Morning Herald*, 8 April 1922, 9. http://trove.nla.gov.au/newspaper/article/15997451
20. *Sydney Morning Herald*, 21 August 1922, 4. http://trove.nla.gov.au/newspaper/article/16020037
21. *Sunday Times*, 29 January 1922, 3. http://trove.nla.gov.au/newspaper/article/128211489
22. *Sunday Times*, 12 March 1922, 2. https://trove.nla.gov.au/newspaper/article/128218179
23. Until 1933 the members of the Legislative Council (the upper house) were nominated by the Governor. In 1933, the Council was reconstituted as a body elected by the members of both Houses of Parliament voting as a single electoral college.
24. *Truth* (Brisbane), 8 January 1929, 11. http://trove.nla.gov.au/newspaper/article/198976923
25. *Sydney Morning Herald*, 3 March 1922, 10. http://trove.nla.gov.au/newspaper/article/15983949
26. *Sydney Morning Herald*, 3 March 1922, 11. https://trove.nla.gov.au/newspaper/article/15983986
27. *Sydney Morning Herald* 10 March 1922, 10. http://trove.nla.gov.au/newspaper/article/15992170
28. *Truth*, 26 March 1922, 8. http://trove.nla.gov.au/newspaper/article/169190126
29. *The Sun*, 12 May 1922, 1. http://trove.nla.gov.au/newspaper/article/223955476
30. *Goulburn Evening Penny Post*, 23 May 1922, 1. http://trove.nla.gov.au/newspaper/article/99205216
31. *Table Talk*, 18 May 1922, 10. http://trove.nla.gov.au/newspaper/article/147419676
32. *The Sun*, 27 March 1922, 1. http://trove.nla.gov.au/newspaper/article/225221205
33. *The Argus*, 9 March 1922, 7. http://trove.nla.gov.au/newspaper/article/4689410
34. *The Argus*, 6 April 1922, 8. http://trove.nla.gov.au/newspaper/article/4671019
35. *The Sun*, 26 November 1922, 17. http://trove.nla.gov.au/newspaper/article/224163090
36. *The Sun*, 26 November 1922, 17. http://trove.nla.gov.au/newspaper/article/224163090
37. *Evening News*, 6 September 1922, 12. http://trove.nla.gov.au/newspaper/article/118828207
38. *Sydney Morning Herald*, 20 December 1923, 9. http://trove.nla.gov.au/newspaper/article/16107699 Later Millicent would learn that Ley was implicated in unsavoury political actions and after his return to England was convicted of the Chalkpit

Murders in the Old Bailey, declared insane and died in Broadmoor Asylum for the Criminally Insane.
39. *The Sun*, 29 April 1924, 13. http://trove.nla.gov.au/newspaper/article/223399824
40. Diana Wyndham, *Striving for National Fitness: Eugenics in Australia 1910s to 1930s*. PhD Thesis University of Sydney 1996, 196. http://www.kooriweb.org/foley/resources/AEK1201/eugenics/eugenics1.pdf
41. *The Register*, 10 June 1924, 8. http://trove.nla.gov.au/newspaper/article/57382644
42. *The Sun*, 1 June 1924, 5. http://trove.nla.gov.au/newspaper/article/223399277
43. *Sydney Morning Herald*, 14 August 1924, 9. http://trove.nla.gov.au/newspaper/article/16162502
44. *Sydney Morning Herald*, 19 April 1924, 10. http://trove.nla.gov.au/newspaper/article/16138991
45. SANSW: NRS 302/NRS 333, [7/7167.2] 30/2348
46. *The Sun*, 30 April 1924, 9. http://trove.nla.gov.au/newspaper/article/223398192
47. *Sydney Morning Herald*, 12 April 1924, 14. http://trove.nla.gov.au/newspaper/article/16145171
48. *Sydney Morning Herald*, 15 April 1924, 11. http://trove.nla.gov.au/newspaper/article/16137373
49. SANSW: NRS12060, [0/4911A] A24/938 'Letter to Premier from Emelie Polini Ellis, 17 April 1924'.
50. Gail Griffiths, 'The Feminist Club of NSW, 1914-1970: A History of Feminist Politics in Decline', *Hecate*, 14, 1, 1988, 58.
51. *Sydney Morning Herald*, 1 May 1924, 12. http://trove.nla.gov.au/newspaper/article/16139118
52. *Brisbane Courier*, 21 April 1924, 5. http://trove.nla.gov.au/newspaper/article/20671581

Chapter 4

1. *Sydney Morning Herald*, 27 June 1925, 14. http://trove.nla.gov.au/newspaper/article/16226747
2. *The Sun*, 1 September 1924, 8. http://trove.nla.gov.au/newspaper/article/ 222304842
3. *The Advertiser*, 7 October 1924, 6. http://trove.nla.gov.au/newspaper/article/43240795
4. *Sydney Morning Herald*, 6 October 1924, 2. http://trove.nla.gov.au/newspaper/article/28071257
5. *Australian Worker*, 3 December 1924, 1. http://trove.nla.gov.au/newspaper/article/145949690
6. *Sydney Morning Herald*, 27 October 1924, 4. http://trove.nla.gov.au/newspaper/article/ 16157749
7. *Sydney Morning Herald*, 28 November 1924, 10. http://trove.nla.gov.au/newspaper/article/16172820
8. *The Sun*, 14 March 1925, 5. http://trove.nla.gov.au/newspaper/article/222934574; Compulsory voting was introduced in NSW in 1928.

9. *Table Talk*, 2 April 1925, 10. https://trove.nla.gov.au/newspaper/article/146555979 Dame Clara Butt DBE, an English contralto was known for her deep, powerful voice.
10. *The Sun*, 10 May 1925, 2. https://trove.nla.gov.au/newspaper/article/224052264
11. *Sydney Morning Herald*, 7 May 1925, 12. https://trove.nla.gov.au/newspaper/article/16222308
12. *The Daily Mail*, 9 May 1925, 14. https://trove.nla.gov.au/newspaper/article/218252182
13. *Sydney Morning Herald*, 7 May 1925, 12. https://trove.nla.gov.au/newspaper/article/16222308
14. Helen Bourke, 'Weaver, Reginald Walter (1876–1945)', *Australian Dictionary of Biography*, National Centre of Biography, Australian National University, http://adb.anu.edu.au/biography/weaver-reginald-walter-9022/text15887
15. *Daily Telegraph*, 17 September 1925, 4. https://trove.nla.gov.au/newspaper/article/245246392
16. Millicent Preston Stanley Papers, NLA MS 9062.
17. *The Australian Worker*, 11 February 1925, 16. https://trove.nla.gov.au/newspaper/article/145956522
18. *Sydney Morning Herald*, 29 May 1925, 10. http://trove.nla.gov.au/newspaper/article/16226668
19. *The Australian Worker*, 25 February 1925, 5. https://trove.nla.gov.au/newspaper/article/145953071
20. *The Australian Worker*, 18 March 1925, 18. https://trove.nla.gov.au/newspaper/article/145956271
21. *The Australian Worker*, 25 February 1925, 5. https://trove.nla.gov.au/newspaper/article/145953071
22. *Sunday Times*, 17 May 1925, 2. https://trove.nla.gov.au/newspaper/article/128169414
23. *Sydney Morning Herald*, 16 May 1925, 12. http://trove.nla.gov.au/newspaper/article/16210122
24. *The Sun*, 12 May 1925, 13. https://trove.nla.gov.au/newspaper/article/224046458
25. *Sydney Morning Herald*, 26 May 1925, 10. http://trove.nla.gov.au/newspaper/article/16225714
26. *Daily Telegraph*, 26 May 1925, 7. https://trove.nla.gov.au/newspaper/article/245227734
27. *The Catholic Press*, 14 May 1925, 21. https://trove.nla.gov.au/newspaper/article/107349591
28. *The Freeman's Journal*, 14 May 1925, 24. http://trove.nla.gov.au/newspaper/article/116791665/13259062
29. *The Australian Worker*, 22 April 1925, 1. https://trove.nla.gov.au/newspaper/article/145956976
30. *The Australian Worker*, 6 May 1925, 1. http://trove.nla.gov.au/newspaper/article/145953452
31. *The Daily Telegraph*, 12 May 1925, 2. https://trove.nla.gov.au/newspaper/article/245230925
32. *The Daily Telegraph*, 12 May 1925, 2. https://trove.nla.gov.au/newspaper/article/245230925

33. *The Daily Telegraph*, 12 May 1925, 2. https://trove.nla.gov.au/newspaper/article/245230925
34. *Daily Telegraph*, 1 June 1925, 7. https://trove.nla.gov.au/newspaper/article/245235604
35. *Daily Telegraph*, 1 June 1925, 7. https://trove.nla.gov.au/newspaper/article/245235604
36. Millicent Preston Stanley Papers, NLA MS9062.
37. *The Australian Worker*, 13 May 1925, 9. http://trove.nla.gov.au/newspaper/article/145954704
38. *The Australian Worker*, 13 May 1925, 11. http://trove.nla.gov.au/newspaper/article/145954692
39. *Daily Telegraph*, 1 June 1925, 7. https://trove.nla.gov.au/newspaper/article/245235604
40. Millicent Preston Stanley Papers, NLA MS 9062.
41. *Daily Telegraph*, 1 June 1925, 7. https://trove.nla.gov.au/newspaper/article/245235604
42. *The Sun*, 24 June 1925, 13. http://trove.nla.gov.au/newspaper/article/224049532
43. *The Sun*, 1 June 1925, 10. http://trove.nla.gov.au/newspaper/article/224047398
44. *Sydney Mail*, 17 June 1925, 20. http://trove.nla.gov.au/newspaper/article/159722297
45. *Sydney Mail*, 17 June 1925, 20. http://trove.nla.gov.au/newspaper/article/159722297
46. *Mullumbimby Star*, 25 June 1925, 3. http://trove.nla.gov.au/newspaper/article/125183040
47. *Sydney Morning Herald*, 24 June 1925, 6. http://trove.nla.gov.au/newspaper/article/16220461
48. *Daily Mail* (Brisbane), 22 August 1925, 11. http://trove.nla.gov.au/newspaper/article/218260733 Richmond Villa was built by the Colonial Architect, Mortimer Lewis in 1849 as his residence. From 1893 Richmond Villa provided an annexe to Parliament House, although in 1975 it was dismantled and reassembled in Kent Street at Millers Point, where it remains the home of the Australian Society of Genealogists. The decision to situate Millicent's office there rather than in the Macquarie Street building may not have been a deliberate act of discrimination but rather an attempt to save her from having to share a cramped office in the parliament building with a male member.
49. *The Sun*, 30 November 1926, 11. http://trove.nla.gov.au/newspaper/page/24504858
50. The Domain, inaugurated by Governor Macquarie in 1816 was a large grassed area fringed with Morton Bay Fig trees, which became the location for balloon ascents, parades, picnics, a soap box arena akin to London's Hyde Park Speakers' Corner.
51. *Northern Star*, 19 August 1925, 9. http://trove.nla.gov.au/newspaper/article/93531989
52. *The Age*, 18 August 1925, 6. http://trove.nla.gov.au/newspaper/article/155809874
53. *North West Champion*, 29 June 1925, 6. https://trove.nla.gov.au/newspaper/article/181564883
54. *Sydney Morning Herald*, 26 August 1925, 12. http://trove.nla.gov.au/newspaper/article/162379388
55. *The Sun*, 16 August 1925, 20. http://trove.nla.gov.au/newspaper/article/223733375
56. Ottoman silk with its pronounced ribbed effect is an elegant fabric used primarily for formal attire and legal gowns.
57. *Sydney Morning Herald*, 14 August 1925, 8. https://trove.nla.gov.au/newspaper/

article/16235453 Irene Vanbrugh was a celebrated English actress. J M Barrie, Bernard Shaw and Noel Coward wrote leading roles for her.
58. *National Advocate*, 13 August 1925, 2. http://trove.nla.gov.au/newspaper/article/158953326
59. *Truth*, 16 August 1925, 10. http://trove.nla.gov.au/newspaper/article/168715243
60. *Cessnock Eagle and South Maitland Recorder*, 18 August 1925, 8. http://trove.nla.gov.au/newspaper/article/99367675
61. *The Inverell Times*, 7 August 1925, 3. http://trove.nla.gov.au/newspaper/article/184196950 *The Sun*, 20 August 1925, 11. http://trove.nla.gov.au/newspaper/article/223732729
62. *National Advocate*, 13 August 1925, 2. http://trove.nla.gov.au/newspaper/article/158953326
63. NSWPD, 26 August 1925, 368.
64. NSWPD, 19 August 1925, 205.
65. NSWPD, 12 August 1925, 66
66. *The Sun*, 21 August 1925, 9. http://trove.nla.gov.au/newspaper/article/223741437
67. *Evening News*, 21 August 1925, 6. http://trove.nla.gov.au/newspaper/article/113929323
68. *The Mercury*, 21 August 1925, 6. http://trove.nla.gov.au/newspaper/article/29110411
69. *The Sun*, 23 August 1925, 5. http://trove.nla.gov.au/newspaper/article/223736639
70. *Truth*, 30 August 1925, 8. http://trove.nla.gov.au/newspaper/article/168717007

Chapter 5

1. *The Sun*, 26 August 1925, 10. http://trove.nla.gov.au/newspaper/article/223732911
2. NSWPD, 26 August 1925, 368.
3. Inaugural speeches today are short, and generally include reference to family members, motivations for seeking election and acknowledgement of supporters. In 2007 in her inaugural speech, the Hon Marie Ficarra paid tribute to the 'first woman to serve in this Parliament' describing Millicent as 'a woman who never gave up'. NSWPD, 5 June 2007, 723. The Hon Dawn Walker, in her inaugural speech in 2017, acknowledged the 'courage and tenacity' of all the inspirational women who had preceded her. NSWPD, 6 March 2017, 52.
4. *Uralla Times*, 27 August 1925, 2. http://trove.nla.gov.au/newspaper/article/175998598
5. In the 2007 Standing Orders, the term, 'maiden' speech was replaced by the word, 'inaugural' and both the Speaker of the Legislative Assembly and the President of the Legislative Council now request unspecified 'courtesies' be followed, assumed to be listening in silence.
6. *The Sun*, 26 August 1925, 10. http://trove.nla.gov.au/newspaper/article/223732911
7. Adela became an organiser for Vida Goldstein in the Women's Political Association and the Women's Peace Army, was gaoled for leading a demonstration in Melbourne, promoted an anti-war, anti-conscription agenda, with her husband Tom Walsh, became one of the founders of the Communist Party of Australia, although she left that party and moved to the right, in 1928 founding the Australian Women's Guild of Empire and finally embraced the Australia First Movement.

8. *Sydney Morning Herald*, 29 August 1925, 19. http://trove.nla.gov.au/newspaper/article/ 28063766
9. *Sydney Morning Herald*, 29 May 1925, 7. http://trove.nla.gov.au/newspaper/article/ 16226612
10. Deborah Brennan, 'Women in the "Mother Parliament": Inaugural Impressions' in Deborah Brennan and Louise Chappell (eds) *'No Fit Place for Women'?: Women in New South Wales Politics, 1856-2006*, 2006, 23.
11. ¹NSWPD, 26 August 1925, 383.
12. NSWPD, 26 August 1925, 390.
13. Cecil's sister, Edith was the widow of Millicent's brother, Victor.
14. NSWPD, 26 August 1925, 403-404.
15. *Tweed Daily*, 27 August 1925, 3. http://trove.nla.gov.au/newspaper/article/191405650
16. *The Land*, 28 August 1925, 14. http://trove.nla.gov.au/newspaper/article/1030389398
17. *National Advocate* (Bathurst), 27 August 1925, 2. http://trove.nla.gov.au/newspaper/article/158958529
18. *Sydney Morning Herald*, 27 August 1925, 8. http://trove.nla.gov.au/newspaper/article/ 16238455
19. *Daily Examiner* 27 August 1925, 4. http://trove.nla.gov.au/newspaper/article/ 195403205
20. *Australasian*, 12 September 1925, 61. http://trove.nla.gov.au/newspaper/article/ 140719873
21. *The Mercury*, 27 August 1925, 6. http://trove.nla.gov.au/newspaper/article/29111055
22. *Sydney Morning Herald*, 27 August 1925, 8. https://trove.nla.gov.au/newspaper/article/ 16238420
23. *Barrier Miner*, 26 August 1925, 4. http://trove.nla.gov.au/newspaper/article/ 45882441
24. *The Bulletin*, 5 September 1925, 29.
25. *Truth*, 30 August 1925, 8. http://trove.nla.gov.au/newspaper/article/168717005
26. *The Labor Daily*, 27 August 1925, 5. https://trove.nla.gov.au/newspaper/article/ 238120432
27. *The Labor Daily*, 28 August 1925, 4. https://trove.nla.gov.au/newspaper/article/ 238124988
28. *Sunday Times*, 30 August 1925, 6. http://trove.nla.gov.au/newspaper/article/128167180
29. *Sunday Times*, 6 September 1925, 1. https://trove.nla.gov.au/newspaper/article/ 128166964
30. NSWPD, 1 September 1925, 464.
31. NSWPD, 16 September 1925, 806.
32. Notices of Motion and Orders of the Day, 17 September 1925.
33. NSWPD, 29 September 1925, 1081.
34. NSWPD, 30 September 1925, 1179-1180.
35. Executor, Trustee and Agency Company of South Australia Limited bill.
36. NSWPD, 6 October 1925, 1251-1253.

37. *The Farmer and Settler*, 9 October 1925, 2. https://trove.nla.gov.au/newspaper/article/118021600
38. *The Labor Daily*, 7 October 1925, 1. https://trove.nla.gov.au/newspaper/article/238114470
39. *Sydney Morning Herald*, 8 October 1925, 10. https://trove.nla.gov.au/newspaper/article/16247019
40. NSWPD, 20 October 1925, 1651.
41. *The Sun*, 1 October 1925, 12. https://trove.nla.gov.au/newspaper/article/223926692
42. NSWPD, 20 October 1925, 1656.
43. NSWPD, 26 November 1925, 2593.
44. *Sydney Morning Herald*, 3 December 1925, 10. https://trove.nla.gov.au/newspaper/article/16258744
45. NSWPD, 2 December 1925, 2782-2798.
46. *The Sun*, 12 January 1926, 10. https://trove.nla.gov.au/newspaper/article/224072732
47. *Daily Examiner*, 7 January 1926, 4. https://trove.nla.gov.au/newspaper/article/195644047
48. *The Daily Mail*, 10 June 1926, 21. https://trove.nla.gov.au/newspaper/article/220620680
49. *The Daily Telegraph*, 28 December 1925, 4. https://trove.nla.gov.au/newspaper/article/245054623 *Sydney Morning Herald*, 28 December 1925, 6. https://trove.nla.gov.au/newspaper/article/16275830
50. *Morning Bulletin*, 12 January 1926, 10. https://trove.nla.gov.au/newspaper/article/55251166
51. *Sydney Morning Herald*, 31 December 1925, 4. https://trove.nla.gov.au/newspaper/article/16270873
52. *Daily Examiner*, 1 February 1926, 3. https://trove.nla.gov.au/newspaper/article/195644020

Chapter 6

1. *The Blue Mountains Echo*, 22 January 1926, 6. https://trove.nla.gov.au/newspaper/article/108959584
2. *The Daily Telegraph*, 21 January 1926, 1. https://trove.nla.gov.au/newspaper/article/245840681
3. *The Sun*, 20 January 1926, 13. https://trove.nla.gov.au/newspaper/article/224061792
4. *The Daily Telegraph*, 21 January 1926, 1. https://trove.nla.gov.au/newspaper/article/245840688
5. *The Daily Telegraph*, 25 June 1926, 14. https://trove.nla.gov.au/newspaper/article/245758524
6. *The Daily Telegraph*, 10 March 1926, 2. https://trove.nla.gov.au/newspaper/article/245846977
7. W Hughes, 'Preface'. M Preston Stanley, *My Daily Message*, Sydney; Cornstalk Publishing Co, 1926.

8. *Canberra Times*, 20 January 1927, 13. http://trove.nla.gov.au/newspaper/article/1210469
9. *The Daly Telegraph*, 15 May 1926, 2. https://trove.nla.gov.au/newspaper/article/245760687
10. *The Methodist*, 18 September 1926, 12. https://trove.nla.gov.au/newspaper/article/155359727
11. *The Daily Telegraph*, 23 September 1926, 5 https://trove.nla.gov.au/newspaper/article/246347484
12. NSWPD, 14 October 1926, 293.
13. NSWPD, 19 October 1926, 347.
14. NSWPD, 19 October 1926, 351-352.
15. Colin James, 'Winners and Losers: the Father Right Factor in Australian Child Custody Law' *ANZLHE-Journal*, 2005. http://www.anzlhsejournal.auckland.ac.nz/pdfs_2005/James.pdf
16. *Sydney Morning Herald*, 19 April 1924, 10. http://trove.nla.gov.au/newspaper/article/16138991
17. NSWPD, 2 November 1926, 693ff.
18. NSWPD, 9 November 1926, 921ff.
19. Tonge not only contested the seat of Canterbury in 1927, but won it.
20. *Evening News*, 10 November 1926, 7. http://trove.nla.gov.au/newspaper/article/117324439
21. *The Sun*, 10 November 1926, 7. http://trove.nla.gov.au/newspaper/article/224117630
22. NSWPD, 29 November 1926, 1415ff.
23. Ibid., 1415.
24. Ibid., 1416.
25. Ibid., 1418.
26. Ibid., 1419.
27. Ibid., 1421.
28. *Sydney Morning Herald*, 30 November 1926, 10. http://trove.nla.gov.au/newspaper/article/28059805
29. *The Sun*, 30 November 1926, 10. http://trove.nla.gov.au/newspaper/article/224116780
30. *Sunday Times*, 9 January 1927, 4. http://trove.nla.gov.au/newspaper/article/128514678

Chapter 7

1. *Sun*, 7 August 1927, 13. https://trove.nla.gov.au/newspaper/article/168690811
2. Notices of Motion and Orders of the Day.
3. NSWPD, 19 January 1927, 487.
4. NSWPD, 28 January 1927, 741.
5. Baiba Berzins, 'Ley, Thomas John (Tom) (1880–1947)', *Australian Dictionary of Biography*, National Centre of Biography, Australian National University, http://adb.anu.edu.au/biography/ley-thomas-john-tom-7191/text12435
6. NSWPD. 2 February 1927, 831.

7. NSWPD, 8 February 1927, 1037ff.
8. *Sun*, 7 August 1927, 13. https://trove.nla.gov.au/newspaper/article/168690811
9. *Hebrew Standard of Australasia*, 7 October 1927, 4. http://trove.nla.gov.au/newspaper/article/120817928
10. *Sydney Morning Herald*, 13 September 1927, 12. http://trove.nla.gov.au/newspaper/article/16403532
11. *Sunday Times*, 16 October 1927, 5. http://trove.nla.gov.au/newspaper/article/128512297
12. *The Examiner* (Tasmania), 20 October 1927, 7. http://trove.nla.gov.au/newspaper/article/51445157
13. *Daily Examiner* (Grafton), 21 June 1928, 3. http://trove.nla.gov.au/newspaper/article/195224458
14. *Daily Examiner* (Tasmania), 3 March 1928, 6. http://trove.nla.gov.au/newspaper/article/153851941
15. *The Sun*, 15 August 1929, 15. http://trove.nla.gov.au/newspaper/article/222950116
16. *Newcastle Morning Herald*, 16 August 1929, 11. http://trove.nla.gov.au/newspaper/article/134493641
17. *Sydney Morning Herald*, 16 August 1929, 14. http://trove.nla.gov.au/newspaper/article/16576054
18. *Sydney Morning Herald*, 26 August 1929, 5. http://trove.nla.gov.au/newspaper/article/16578419
19. *Sydney Morning Herald*, 31 August 1929, 14. http://trove.nla.gov.au/newspaper/article/16580215
20. *Barrier Miner*, 30 August 1929, 4. http://trove.nla.gov.au/newspaper/article/46073496
21. *The Sun*, 13 February 1930, 25. https://trove.nla.gov.au/newspaper/article/226022972
22. *The Sun*, 19 February 1930, 5. http://trove.nla.gov.au/newspaper/article/226032091
23. *Sunday Times*, 2 March 1930, 13. http://trove.nla.gov.au/newspaper/article/132062505
24. *Sunday Times*, 20 April 1930, 15. http://trove.nla.gov.au/newspaper/article/132058808
25. *Daily Pictorial*, 7 May 1930, 20. https://trove.nla.gov.au/newspaper/article/246183158
26. *Evening News*, 20 June 1930, 10. https://trove.nla.gov.au/newspaper/article/117476727
27. *Sydney Morning Herald*, 22 August 1930, 5. http://trove.nla.gov.au/newspaper/article/16693309
28. *Sydney Morning Herald*, 23 July 1930, 8. http://trove.nla.gov.au/newspaper/article/16698051
29. *Evening News*, 29 August 1930, 10. http://trove.nla.gov.au/newspaper/article/115683631
30. *Sydney Morning Herald*, 28 August 1930, 4. http://trove.nla.gov.au/newspaper/article/16688533
31. *Sydney Morning Herald*, 10 December 1930, 1. http://trove.nla.gov.au/newspaper/article/16737243
32. *Sydney Mail*, 17 December 1930, 20. http://trove.nla.gov.au/newspaper/article/159658227

33. *Sydney Morning Herald*, 16 January 1931, 4. http://trove.nla.gov.au/newspaper/article/16746099
34. *Evening News*, 5 February 1931, 9. http://trove.nla.gov.au/newspaper/article/115400211
35. *The Sun*, 7 March 1931, 8. http://trove.nla.gov.au/newspaper/article/224670411
36. *Australian Worker*, 17 December 1930, 7. https://trove.nla.gov.au/newspaper/article/145974530
37. *Sydney Morning Herald*, 24 July 1931, 8. http://trove.nla.gov.au/newspaper/article/28040391
38. *The Australian Worker*, 23 December 1931, 18. http://trove.nla.gov.au/newspaper/article/145996318
39. *The Sun*, 30 December 1931, 6. http://trove.nla.gov.au/newspaper/article/224283187

Chapter 8

1. Millicent Preston Stanley Papers NLA MS 9062.
2. The Legislative Council was established as a unicameral parliament in 1823 to advise the Governor. Following the establishment of the bicameral parliament in 1855, the Council was appointed by the Governor on the advice of the government of the day with similar powers to the Legislative Assembly. Members of the Council tended to be more conservative than the elected members of the Assembly which resulted in frequent clashes between the two Houses. In 1933, Members of the Council were indirectly elected and from 1978 directly elected.
3. *Sydney Morning Herald*, 23 March 1932, 13. https://trove.nla.gov.au/newspaper/article/16850128
4. Although Game's action was justifiable socially and politically, constitutionally it was problematic since courts, not the Governor, are charged with determining illegality.
5. *Sydney Morning Herald*, 6 June 1932, 8. http://trove.nla.gov.au/newspaper/article/16915320
6. *Sydney Morning Herald*, 8 June 1932, 12. http://trove.nla.gov.au/newspaper/article/16904234
7. *Sydney Morning Herald*, 22 July 1932, 10. https://trove.nla.gov.au/newspaper/article/16914653
8. *Sydney Morning Herald*, 13 October 1932, 9. https://trove.nla.gov.au/newspaper/article/16919686
9. *Sydney Morning Herald*, 23 February 1932, 7. https://trove.nla.gov.au/newspaper/article/16842757
10. *Sydney Morning Herald*, 17 May 1934, 12. http://nla.gov.au/nla.news-article17051996
11. *The Mail*, 9 June 1934, 19. http://trove.nla.gov.au/newspaper/article/58853140
12. 'The Price'. *Hospital Saturday News*, 19 April 1930, 5. http://trove.nla.gov.au/newspaper/article/1880644353.3
13. 'The Willow Tree'. *Sydney Morning Herald*, 21 November 1931, 9. http://trove.nla.gov.au/newspaper/article/16801272.5; 'Pines at Manly'. *Sydney Morning Herald*, 21 May 1932, 9. https://trove.nla.gov.au/newspaper/article/16865252 ; 'The Phantom of the Mists'. *Sydney Morning Herald*, 20 February 1932, 9. http://trove.nla.gove.au/

newspaper/rendition/nla.news-article16842186.5; 'A Cobweb in the Sun'. *Sydney Morning Herald*, 19 March 1932, 9. http://trove.nla.gove.au/newspaper/rendition/nla.news-article28034366.5

14. 'The Bridge at Evening'. *The Australasian*, 19 March 1932, 12. http://trove.nla.gov.au/newspaper/article/142423673 ; 'Sydney Harbour from the Bridge'. *Sydney Morning Herald*, 9 April 1932, 9. http://trove.nla.gove.au/newspaper/rendition/nla.news-article16854669.5

15. *Sydney Morning Herald*, 31 December 1932, 5. http://trove.nla.gov.au/newspaper/article/16942095

16. *The Labor Daily*, 14 May 1932, 7. https://trove.nla.gov.au/newspaper/article/236985089

17. *Sydney Morning Herald*, 28 November 1932, 4. https://trove.nla.gov.au/newspaper/article/16933737

18. Portrait of Emélie Polini [holding baby Patricia / Mary Moore 1922 Part of Lady Viola Tait Collection, National Library of Australia.

19. Translated by Aaron Green from original Czech lyrics by Adolf Heyduk.

20. *Sydney Morning Herald*, 10 September 1932, 8. http://trove.nla.gov.au/newspaper/article/16911000

21. *Sydney Morning Herald*, 12 November 1932, 8. http://trove.nla.gov.au/newspaper/article/16930303

22. *Wellington Times*, 17 November 1932, 10. http://trove.nla.gov.au/newspaper/article/143129951

23. *Sydney Morning Herald*, 12 November 1932, 8. http://trove.nla.gov.au/newspaper/article/16930303

24. These fashionable stores offered elegant reception rooms with quality catering services.

25. *Sydney Morning Herald*, 21 November 1932, 1. http://trove.nla.gove.au/newspaper/article2802981 *Sydney Morning Herald*, 24 November 1932, 1. http://trove.nla.gov.au/newspaper/article/16932535

26. *The Mail*, 9 June 1934, 19. http://trove.nla.gov.au/newspaper/article/58853140

27. Lady Game was in the audience although Sir Philip attended another event in Newcastle that night.

28. *Sydney Morning Herald*, 28 November 1932, 8. http://trove.nla.gov.au/newspaper/article/16933605

29. *Sydney Morning Herald*, 15 November 1934, 4. http://trove.nla.gov.au/newspaper/article/17141064

30. *Sydney Morning Herald*, 28 November 1932, 4. http://trove.nla.gov.au/newspaper/article/16933737

31. *The Sun*, 20 November 1932, 24. http://trove.nla.gov.au/newspaper/article/230574443

32. *Sydney Morning Herald*, 28 November 1932, 10. http://trove.nla.gov.au/newspaper/article/16933750

33. *Sydney Morning Herald*, 17 May 1934, 12. http://trove.nla.gov.au/newspaper/article/17051996

34. *The Australasian*, 30 September 1933, 14. http://trove.nla.gov.au/newspaper/article/141381150 accessed 20 October 2017.

35. *Daily Examiner*, 29 September 1932, 4. http://trove.nla.gov.au/newspaper/article/193558945
36. *Sydney Morning Herald*, 19 November 1932, 8. http://trove.nla.gov.au/newspaper/article/16932056
37. *Newcastle Morning Herald*, 19 November 1932, 9. http://trove.nla.gov.au/newspaper/article/135489768
38. *Sydney Morning Herald*, 24 November 1932, 13. http://trove.nla.gov.au/newspaper/article/16932585
39. *Sydney Morning Herald*, 23 November 1932, 11. http://trove.nla.gov.au/newspaper/article/28029762
40. *Sydney Morning Herald*, 25 November 1932, 12. https://trove.nla.gov.au/newspaper/article/16933097

Chapter 9

1. *Sydney Morning Herald*, 15 November 1934, 4. https://trove.nla.gov.au/newspaper/article/17141064
2. *Sydney Morning Herald*, 21 August 1933, 9. https://trove.nla.gov.au/newspaper/article/ 16999886
3. *Northern Star*, 31 August 1933, 6. http://trove.nla.gov.au/newspaper/article/94230765
4. Correspondence Mrs Bernard Muscio to Minister of Justice 24 November 1932 NSW State Archives 7/7167
5. *The Sun*, 10 September 1933, 28. http://trove.nla.gov.au/newspaper/article/229157104
6. *Sydney Morning Herald*, 16 May 1934, 12. http://trove.nla.gov.au/newspaper/article/17053606
7. *The Sun*, 16 May 1934, 21. http://trove.nla.gov.au/newspaper/article/229216301
8. *The Sun*, 10 May 1934, 11. http://trove.nla.gov.au/newspaper/article/229207956
9. *Sydney Morning Herald*, 10 May 1934, 6. http://trove.nla.gov.au/newspaper/article/17078132
10. *Truth*, 13 May 1934, 30. http://trove.nla.gov.au/newspaper/article/169326162
11. *Sydney Morning Herald*, 17 May 1934, 12. http://trove.nla.gov.au/newspaper/article/17051996
12. *Truth*, 20 May 1934, 15 https://trove.nla.gov.au/newspaper/article/169328711
13. *The Canberra Times*, 1 June 1934, 6. http://trove.nla.gov.au/newspaper/article/2355944
14. *Evening News*, 6 June 1934, 3. http://trove.nla.gov.au/newspaper/article/198826536
15. *Sydney Morning Herald*. 1 June 1934, 15. http://trove.nla.gov.au/newspaper/article/17067771
16. *Voice* (Hobart), 14 July 1934, 7. http://trove.nla.gov.au/newspaper/article/218830163
17. *The Mercury* (Hobart), 20 October 1934, 15. http://trove.nla.gov.au/newspaper/article/29163744
18. *Sydney Morning Herald*, 10 October 1934, 10. http://trove.nla.gov.au/newspaper/article/17118784
19. *The Sun*, 24 October 1934, 10. http://trove.nla.gov.au/newspaper/article/230316235

20. *Barrier Miner*, 6 November 1934, 3. http://trove.nla.gov.au/newspaper/article/49524556
21. *Catholic Freeman's Journal*, 8 November 1934, 21. http://trove.nla.gov.au/newspaper/page/17320030
22. *The Australasian*, 24 November 1934, 13. http://trove.nla.gov.au/newspaper/article/145244441
23. *Australian Women's Weekly*, 3 November 1934, 26. http://trove.nla.gov.au/newspaper/article/47215475
24. Justice Harvey, now Sir John Musgrave Harvey was critical of the bill. Reflecting on his career in 1936 Harvey proclaimed that the Act had done nothing more than 'emphasise the law as it stood' because the 'welfare of the child' remained as the only factor in determining such cases. He said there had been a 'great deal of misunderstanding' about his judgement but he had determined the Polini case on what was in the child's interest. (*Goulburn Evening Penny Post*, 6 February 1936, 1. http://trove.nla.gov.au/newspaper/article/99565310) Unfortunately, he did not live long enough to learn that his judgment about the best interests for Polini's child, Patricia, was fatally flawed. Patricia, deprived of her mother, lived a somewhat unsettled life – never marrying, devoting her mother's inheritance to her dogs, becoming severely obese and dying of cancer in Sydney Hospital on 19 June 1981. (Interview with Judith Channon, life-long friend of Patricia Ellis on 23 April 2012.)
25. *Sydney Morning Herald*, 15 November 1934, 4. https://trove.nla.gov.au/newspaper/article/17141064
26. *Dubbo Liberal and Macquarie Advocate*, 27 December 1934, 4. http://trove.nla.gov.au/newspaper/article/131588125

Chapter 10

1. *The Argus*, 29 May 1934, 10. http://trove.nla.gov.au/newspaper/article/10941467
2. *Australian Women's Weekly*, 2 June 1934, 2. http://trove.nla.gov.au/newspaper/article/46467498
3. *The Sun*, 27 May 1934, 1. http://trove.nla.gov.au/newspaper/article/229212816
4. *The Northern Miner*, 31 May 1934, 2. http://trove.nla.gov.au/newspaper/article/81446347
5. *Sunday Times* (Perth), 10 June 1934, 6. http://trove.nla.gov.au/newspaper/article/61196881
6. *The Sun*, 1 June 1934, 11. http://trove.nla.gov.au/newspaper/article/229215045
7. *The Argus*, 30 May 1934, 5. https://trove.nla.gov.au/newspaper/article/10941831
8. *The Advertiser*, 15 February 1935, 19. https://trove.nla.gov.au/newspaper/article/37267052
9. *Australian Women's Weekly*, 12 January 1935, 22. http://trove.nla.gov.au/newspaper/article/47232377
10. *Sunday Times*, 10 June 1934, 6. https://trove.nla.gov.au/newspaper/article/61196881
11. *Tweed Daily*, 10 October 1935, 7. http://trove.nla.gov.au/newspaper/article/192409628
12. Evelyn had distinguished herself as a public speaker who was often called on to address meetings. She published short stories and novels and was a member of

the Women's Non-Party Political Association. During WWI she was actively involved in recruiting programs, accompanied Crawford to America and was awarded an OBE for her patriotic services.

13. *The Sun*, 16 February 1930, 20. http://trove.nla.gov.au/newspaper/article/132058343
14. *Sydney Morning Herald*, 14 August 1930, 3. http://trove.nla.gov.au/newspaper/article/16673405
15. *News* (Adelaide), 4 December 1931, 5. http://trove.nla.gov.au/newspaper/article/129016092
16. *News* (Adelaide), 15 December 1931, 9. http://trove.nla.gov.au/newspaper/article/129019174
17. *Sydney Morning Herald*, 14 May 1931, 6. https://trove.nla.gov.au/newspaper/article/16777595
18. *Smith's Weekly*, 28 July 1934, 10. https://trove.nla.gov.au/newspaper/article/235491430
19. *The Argus*, 29 May 1934, 10. http://trove.nla.gov.au/newspaper/article/10941467
20. *The Sun*, 13 April 1939, 23. https://trove.nla.gov.au/newspaper/article/231109089
21. *Goulburn Evening Post*, 10 September 1934, 13. https://trove.nla.gov.au/newspaper/article/103666614
22. *Sydney Morning Herald*, 1 July 1929, 12. https://trove.nla.gov.au/newspaper/article/16559409
23. *Australian Women's Weekly*, 2 June 1934, 2. https://trove.nla.gov.au/newspaper/article/ 46467498
24. *Sydney Morning Herald*, 7 September 1934, 15. https://trove.nla.gov.au/newspaper/article/17108681
25. *National Advocate* (Bathurst), 10 September 1934, 3. https://trove.nla.gov.au/newspaper/article/159749918
26. *Sydney Morning Herald*, 10 September 1934, 13. https://trove.nla.gov.au/newspaper/article/17086817
27. *Sydney Morning Herald*, 13 September 1934, 16. https://trove.nla.gov.au/newspaper/article/17082104
28. *Sydney Morning Herald*, 10 September 1934, 8. http://trove.nla.gov.au/newspaper/article/17086961
29. Rookwood Cemetery Zone C, Section 6, Allotment 572.
30. M Preston Stanley, 'My Daily Message. 'Motherhood'. *Daily Telegraph*, 2 February 1926, p.2. https://trove.nla.gov.au/newspaper/article/245857474
31. *Sunday Times*, 31 January 1915, 5. https://trove.nla.gov.au/newspaper/article/120809917
32. *Sydney Morning Herald*, 8 December 1920, 18. https://trove.nla.gov.au/newspaper/article/16878690
33. *Evening News*, 12 April 1921, 5. https://trove.nla.gov.au/newspaper/article/118909081
34. *Evening News* 11 September 1924, 13. https://trove.nla.gov.au/newspaper/article/119964673
35. *The Sun*, 25 July 1925, 9. https://trove.nla.gov.au/newspaper/article/223730500
36. *The Sun*, 15 November 1925, 2. https://trove.nla.gov.au/newspaper/article/223939153

37. *The Daily Telegraph*, 15 December 1934, 10. https://trove.nla.gov.au/newspaper/article/ 247000300
38. *The Daily Telegraph*, 27 October 1934, 6. https://trove.nla.gov.au/newspaper/article/ 246679617

Chapter 11

1. *Truth*, 1 September 1935, 22. http://trove.nla.gov.au/newspaper/article/169343784
2. *Truth*, 1 September 1935, 22. http://trove.nla.gov.au/newspaper/article/169343784
3. *Courier Mail* (Brisbane), 5 August 1935, 17. https://trove.nla.gov.au/newspaper/article/36762859
4. *Newcastle Sun*, 17 September 1935, 5. https://trove.nla.gov.au/newspaper/article/166148181
5. *Australian Women's Weekly*, 7 November 1936, 39. http://trove.nla.gov.au/newspaper/article/47478535
6. *The Sun*, 24 May 1937, 9. https://trove.nla.gov.au/newspaper/article/229410501
7. *National Advocate* (Bathurst), 3 August 1937, 1. http://trove.nla.gov.au/newspaper/article/160570651
8. *The Sun*, 2 August 1937, 10. https://trove.nla.gov.au/newspaper/article/231085389
9. *Sydney Morning Herald*, 15 July 1937, 18. http://trove.nla.gov.au/newspaper/article/17382261
10. *Sydney Morning Herald*, 9 September 1937, 22. https://trove.nla.gov.au/newspaper/article/17403662
11. *Sydney Morning Herald*, 15 July 1937, 18. https://trove.nla.gov.au/newspaper/article/17382261
12. *The Workers' Weekly*, 12 November 1937, 4. http://trove.nla.gov.au/newspaper/article/ 211823425
13. *Sydney Morning Herald*, 3 November 1937, 19. http://trove.nla.gov.au/newspaper/article/17534564
14. *Sydney Morning Herald*, 28 December 1938, 8. http://trove.nla.gov.au/newspaper/article/17544931
15. *The Sun*, 31 October 1937, 15. http://trove.nla.gov.au/newspaper/article/229450647
16. *The Grenfell Record and Lachlan District Advertiser*, 16 May 1938, 4. https://trove.nla.gov.au/newspaper/article/115445756
17. *Australian Women's Weekly*, 29 January 1938, 35. https://trove.nla.gov.au/newspaper/article/45657401
18. *Sydney Morning Herald*, 15 February 1938, 12. https://trove.nla.gov.au/newspaper/article/17431019
19. *The Daily Telegraph*, 5 November 1938, 10. https://trove.nla.gov.au/newspaper/article/ 247438149
20. *Sydney Morning Herald*, 22 January 1938, 7. http://trove.nla.gov.au/newspaper/article/ 17434208
21. *Australian Women's Weekly*, 6 November 1937, 12. http://trove.nla.gov.au/newspaper/article/52246211

22. *Sydney Morning Herald*, 5 November 1938, 19. https://trove.nla.gov.au/newspaper/article/17534564
23. *Northern Star*, 10 November 1938, 7. https://trove.nla.gov.au/newspaper/article/94715047
24. *Sydney Morning Herald*, 28 December 1938, 8. https://trove.nla.gov.au/newspaper/article/17544931
25. *The Evening News* (Rockhampton), 11 February 1939, 6. https://trove.nla.gov.au/newspaper/article/198300436
26. Mary Quirk was elected in January 1939.
27. No woman was sitting in any Legislative Council in any state in 1939.
28. *Daily News*, 13 April 1939, 2. https://trove.nla.gov.au/newspaper/article/236278623
29. *Sydney Morning Herald*, 4 July 1939, 4. https://trove.nla.gov.au/newspaper/article/17595284
30. *The Daily Telegraph*, 4 September 1939, 4. https://trove.nla.gov.au/newspaper/article/ 247811173
31. *Sydney Morning Herald*, 28 December 1939, 6. http://trove.nla.gov.au/newspaper/article/17635936
32. *Sydney Morning Herald*, 28 December 1939, 8. https://trove.nla.gov.au/newspaper/article/17635936
33. *The Sun*, 8 December 1939, 11. https://trove.nla.gov.au/newspaper/article/231499269
34. *Daily Advertiser* (Wagga Wagga), 24 October 1940, 3. http://trove.nla.gov.au/newspaper/article/144319630
35. *Newcastle Morning Herald & Miners Advocate*, 6 November 1940, 6. http://trove.nla.gov.au/newspaper/article/132802752
36. David Dufty, *Radio Girl*. Sydney; Allen & Unwin. 2020, 190.
37. *The Daily Telegraph*, 13 October 1940, 7. https://trove.nla.gov.au/newspaper/article/247612874
38. *Sydney Morning Herald*, 23 October 1940, 13. https://trove.nla.gov.au/newspaper/article/17698280
39. *The Sun*, 24 May 1937, 8. https://trove.nla.gov.au/newspaper/article/17707320
40. *The Daily Telegraph*, 19 January 1941, 2. https://trove.nla.gov.au/newspaper/article/247512453
41. *The Sun*, 8 November 1940, 9. https://trove.nla.gov.au/newspaper/article/231154267
42. 'Harbour Ferries by Night', *Sydney Morning Herald*, 27 June 1936, 13. https://trove.nla.gov.au/newspaper/article/17246603; 'Jacaranda Blossoms', *Sydney Morning Herald*, 26 December 1937, 7. https://trove.nla.gov.au/newspaper/article/17307158
43. Hold your girl' (1935), NAA 27147, 'The Madonna of Mean Street' (1936), NAA 32342, 'The Call of the Magpie' (1936), co-authored with Crawford, NAA 28115, 'The Little Brown House' (1940), musical co-written with Richard Hans Forst, NAA 34172, 'Australia Marches On' (1938), literary work, NAA 32342, 'The Other Woman' (undated), NLA MS 9062, Return to Carthage' (1943), NLA MS 9062.
44. *The Sun*, 20 February 1940, 7. https://trove.nla.gov.au/newspaper/article/231239619
45. M Preston Stanley, *Pulse of Victory*, Sydney: Frank Johnson, 1942.

46. Winston Churchill's 'Their Finest Hour Speech'. https://winstonchurchill.org/resources/speeches/1940-the-finest-hour/their-finest-hour/
47. M Preston Stanley, *Pulse of Victory*. Sydney: Frank Johnson, 1942.
48. *Sydney Morning Herald*, 21 June 1939, 7. https://trove.nla.gov.au/newspaper/article/17605769
49. *The Mail*, 11 April 1914, 8. https://trove.nla.gov.au/newspaper/article/59647857
50. *Sydney Morning Herald*, 2 August 1939, 11. https://trove.nla.gov.au/newspaper/article/ 17601162
51. Crawford Vaughan, *Golden Wattle Time*, Sydney, Frank Johnson, 1942, https://nla.gov.au/nla.obj-365180902/view?partId=nla.obj-365181311 ; In 1946 Dorothy Vaughan, Crawford's sister presented a copy to Gordon's historic home, Dingley Dell. *News*, 13 August 1946, 2. https://trove.nla.gov.au/newspaper/article/130855245
52. *Daily Advertiser*, 29 May 1944, 3. https://trove.nla.gov.au/newspaper/article/144231004
53. *The Daily Telegraph*, 9 May 1940, 10. https://trove.nla.gov.au/newspaper/article/247769600
54. *Sydney Morning Herald*, 14 February 1944, 7. https://trove.nla.gov.au/newspaper/article/17885402
55. *The Daily Telegraph*, 9 November 1943, 7. https://trove.nla.gov.au/newspaper/article/ 247807866
56. http://www.liberals.net/theforgottenpeople.htm
57. *Queensland Times*, 14 October 1944, 1. https://trove.nla.gov.au/newspaper/article/115490579
58. *The Australasian*, 28 October 1944, 17. https://trove.nla.gov.au/newspaper/page/12685844
59. *The Daily Telegraph*, 15 December 1944, 5. https://trove.nla.gov.au/newspaper/article/248066711

Chapter 12

1. *Daily Advertiser*, 4 May 1948, 4. https://trove.nla.gov.au/newspaper/article/144744229
2. https://www.orwellfoundation.com/the-orwell-foundation/orwell/essays-and-other-works/you-and-the-atom-bomb/
3. *Sydney Morning Herald*, 11 September 1947, 2. http://trove.nla.gov.au/newspaper/article/27896711
4. *Sydney Morning Herald*, 11 September 1947, 2. http://trove.nla.gov.au/newspaper/article/27896711
5. Millicent Preston Stanley Papers, NLA, MS 9062. *Sydney Morning Herald*, 23 September 1947, 7. http://trove.nla.gov.au/newspaper/article/18045618
6. *The Sun*, 25 September 1947, 10. http://trove.nla.gov.au/newspaper/article/228967096
7. The AWMAS was initially called the United Women Citizen's Movement Against Socialisation.
8. *Sydney Morning Herald*, 11 September 1947, 2. https://trove.nla.gov.au/newspaper/article/27896711

9. Warwick Eather, 'The Liberal Party of Australia and the Australian Women's Movement Against Socialisation 1947-54', *Australian Journal of Politics and History* 2002, 201.
10. *Townsville Daily Bulletin*, 25 October 1947, 1. https://trove.nla.gov.au/newspaper/article/62907497
11. *Sydney Morning Herald*, 23 October 1947, 1. http://trove.nla.gov.au/newspaper/article/18038162
12. *Advocate* (Burnie), 23 October 1947, 5. https://trove.nla.gov.au/newspaper/article/69027601
13. *The Sun*, 26 October 1947, 35. http://trove.nla.gov.au/newspaper/article/228976712
14. *Sydney Morning Herald*, 27 October 1947, 2. http://trove.nla.gov.au/newspaper/article/18038008
15. *The Sun*, 28 July 1949, 18. http://trove.nla.gov.au/newspaper/article/231051972
16. *The Argus*, 13 November 1947, 8. http://trove.nla.gov.au/newspaper/article/22519689
17. *The Sun*, 28 July 1949, 18. http://trove.nla.gov.au/newspaper/article/231051972
18. *Sydney Morning Herald*, 1 November 1947, 2. https://trove.nla.gov.au/newspaper/article/18048302
19. *Daily Advertiser*, 7 November 1947, 3. https://trove.nla.gov.au/newspaper/article/144834512
20. *The Advertiser*, 19 December 1947, 2. http://trove.nla.gov.au/newspaper/article/43748836
21. *Recorder*, 12 January 1948, 3. http://trove.nla.gov.au/newspaper/article/96233582
22. Millicent was not successful in having any of Crawford's other works published, or in securing a production of the dramatic adaptation of the novel, 'On the Sheep's Back', which was annotated as 'Depicting the struggle in 1807/8 between Captain John Macarthur and Capt William Bligh'. Nor was she able to secure funding for the Australian film company Crawford had hoped to establish, although this was not for want of effort on her part.
23. Mrs Howie claimed Millicent's cheque for £200 for repayment of her loan of £255 was dishonoured by the bank. *Sydney Morning Herald*, 9 September 1927, 8. https://trove.nla.gov.au/newspaper/page/1206377
24. *Daily Advertiser*, 3 March 1948, 3. http://trove.nla.gov.au/newspaper/article/144748459
25. *West Australian*, 22 May 1948, 5. http://trove.nla.gov.au/newspaper/article/46911353
26. http://monologues.co.uk/musichall/Songs-N/No-No-A-Thousand-Times-No.htm
27. *The Sun*, 21 May 1948, 2. http://trove.nla.gov.au/newspaper/article/228805741
28. *West Australian*, 22 May 1948, 5. http://trove.nla.gov.au/newspaper/article/46911353
29. *The Land*, 4 June 1948, 22-3. http://trove.nla.gov.au/newspaper/article/105811861
30. *The Land*, 4 June 1948, 23. http://trove.nla.gov.au/newspaper/article/105811861/11393417
31. ³*Lithgow Mercury*, 29 July 1948, 6. http://trove.nla.gov.au/newspaper/article/219737390
32. *Lithgow Mercury*, 29 July 1948, 4. http://trove.nla.gov.au/newspaper/article/219737390
33. *The Sun*, 4 March 1949, 11. http://trove.nla.gov.au/newspaper/article/231070314
34. *Sydney Morning Herald*, 10 August 1949, 4. http://trove.nla.gov.au/newspaper/article/18124902

35. *Blue Mountains Advertiser*, 21 October 1949, 10. http://trove.nla.gov.au/newspaper/article/189918419
36. *Tribune*, 19 January 1949, 7. https://trove.nla.gov.au/newspaper/article/209386712
37. *Daily Examiner*, 21 July 1949, 1. http://trove.nla.gov.au/newspaper/article/195730982
38. *Courier Mail*, 21 July 1949, 1. http://trove.nla.gov.au/newspaper/article/49691360
39. *Sydney Morning Herald*, 21 July 1949, 4. http://trove.nla.gov.au/newspaper/article/27583305
40. *Sydney Morning Herald*, 26 July 1949, 2. http://trove.nla.gov.au/newspaper/article/18123449
41. *Tribune*, 23 July 1949, 6. http://trove.nla.gov.au/newspaper/article/209390100
42. *The Sun*, 24 July 1949, 9. https://trove.nla.gov.au/newspaper/article/231055999
43. *The Sun*, 3 November 1949, 8. http://trove.nla.gov.au/newspaper/article/229233565
44. *Courier Mail*, 5 November 1949, 4. http://trove.nla.gov.au/newspaper/article/49710849
45. *Sydney Morning Herald*, 24 October 1938, 4. https://trove.nla.gov.au/newspaper/article/17530594
46. 'Churchill and Women', Churchill Archive. http://www.churchillarchive.com/collection-highlights/churchill-and-women.
47. *The West Australian*, 19 November 1949, 11. http://trove.nla.gov.au/newspaper/article/47684078
48. *Australian Worker*, 9 November 1949, 3. http://trove.nla.gov.au/newspaper/article/146170625
49. *The Sun*, 5 December 1949, 4. https://trove.nla.gov.au/newspaper/article/230740879
50. *Cumberland Argus & Fruitgrowers Advocate*, 30 November 1949, 6. http://trove.nla.gov.au/newspaper/article/111527911
51. *The Sun*, 7 December 1949, 33. http://trove.nla.gov.au/newspaper/article/230738087
52. *The Sun*, 7 December 1949, 7. http://trove.nla.gov.au/newspaper/article/230738001
53. *The Sun*, 7 December 1949, 33. http://trove.nla.gov.au/newspaper/article/230738087
54. *Sydney Morning Herald*, 13 December 1949, 2. http://trove.nla.gov.au/newspaper/article/18138316
55. *Construction*, 21 December 1949, 1. https://trove.nla.gov.au/newspaper/article/222884001
56. *The Farmer and Settler*, 30 December 1949, 1. https://trove.nla.gov.au/newspaper/article/117396171
57. AWMAS, *Second Annual Report*, 15 March 1950, IPA (NSW) records, The Sydney Institute.
58. *The Land*, 24 March 1950, 34. https://trove.nla.gov.au/newspaper/article/105720950
59. Mrs O'Malley Wood was active in many organisations and held a number of executive positions including Patron, Pioneer Battalions, President Pioneer Ladies of Australia, President Feminist Club, Treasurer Girl Guides.
60. *The Sun*, 13 December 1950, 29. https://trove.nla.gov.au/newspaper/article/230875770
61. *Daily Mercury*, 31 December 1949, 7. https://trove.nla.gov.au/newspaper/article/171478622

Chapter 13

1. Lyndall Ryan, 'Remembering the Australian Women's Weekly in the 1950s', in Susan Sheridan with Barbara Baird, Kate Borrett and Lyndall Ryan, *Who Was That Woman? The Australian Women's Weekly in the Postwar Years*. Sydney: UNSW Press, 2001, 56.
2. Mary Edwards was also known as Mary Edwell-Burke, Mary Edwell Burke, Maisie Edwards and Mary E Burke.
3. http://www.artgallery.nsw.gov.au/prizes/archibald/
4. In 1943, along with Joseph Wolinski Edwards challenged the decision to award the Archibald Prize to William Dobell for his portrait of Joshua Smith. Their challenge resulted in a court case, with the court upholding the judges' decision.
5. *Sydney Morning Herald* 9 October 1945, 3. https://trove.nla.gov.au/newspaper/article/17955770
6. *Sydney Morning Herald*, 11 December 1945, 6. https://trove.nla.gov.au/newspaper/article/17962546
7. *News*, 12 October 1945, 3. https://trove.nla.gov.au/newspaper/article/128320557
8. *Morning Bulletin*, 8 December 1945, 7. https://trove.nla.gov.au/newspaper/article/56440044
9. When the Feminist Club closed in the 1970s the painting was relocated to the Mitchell Library where it was stored in the archives until 2019 when it was restored and hung in the new Mitchell Galleries. Mary Edwards added the pair of blue spectacles to the portrait in 1952 to 'match those now worn' by Millicent. *Sydney Morning Herald*, 6 August 1952, 7. https://trove.nla.gov.au/newspaper/article/18276369
10. *The Advertiser*, 2 January 1952, 11. https://trove.nla.gov.au/newspaper/article/47385065
11. *Sydney Morning Herald*, 20 December 1951, 11. https://trove.nla.gov.au/newspaper/article/18245148
12. Jack Lang, 'Politics from the Inside', *Truth*, 24 October 1954, 40. https://trove.nla.gov.au/newspaper/article/168414330
13. *Forbes Advocate*, 9 August 1949, 2. https://trove.nla.gov.au/newspaper/article/218702084
14. Sir John Latham's Extra-Judicial Advising' (2011) 35 *Melbourne University Law Review* 6 http://www.austlii.edu.au/au/journals/MelbULawRw/2011/22.html
15. George Williams, 'The Communist Party Dissolution Bill and its Aftermath', *Australian Society for the Study of Labour History*, http://labourhistorycanberra.org/2015/05/the-communist-party-dissolution-bill-and-its-aftermath/ accessed 9 January 2018.
16. *The Sun*, 1 August 1950, 18. https://trove.nla.gov.au/newspaper/article/230933213
17. *Truth*, 23 July 1950, 42. https://trove.nla.gov.au/newspaper/article/167985026
18. *Illawarra Daily Mercury*, 15 February 1951, 6. https://trove.nla.gov.au/newspaper/article/133993022
19. *Courier Mail* (Brisbane), 24 February 1951, 5. https://trove.nla.gov.au/newspaper/article/50113103

20. *The Canberra Times*, 15 February 1951, 5. https://trove.nla.gov.au/newspaper/article/2821021
21. *Sydney Morning Herald*, 15 February 1951, 13. https://trove.nla.gov.au/newspaper/article/18199329
22. *Gosford Times and Wyong District Advocate*, 17 April 1951, 5. https://trove.nla.gov.au/newspaper/article/167220980
23. Millicent Preston Stanley Papers, NLA, MS 9062.
24. *Sydney Morning Herald*, 27 May 1953, 7. https://trove.nla.gov.au/newspaper/article/18372307
25. *Sydney Morning Herald*, 6 May 1953, 9. https://trove.nla.gov.au/newspaper/article/18365671
26. *Sydney Morning Herald*, 2 December 1953, 5. http://trove.nla.gov.au/newspaper/article/18399208
27. *The Sun*, 22 June 1953, 10. https://trove.nla.gov.au/newspaper/article/230725529
28. *The Sun*, 22 June 1953, 10. https://trove.nla.gov.au/newspaper/article/230725529
29. *The Sun*, 22 June 1953, 10. https://trove.nla.gov.au/newspaper/article/230725529
   The Sun 28 June 1953, 14. https://trove.nla.gov.au/newspaper/article/230727307
30. *Barrier Miner*, 29 July 1953, 6. https://trove.nla.gov.au/newspaper/article/49272423
31. *Sydney Morning Herald*, 24 September 1953, 4. https://trove.nla.gov.au/newspaper/article/18379379
32. *Daily Advertiser*, 6 October 1953, 1. https://trove.nla.gov.au/newspaper/article/145660648
33. *Newcastle Sun*, 28 June 1954, 6. https://trove.nla.gov.au/newspaper/article/161615779
34. *Sydney Morning Herald*, 11 August 1954, 4. https://trove.nla.gov.au/newspaper/article/18431576
35. *Sydney Morning Herald*, 26 November 1954, 2. https://trove.nla.gov.au/newspaper/article/18443074
36. *Daily Telegraph*, 14 July 1954, 11. https://trove.nla.gov.au/newspaper/article/248935927
37. *The Sun*, 2 September 1954, 29. https://trove.nla.gov.au/newspaper/article/229900636
38. *Newcastle Sun*, 26 August 1954, 25. https://trove.nla.gov.au/newspaper/article/163299273
39. *Sydney Morning Herald*, 22 September 1953, 4. http://trove.nla.gov.au/newspaper/article/18389076
40. *The Sun*, 27 September 1953, 47. https://trove.nla.gov.au/newspaper/article/230752442
41. *Australian Women's Weekly*, 7 October 1953, 18. http://trove.nla.gov.au/newspaper/article/41079921
42. *Sydney Morning Herald*, 9 March 1954, 15. https://trove.nla.gov.au/newspaper/article/18413624
43. *The Canberra Times*, 5 March 1955, 2. http://trove.nla.gov.au/newspaper/article/91194270
44. *The Canberra Times*, 11 October 1955, 1. https://trove.nla.gov.au/newspaper/article/91210242

45. *Australian Women's Weekly*, 26 October 1955, 20. https://trove.nla.gov.au/newspaper/article/41856487
46. *The Argus*, 12 October 1955, 1. https://trove.nla.gov.au/newspaper/article/71700852

Chapter 14

1. *The Sun*, 13 December 1954, 22. https://trove.nla.gov.au/newspaper/article/232002276
2. *The Sun*, 13 December 1954, 22. https://trove.nla.gov.au/newspaper/article/232002276
3. Darling Point, St Mark's Burial Register, 6 September 1950-24 December 1960, 24 June 1955 Sydney Diocesan Archives.
4. *Australian Dictionary of Evangelical Biography* http://webjournals.ac.edu.au/ojs/index.php/ADEB/article/view/1183/1180
5. Northern Suburbs Memorial Gardens East Terrace, Area 2 Section Wall 21.
6. *The Argus*, 24 June 1955, 10. http://trove.nla.gov.au/newspaper/article/71889904
7. *Canberra Times*, 24 June 1955, 2. https://trove.nla.gov.au/newspaper/article/91203879
8. *Construction*, 27 December 1951, 3. http://trove.nla.gov.au/newspaper/article/222888009 This article also repeated the erroneous statements about Millicent being the first woman parliamentarian in Australia and that her portrait would be hung in the Parliament building in Canberra.
9. Email correspondence and personal conversations with Elizabeth Yager, Tony Preston Stanley, Judi Preston Stanley, Margaret Cutler.
10. Elizabeth Faye Smith, 'Millicent Preston Stanley: A Feminist in Politics', BA Hons Thesis, University of Sydney, 1977.
11. Heather Radi, 'Preston Stanley, Millicent Fanny (1883–1955)', Australian Dictionary of Biography, National Centre of Biography, Australian National University, http://adb.anu.edu.au/biography/preston-stanley-millicent-fanny-8107/text14153 , accessed online 21 June 2018.
12. https://web.archive.org/web/20141031055642/http://womenshistory.net.au/2009/ 02/03/millicent-preston-stanley-mla-nsw-1925-27/ Margaret Fitzherbert, *Liberal Women: Federation to 1949*, Sydney: Federation Press, 2004, 155.
13. Cathy Jenkins, *No Ordinary Lives: Pioneering Women in Australian Politics*, Melbourne: Australian Scholarly Publishing, 2008, 47.
14. Gail Griffiths, 'The Feminist Club of NSW, 1914-1970: A History of Feminist Politics in Decline', *Hecate*, 14, 1, 1988, 56-67.
15. Michael Hogan, 'Millicent Preston Stanley: Organising for Women's Representation', in Ken Turner & Michael Hogan, eds, *The Worldly Art of Politics*, Sydney: Federation Press, 2006, 91.
16. 'Millicent Preston Stanley MLA NSW 1925-1927', https://womenshistory.net.au/2009/02/03/millicent-preston-stanley-mla-nsw-1925-27/
17. The Australian Women's Register, https://www.womenaustralia.info/biogs/AWE1021b.htm
18. Barry, Elaine 'Women, Law and Literature: Representations of Women and the Law in American and Australian Fiction' in Turner, J. Neville and Williams, Pamela. eds. *The Happy Couple: Law and Literature*, Sydney: The Federation Press, 1994, 112.

19. Gail Griffiths, 'The Feminist Club of NSW, 1914-1970: A History of Feminist Politics in Decline', *Hecate*, 14, 1, 1988, 60.
20. Elizabeth Faye Smith, 'Millicent Preston Stanley: A Feminist in Politics' BA Hons Thesis, University of Sydney, 1977, 51.
21. Warwick Eather, '"Every woman! This is your business": the Australian Women's Movement Against Socialisation', *Journal of Interdisciplinary Gender Studies*, Vol 3 Issue, 1997, 57-75.
22. Warwick Eather and Drew Cottle, 'Capital's foot soldiers: the war against the Australian Labor Party during the 1940s', *Journal of the Royal Australian Historical Society*, 99, 2013, 18-35.
23. Anthony Russell Smith, 'Gender in the Fifty-First New South Wales Parliament', PhD Thesis, University of Sydney, 2002, 3.
24. Deborah Brennan, 'Women in the Bear Pit', Refereed Paper presented at the Australasian Political Studies Association Conference, University of Newcastle, 25-29 September, 2006.
25. Marian Sawer and Marian Simms, *A Woman's Place: Women and Politics in Australia*, Sydney: Allen & Unwin, 1993, 99.
26. Tony Smith, 'The sacrosanct seats of the lords of creation': Preston-Stanley on the prospects for women MPs', *Australian Review of Public Affairs*, 2005, http://www.australianreview.net./digest/2005/08.smith2.html
27. NSWPD, 26 August 1925, 369.
28. Dixson Galleries, State Library of New South Wales, Call No DG 396. This portrait is reproduced in Richard Neville, *Faces of Australia: Image, Reality and the Portrait*. Sydney; State Library of NSW, 1992.
29. Preston Stanley Room, NSW Parliament, https://parliamentarycatering.com.au/venue/preston-stanley-room/
30. The Hon Shelley Hancock MP & The Hon John Ajaka MLC, 'Foreword', *A Fit Place for Women: NSW Parliament*. Sydney; Parliament of NSW, 2017, 5.
31. 'Bearpit sexist, says new MP Goward', *The Sydney Morning Herald*, 10 May 2007. https://www.smh.com.au/national/bearpit-sexist-says-new-mp-goward-20070510-gdq3qw.html
32. Jenny Aitchison MP, 'Amazon Women Warriors – Beyond the myth of women as politicians, advocates and decision makers' in *Visions of Sydney + In the Aftermath of the The First World War: The Women's Legal Status Act 1918 (NSW)*, Sydney; ISAA. 2018, 62.
33. Lisa Martin, 'Julie Bishop laments "gender deafness" during her time in politics', *The Guardian*, 13 August 2019. https://www.theguardian.com/australia-news/2019/aug/13/julie-bishop-laments-gender-deafness-during-her-time-in-politics
34. Senator The Hon Penny Wong, 'Speech to the Adelaide International Women's Day Breakfast', 6 March 2020. https://parlinfo.aph.gov.au/parlInfo/search/display/display.w3p;query=Id%3A%22media%2Fpressrel%2F7223732%22;src1=sm1
35. Transcript of Julia Gillard's Speech. *The Sydney Morning Herald*, 10 October 2012. https://www.smh.com.au/politics/federal/transcript-of-julia-gillards-speech-20121010-27c36.html
36. Millicent Preston Stanley Papers, NLA, MS 9062.

Acknowledgements

Battle-axe in the Bear Pit: Millicent Preston Stanley MP is the end point of a decade-long research and writing process, which commenced with my encounter with Millicent's political play, *Whose Child*. This play aroused my interest in her personal and public life and her political ambitions and began my quest to uncover the life story of the first woman to grace the benches of the New South Wales Bear Pit. It has been a challenging task partly because Millicent had gone to considerable lengths to avoid scrutiny of her family life which might have disqualified her from her social and political ambitions and partly because she kept few personal records of her many public activities or no significant correspondence about any of her endeavours. Fortunately Trove has provided invaluable documentation of her public activities and the newspapers of the time often reproduced her speeches in full – including interjections from her audiences.

Many people have contributed to my journey to uncover and narrate Millicent's story. I am grateful to the staff at the National Library of Australia, the National Archives of Australia, the NSW State Archives, the NSW Parliamentary Library and the State Library of New South Wales, particularly the former State Librarian Dr John Vallance AM and Susan Hunt, Director, State Library of NSW Foundation, who supported the restoration and rehanging of the 1950 Mary Edwards Archibald portrait of Millicent that had been lying unseen in the bowels of the library for some decades. It now hangs in the Exhibition Galleries, Dixson Galleries, State Library of New South Wales.

The 2017 NSW Parliament exhibition, *A Fit Place for Women*, also provided a useful resource and an opportunity to share some of my research into Millicent's political endeavours. I am grateful for the encouragement of The Hon Shelley Hancock OAM and the Hon John Ajaka who offered opportunities for advancing my work and who ensured a room in Parliament House - the former Members' Bar – was renovated and re-named the Preston Stanley Room after the first woman parliamentarian in New South Wales - a committed temperance advocate.

I have been particularly fortunate to have had the support and encouragement of many colleagues who have engaged in exploratory discussions with me about ways of telling Millicent's story and who have read and commented on multiple drafts. These include the late Professor Lyndall Ryan AM FAHA, Professor Penny Russell FAHA, Professor Emerita Eileen Baldry AO, Associate Professor Caroline Webb, Professor Shirley Randell AO, Associate Professor Josephine May, Associate Professor Nancy Cushing, Dr Jill Bough, Dr Jennifer Debenham, Dr Patricia Holt, Dr Margaret Kelly, Associate Professor Zora Simic, Emeritus Professor Murray Goot, Associate Professor Richard White, Dr Michael Kilminster.

I have also benefitted from the opportunities to present papers at seminars and conferences of several professional organisations and to gain productive feedback from a wider audience. These organisations include the Australian Women's History Network, the Sydney Feminist History Network, Australian Graduate Women, The Australian Historical Association, Independent Scholars Association of Australia; Royal Historical Association, Women's Electoral Lobby and the National Council of Women NSW.

Although Millicent did not have any children, I have been fortunate to make contact with some of her great nieces and a great nephew, who willingly shared their childhood memories of Millicent, which helped to put flesh on the bones. Especial thanks to Elizabeth Yager, Tony Preston Stanley, Judi Preston Stanley, Diana Pierce and Margaret Cutler.

Thank you Anthony Cappello, founder and publisher of Connor Court and Michael Gilchrist for your meticulous work on the manuscript. Thank you also Ian Yager for your careful proof reading and Dr Patricia Holt for your valuable advice about indexing.

Finally, I appreciate the support of many friends who encouraged me to keep going even when I seemed to be caught in a *cul de sac*. Thank you Professor Emeritus Trevor Parmenter AM, Marie Parmenter, Associate Professor Rosemary Huisman, Professor Tony Blackshield AO, Dr Saba Vasefi, Angela Bowne SC, Virginia Milson, Pauline Plumb, Dr Desmond McDonnell, Susan Wilson, Thalia Stevens, Sheelagh Scott and Heather Roland. Thank you also to my sons, Selwyn, Owen and Evan and my granddaughters Phoebe and Sage for your encouragement.

INDEX

abdication, King Edward VIII, 147
Abyssinian crisis, 145
Address in Reply, 53, 54, 55, 58
Adelaide News, 133
Aitchison, Jenny, 193
Ajaka, The Hon John, 223
alcoholism, 4, 5, 16
Alliance for the Suppression of Intemperance, 16, 17
All for Australia League, 100
anonymous, 14-15, 46, 47-8, 69-70
Anti-Conscription League, 19
Aorangi MV, 149
Appleton, Benita, 111
Archibald, J F, 176
Ardill, Katie Louisa, 163
Arkins, James, 59, 65, 71, 78
Argus, The, 132, 190
Armistice 1918, The, 28
Ashton, Queenie, 179
Astor, Lady Nancy, 1, 49
Atkinson, Meredith, 16
Australian Council of Trade Unions, 183
Australian Party, 100
Australian Women's Guild of Empire, 115
Australian Women's Movement Against Socialisation, 162-174
Australian Women's Weekly, The, 127-8, 132, 150
Australian Worker, The, 43, 45, 46, 100, 171
Australasian, The, 127

Autumn Crocus, 112
Baddeley, John, 90
Baker-Young, Mrs, 29
Balmain electorate, 43
bank nationalisation, 162
Barton, Edmund, 6
battle-axe, *xi*, *xii*, 32, 193
Bavin, Thomas, 36, 70-71, 80, 89, 95, 96
bear garden, 26, 27
Bear Pit, *vii*, *viii*, *xi*, *xii*, 2, 33, 49, 51, 57, 61, 160, 182, 191, 193, 222
Beeby, George, 22
Bennett, Emily, 99, 115
Bennett White, Meta, 111
Bishop, Julie, 193
Black Monday Riots 1916, 17
Blackstone, William, 77
Bluett, G C, 17
Bondi, 88, 93, 133
Booth, Dr Mary, 21, 28, 30, 198
Boyce, Archbishop Francis, 17
Boyce, Attorney General Francis, 17, 94, 96, 99, 117, 129
British American Co-operation Movement, 146-150
British Australian Cotton Growing Association, 133
British Empire, 146, 155, 156
British House of Commons, 1, 54
Brookes, Lady Mabel, 164
Bruce, Prime Minister Stanley Melbourne, 36
Bruntnell, Albert, 54

Bruxner, Michael, 157
Bryan, Owen Ruth, 157
Bulbeck, Rev A L, 166
Bulletin, The, 63
Business Women's Prohibition League, 34
Butler, Maude, 18
Butt, Dame Clara, 29, 43
Buttenshaw, Ernest, 92
Byles, Marie, 99, 100

camels, 161, 167, 172, 179
Canberra Times, 124, 190
Cann, George, 59, 65, 67, 75-76, 81-86, 109
Catholic Freeman's Journal, 127
Catholic Press, The, 44-45
Cavell, Edith, 18
Chaffey, Frank, 71, 80,
Chauvel, Lieutenant General Sir Harry, 112
Chifley, Ben, 161-162, 164, 169, 173, 178
child custody, 36, 39, 95, 114, 115, 185, 207
Chocolate Soldier, The, 112
Christy, Janice, 172-173
Churchill, Winston, 156, 171, 216
Coates, Joseph, 96
Cocks, Joyce, 99
Cold War, *xii*, 159, 160, 161, 162, 168, 169
Commonwealth Franchise Act 1901, 9
communism, 145, 159, 167, 168, 169, 170, 178, 179, 181, 191

Communist Party, 148, 163, 169, 177-178, 204, 219
Communist Party Dissolution Act, 178
Connell, Hugh, 62
Constance, Rubina, 166
Constitution Amendment Act (Legislative Council Elections) 1933, 70-71,120
Cook, Prime Minister Joseph, 13
Cornstalk Publishing, 74, 206
Coronation Luncheon, 181
Cowan, Edith, 41, 49
Crimes Bill, 36
Criterion Theatre, 110
Crowdy OBE, Isabel, 112
Cunningham, John, 27
Currie, Gordon, 172
Curtin, John, 146, 158, 161

Daily Telegraph, The, 45, 133, 135, 143, 154
Daily Telegraph Women's Supplement, 73
Dale, Margaret, 36
D'Alpuget, Lou, 186
D'Arcy, Dame Constance, 163
David Jones (department store), 111, 129
Davies, William, 96
De Chair, Governor Dudley, 48, 50, 52, 95
De Chair, Lady Enid, 52
De Groot, Francis, 103
Democratic Party, 158
Depression, *xii*, 4, 100, 105, 136, 137, 172
disarmament, 142, 146

District Court Act, 98
Dobell, William, 176
Domain Terrace, 50
Domino theory, 178
Donald, Will, 46
Dooley, Mrs Kate, 52
Double-barrelled surname, 6-7
double dissolution election, 13, 178
Douglas, William, 182
Downing, Robert, 183
Drummond, David, 71
Dubbo Liberal and Macquarie Advocate, 130
Dunn, William, 91
Dvořák, Anton, 106
Dwyer, Kate, 23, 43, 49, 55

Eastern Suburbs, 30, 31, 42, 46, 47, 49, 53, 60, 133
Edith Cavell Memorial Fund, 18
Edmonds, Mr Justice, 60
Edwards, Mary, 175-177, 191, 219
Eisenhower, President Dwight, 178
Eisenhower, Mamie, 181
election campaign, *xii*, 13, 28, 44, 68, 92, 133, 137, 138, 139, 174
Ellis v Ellis, 37 -38
Ellis, Patricia, 37, 132
eugenics, 15-16, 197, 201
Evans, Ada, 23
Evatt, Dr Herbert Vere, 22, 29, 39, 54, 77, 172, 179
Evening News, The, 124

Fadden, Arthur, 158

family endowment bill, 90
'Fanella', 33
Federation of Women's Clubs, 149
Feminist Club, *xiii*, 2, 16, 29, 30, 34, 36, 37, 39, 74, 96, 97, 99, 105, 114, 115, 128, 134, 135, 141, 142, 169, 174, 177, 181, 183, 186, 189, 191, 201, 218, 219, 221, 222
Femme Covert, 133
Ferguson, Governor General Sir Ronald Munro, 13
Financial Agreement Reinforcement Act (Cth) 1932, 103
Fisher, Andrew, 14, 19
Fit Place for Women, 192-193
Fitton, Doris, 163
Fitzpatrick, John, 62, 67, 71
Flowers, Mrs Annie, 52
Forde, Frank, 157
forty-four hours bill, 66
Foster, William, 31, 43
Fowler, Lilian, 23
franchise, 9, 13, 42, 71, 157, 158
Freeman's Journal, The, 45
Francis, Susan, 93
Fuller, George, 48, 136

Gag, 81, 109
Galton, Francis, 15
Game, Governor Philip, 103, 112
Game, Lady, 98, 112
Gardiner, Evelyn, 163, 168
Geach, Portia, 163
Gilmore, Mary, 176
Gilpin, David, Mrs, 141

Gladesville Hospital, 189
Glencross, Eleanor, 129, 163
Golden Wattle Time, 156
Goldstein, Hyman, 31, 42
Goodwin, Rector Clive Andrew, 190
Gorden, Florence, 32
Goward, Pru, 193
Gowrie, Lord Alexander, 158
Green, Hetty, 14
Groom, Mrs, 164
guardianship of infants, 65, 67, 76, 84, 88, 92, 95, 101, 104, 112, 115, 116, 118, 120, 125, 126, 127, 128, 132, 136, 139, 143, 153, 157, 186

Hall, Attorney General David, 23
Hammond, Rev Robert, 44
Hancock, The Hon Shelley, x, 222, 223
Harvey, Justice, 37-38, 77-78, 96-97, 119, 121
Heffron, Robert, 119, 121, 186
Hemsley, Alfred, 124
Henley, Thomas, 50, 91
Henry, Alfred, 119, 124
Herron, Justice, 185
Hibberd, Elbert, 74
Hill, Theo, 62, 68, 71, 90
Holden, Thomas, 124
Hollywood Chamber of Commerce, 149
Holman, May, 1
Holman, William, 6
home front, 18, 152, 153, 157
Hordern Bros (department store), 129

Horses Rights for Women, 35, 136
Hoskins, Tom, 71, 85
Housewives Association, 129, 163, 169, 170
Howie, Archibald, 147
Hughes, Prime Minister Billy, 6, 10, 19, 20, 25, 27, 44, 46, 49, 74, 136, 156-157, 166, 176-177, 179
Hughes, Mary, 49
Hurstville Choral Society, 155
Husbands on Parade, 155

Institute of World Affairs, 149
interjections, 60, 61, 63, 69, 82, 108, 139
Isaacs, Governor General Isaac, 103

Jaques, Harold, 31, 42, 53, 66, 93, 97
Jones, Henry Arthur, 110
Justices Act, 97-98

Kay, Alick, 60, 75
Keegan, Thomas, 71
Keller, P J, 105
Kelly, Christopher, 84
Kilmuir, Viscount, 187
Kristallnacht, 149

Labor Daily, 64
Labor Party, 2, 10, 12, 51, 73, 75, 82, 104, 105, 128, 137, 168, 173, 222
Lamaro, Joseph, 82, 94, 100, 104, 105, 119, 121, 128, 137
Lang, Hilda, 52
Lang, Jack, 49, 51, 53, 55, 58, 65-70, 72-75, 86, 88, 92, 97-99, 100, 103-

104, 119-120, 122, 136, 137, 138, 177, 219
Latham, Sir John, 101, 134, 178, 219
Laverty, Elizabeth, 134
Law, Archibald, Dr, 131
Law, Hartland & Herbert, 11
League of Nations, 36, 143, 145, 146, 148
Lee, Charles, 10, 50
Lee, John, 66, 78, 96, 98-99
Legislative Assembly, *xi*, 1, 23, 41, 47, 50, 51, 52, 53, 85, 92, 96, 98, 117, 120, 121, 125, 142, 151, 190, 192, 204, 209
Legislative Council, 23, 31, 43, 50, 52, 58, 64, 96-98, 103, 120-121, 123-126, 134, 142
letters to the editor, *xii*, 10,
Ley, Thomas, 35, 39, 89
Liberal Association, 14
Liberal Party of Australia, 159, 163, 171, 172, 217
Liberal Party Women's Auxiliary, 163
Liberal Reform Association, 2, 12, 13
Liddell, Mary 1, 2, 3, 7, 29, 49, 50
Littlejohn, Linda, 99, 127, 128
Liquor Amendment bill, 88-89
Liquor Referendum/Early Closing Referendum, 17
Lockhart, Grace, 150
Long Innes, Reginald, 95
Loughran, Daisy, 28
Lyons, Enid, 112, 158, 162, 176
Lyons, Joseph, 100, 103, 112, 136, 157
Lynton, Mayne, 110

Lysaght, Andrew, 98
Lysistrata, 180

Macarthur, Douglas, 156
Macarthur-Onslow, Mrs, 21
Macarthur-Onslow, Miss, 21
Macdonald, Jessie, 28
Mace, Gloria, 185
Mace-Murray, 185-187
Macdonald, Jessie, 28
Mackinnon, Eleanor, 134
maiden speech 55, 57, 58, 64, 66, 71, 151, 152, 183, 204
Mair, Alexander, 153, 157
Manfred, Edmund, 138
Manning, Attorney General Henry, 120, 123, 125,
Mao, Zedong, 177
Marks, Captain, 31
Marsh, Anne, 152
Marshall, Valda, 182
Martin, Lewis Ormsby, 112, 113-115, 117, 122-123, 125-6, 127, 129,
Marx, Karl, 169
maternal mortality, 35, 59, 65, 67, 93
McClelland, Justice, 186
McGirr, John, 29, 106
McIntosh, Hugh, 64-65
McKell, William, 88, 118, 121, 157
McKenzie, Violet, 153
McTiernan, Sir Edward, 79
Melba, Dame Nellie, 29
mental hospitals, 189
mentally defective persons 65, 76
Menzies, Robert, 152, 157, 159, 162, 173, 176, 178, 179

Mercury, The, 124
Meta Wilson, Clare, 32-33
Metropolitan Milk Bill, 91
midwifery, 35, 67
Molyneux Parkes, Hilda, 9-10, 160
Moncrieff, Gladys, 112, 155
Monowai HMNZS, 147
Monroe Doctrine, 150
Morris, Dr Emmanuel, 67, 75
Morrison, Sibyl, 23
mother/motherhood, xi, 3, 4, 5, 7, 11, 16, 19, 27, 30, 36, 37, 38, 39, 40, 45, 53, 61, 64, 68, 71, 76, 77, 78, 79, 87, 90, 91, 92, 94, 96, 97, 98, 105, 106, 107, 108, 109, 110, 111, 113, 115, 117, 118, 122, 124, 125, 127, 128, 132, 138, 139, 140, 141, 142, 143, 156, 166, 176, 183, 185, 186, 187, 196, 205, 212, 213
Mowll, Archbishop Howard, 147
Mulcahy, Dan, 172
Munro, Grace, 163
Murray, Joan, 185
Murphy, Cecil, 62, 71
Murphy, Senior Constable, 27
Muscio, Mildred, 44, 114, 115
Mussolini, Benito, 145

Nathan, Jerrold, 177, 191
National Council of Women (NSW), 94, 99
Nationalist Party, 25, 27, 30-31, 35, 36, 39, 41, 42, 46, 47, 89, 91, 92, 93, 101, 133, 134, 177,
National Service Bureau, 20, 21
navigable waters, 88

Neale, Clara, 29
Nehru, Pandit, 182
Ness, John, 122
New Housewives Association, 169-170
New Look, 165, 168
New Theatre, 105
Nicholas, The Hon Harold, 121
'Nimitybelle', 25
'Nomad', 25
Norden, A E, 95
Norrington, H S, 168-169
North Shore, 46, 75, 80
Northern Miner, 26
Northern National Political Union of Queensland, 25, 27
Norton, Caroline, 76
Nowland, Harrie, 41
nuclear tests, 147
Nyland, Mr, 33

Oakes, Charles, 31, 35, 42, 43
obiter dictum, 121
O'Conor, Broughton, 98
Of Mice and Men, 180
O'Malley Wood, Lilla, 174, 177, 218
One Big Union, 26
Onslow, Mrs Arthur, 115
Orwell, George, 161
Overhill, George, 32, 42
Owen, Ruth Bryan, 157

Page, Earle, 138, 157
Palace of Education and Social Economy, 15

Panama-Pacific International Exposition, 14, 15
Pan Pacific Women's Conference, 148
Pankhurst-Walsh, Adela, 60, 115-116
Paris Peace Talks, 25, 146
Parliamentary Electorates and Elections Act, 92-3
Peacock, Millicent, 1
Peloponnesian Wars, 180
Peters, Dorothy, 112
Petrov Affair, 180
Piddington, Marion, 16
Pilgrim, Joan, 173-174
Playfair, Edmund, Mrs, 141
Playford, Sir Thomas, 166
Police Offences Amendment (Drugs) Bill, 79
Polini, Emélie, 37, 77-8, 92, 95-7, 99, 105-7, 110-111, 113, 115, 118-9, 121, 123, 127-8, 130, 132, 187, 201, 210, 212
political action, xii, 103, 105, 110, 113, 200
Porter, Persia, 163
pre-selection, 41, 42, 43
Preston Stanley, Fanny, 3-5, 138-140
Preston Stanley, Harold, 131
Preston Stanley, Joan, 129
Preston Stanley, Millicent
  birth, 3
  death 124, 189, 190
  family, 3-6
  Mmarriage, 131-133,
Premiers Conference, 94, 117
Production of Human Degeneracy, The, 16

Progressive Party, 31, 46, 68, 133
prohibition, 17, 34, 88, 90, 133, 142
Prohibition Alliance, 133
Pulse of Victory, 155, 156
questions without notice, 34, 66, 75, 79, 80, 87
Quigg, Frank, 80

Radio 2GB, 147
Rankin, Annabelle, 162, 164
Raynor, Molly, 111
red scare, 137-138
referendum, 17, 18, 19, 25, 27, 88, 164, 166-8, 178, 179
Reid, Alan, 181-182
Reid, George, 6
Rents and Prices Referendum, 166-168
'Resurgam', 193-4
Rich, Ruby, 29, 92
Richmond Villa, 50, 53, 104,
Rischbieth, Bessie, 34
Robinson, Admiral SS, 142
Robinson, J J, 42
Robson, William, 96, 124
Roosevelt, Eleanor, 149
Roosevelt, Franklin, 156
Royden, Maude, 190
Royal Empire Society, 177
Ryan, Lyndall, 175

sacrifice, 9, 18, 20, 84, 133, 160
Sand Bag Fund, 18
Sarony, Leslie, 167

School of Arts Debating Society, 6, 135,
Scobie, Grace, 28
Scott, Rose, 28, 76, 142
Scullin, James, 100, 136, 137
'Senga', 20
Shall, Theo, 111
Shand, John Wentworth, 187
Shaw, George Bernard, 105, 112
Sheehan, Archbishop Michael, 104
Singapore, 150
Smith, Carlotta, 41
Smith, Dodie, 112
Snowy Mountains Scheme, 161
socialism, 10, 11, 43, 101, 104, 161, 162, 164, 167, 168, 169
Society of Women Writers NSW, 2
Soubeiran, Madame, 29
Southcombe, Eva, 164
Spender, Percy, 176
Stanley, Augustine Gregory, 3, 4, 5, 140
Steinbach, Dr C, 189
Stevens, Bertram, 55, 104, 112, 129, 147, 157
Stewart, Nancy, 110
Stewart, Nellie, 164
Stopford, Dr Robert, 39
Street, Jessie, 99, 128, 170
strike, 20, 46, 60, 169, 170, 179, 180
suffrage, 12, 44, 193
Sun, The, 49, 118, 122, 132, 170, 172
Supply bill, 81, 82, 86
Sydney Morning Herald, The, 122-124, 127, 129, 139-140, 150, 170, 176

Sydney Town Hall, 44, 152, 159, 162, 167, 169, 172
Sunday Times, 64

Talfourd, Sir Thomas, 76
Tangney, Dorothy, 158
Taylor OBE, Florence, 151, 163
Taylor, Frances, 63, 74
Temperance, 5, 15, 16, 17, 34, 44, 74, 88, 89, 94, 131, 133, 192
Theodore, Ted, 100
Tomson, Edward, 26
Tonge, Arthur, 75, 79-81
Toohey, Annie, 28
Treaty of Versailles, 146
Trocadero, 179
Tully, John, 84
Tribune, 170
Truth, 63-64, 123, 145

United Associations of Women, 96, 99, 114, 129
United Australia Party, 100, 150, 158
United Australia Party Women's Co-ordinating Council, 145, 150, 158
Unity Conference, 159
University Labour Club, 104
unmarried mothers, 79, 185, 186

Vanbrugh, Irene, 52
Vaughan, Crawford, 131 ff, 165-166, 171, 216
Vaughan, Evelyn, Maria, 133
'V.H.', 123
Viavi, 11-12

Videon, M C, 99
'Vignette', 85-6
Voice, 124

Wakehurst, Lord John de Vere Loder, 147
Wakehurst, Lady Margaret, 153, 155, 190
Walder, The Hon Samuel, 112
Waley, Frederick, 44
Wall Street crash, 100
war brides, 152
war effort, 18
War Precautions Act, 26
War Savings Certificates Campaign, 20
Ward, Eddie, 100, 164
WEA, 6, 16
Wearne, Walter, 50
Weaver, Reginald, 14-15, 30, 43, 45-46, 94, 158
Webb, Jessie, 36
Webster, Ellen, 120
wedding ring, 184-185
Whose Child, 104, 105, 106, 110, 112, 113, 117, 141, 153, 186
Widows Pension bill, 68-69
Williams, Mrs Jamieson, 50
Williams, Snowy, 27

Willis, Mrs Mary, 52
Wilson, President Woodrow, 146
Win the War League, 20
Wolstenholme Anderson, Maybanke, 11
women in parliament, 30, 41, 108, 182,
Women Justices Association, 34, 42, 100
Women War Workers Depot, 152
Women's Australian National Service (WANS), 153, 154, 155, 190
Women's Co-ordinating Council, 145, 150, 151
Woman's Day, 175
Women's Federation League, 11
Women's Guild of Empire, 115, 204
Women's International League for Peace and Freedom, 19
Women's Legal Status bill, 22
Women's Legal Status Act, 23
Women's Liberal League, 9, 161
Women's Loyal Service Bureau, 2, 21-2, 28, 153
Women's Peace Army, 19
Wong, Penny, 193
Workers Weekly, 148
Wragge, Hugh, 120, 123

Young Liberals Clubs, 12

www.ingramcontent.com/pod-product-compliance
Lightning Source LLC
Chambersburg PA
CBHW070344240426
43671CB00013BA/2396